"Dr. Schwartz perfectly blends the academic principles of science with the abstract possibilities of spirituality, searching to answer the age-old question of what happens after we die. Is there a survival of consciousness? Does love survive? This book is an absolute must-own and must-read for anyone who struggles with faith, love, death and aspects of divinity."

—John Edward, host of
*Crossing Over with John Edward*,
and author of *Crossing Over: The Stories Behind the Stories*

"Professor Schwartz exhibits courage and integrity . . . in his groundbreaking experiments. This book . . . is an important milestone in the scientific research on the survival of consciousness after physical death."

—Richard C. Powell, vice president for research and graduate studies,
University of Arizona

"A compelling read, this book supports with real evidence the existence of a spirit world that many assumed was there, but may now embrace beyond reasonable doubt."

—George E. Dalzell, L.C.S.W.,
author of *Messages: Evidence for Life After Death*

"[A] painstakingly assembled hypothesis followed by rigorous experimentation. Dr. Schwartz has made his case—compellingly, in my view."

—Rustum Roy, Evan Pugh Professor of the Solid State
and professor of geochemistry, Pennsylvania State University

"Anyone who has ever questioned life after death must read *The Afterlife Experiments*. Dr. Schwartz's work finally closes the gulf in our understanding of life and death."

— Joel Rothschild, author of *Signals*

"Gary Schwartz navigates his readers on a journey of discovery. At last we can take another collective step toward affirming that life and love survive physical death. . . . Thanks, Gary!"

— Judy Guggenheim, after-death communication researcher and co-author of *Hello From Heaven!*

"Armed with consummate authority. . . . Schwartz embraces an admirable passion for curious knowledge and adamantly resolves to uphold his survival-of-consciousness hypothesis until research proves otherwise."

— *Publishers Weekly*

# THE AFTERLIFE EXPERIMENTS

Breakthrough Scientific Evidence
of Life After Death

## Gary E. Schwartz, Ph.D.
with William L. Simon
Foreword by Deepak Chopra

**ATRIA** BOOKS
New York London Toronto Sydney

ATRIA BOOKS

1230 Avenue of the Americas
New York, NY 10020

Schwartz, Gary E., 1944–
    The afterlife experiments : breakthrough scientific evidence of life after death
    / Gary E. Schwartz with William L. Simon
        p. cm.
    Includes bibliographical references and index.
    ISBN 0-7434-3658-X (alk. paper)    0-7434-3659-8 (Pbk)
    1. Science and spiritualism.  I. Simon, William L., 1930–  II. Title.

    BF1275.S3 S34 2002
    133.90'01'3—dc21

                                                            2001055175

First Atria Books trade paperback printing March 2003

10   9   8   7

For information regarding special discounts for bulk purchases,
please contact Simon & Schuster Special Sales at 1-800-456-6798 or
business@simonandschuster.com

Designed by Jaime Putorti

Printed in the U.S.A.

*For Howard and Shirley,*
*Linda, Henry and Elayne,*
*Susy and Sam*

*For Arynne, Victoria and David*
*Sheldon, Vincent, and Elena*

*And for everyone's loved ones, here and there,*
*and all of us who care about compassion, wisdom, and truth.*

*In order to disprove the law that all crows are black,*
*it is enough to find one white crow.*
—WILLIAM JAMES, M.D., PSYCHOLOGIST AND PHILOSOPHER (1842–1910)

# •Contents•

# Contents

# • FOREWORD •

There is a wonderful story about a guru and his cranky disciple. Both were getting on in years, and they happened to be sitting one afternoon in a cramped, dingy room waiting for someone to bring them food.

"Why are you any different from me?" the disciple grumbled. "We're just two old men sitting here waiting impatiently for our dinner."

"That's true," the guru said.

"We see the same room," the disciple went on. "We live in the same world. There's no difference at all."

The guru shook his head. "You say we live in the same world, but we don't. Your world is private; no one else can enter it. It is made of personal memories, desires, feelings, and dreams. My world is not private but open to all. It is eternal and unbounded. Nothing exists in it that I claim as my own. Wherever I look I see love, trust, truth, eternity."

The disciple still complained. "If your world is so much better than mine, why do you even bother to be here?"

"Because your world is only a dream," the guru said quietly. "And it gives me pleasure when someone wakes up."

Although beautiful in itself, this story, which I have returned to a dozen times since I first came across it twenty years ago, underlines one of the great truths of spirituality. There is an absolute world that our world dimly mirrors. Saint Paul spoke of seeing this world as if through a glass darkly. That is, we can catch vague glimpses of it, but a full, clear view is rare. Only in flashes of insight, those moments called "going into the light," do we escape our private world of sensation and memory. The rest of the time we seem to be satisfied with accepting very little that goes beyond the five senses.

Even so, a small band of people has never given in to ordinary reality. The great psychiatrist R. D. Laing referred to them as a motley crew of madmen: poets, geniuses, saints, and seers—outsiders whose perception is somehow skewed. We venerate such rebels of the soul, but we have also kept them at arm's length because believing in the material world has become a sort of survival mechanism, identified with being sane.

Only in our lifetime have the keepers of reality come forward to challenge the accepted belief system. The majority were believers to begin with, individuals with a special sensitivity to subtle energies of various kinds—telepaths, mediums, clairvoyants, mystics. But a few have been open-minded rationalists. Their strategy has been to apply the very rules of science to topple some of science's most iron-guarded assumptions.

With his hypothesis of the living soul, Gary Schwartz applies procedures of experimentation that no honest skeptic could argue with. He doesn't start from an assumption that the subtle plane must be real, only from an openness that it might be. His specific interest in this book is to explore and answer questions about the afterlife, and in particular whether we can communicate with the dead.

I consider this visionary book a look-around at one of those high spots, a place where love and memory are bound together, where no one is ever lost to anyone else. A vast domain of knowledge is opened up by even the shortest visit here.

Deepak Chopra, MD

# Are Life and Love Eternal?

*If it is real, it will be revealed.*
*If it is fake, we'll find the mistake.*
—MOTTO OF THE HUMAN ENERGY SYSTEMS LABORATORY

If it could be proved beyond a doubt and in an entirely convincing way, if it could be proved scientifically that life and love are eternal—

would your love be enhanced,
would your fears vanish,
would your purpose in life be magnified?

How would life be different for you if you knew that just as patterns of dynamic light from distant stars continue to expand into the universe, our light, our dynamic information and energy, our soul and spirit not only continue to expand into the universe but live and grow just as we do on the earth? That the living soul can be likened to a dynamic living rainbow, a vibrating spectrum of visible and invisible energies that shimmer and shine forever?

Consider a time when eternal life is an accepted part of our universe. Imagine a time when the continuum for all of our human relationships can be extended beyond the physical years spent on earth.

This book presents the scientific possibility that all this, and more, has been proved and is real. How you handle this information is up to you; even skeptics will begin to evolve as a result of these findings.

## CELEBRATING SCIENTIFIC EXPLORATION OF THE LIVING SOUL

This journey unfolds as a scientific adventure tale investigating life after death. The story illustrates the capacity of humans to cherish the process of scientific exploration and to follow the discoveries wherever they may lead. It is a story about the inherent potential in all of us to love people, nature, and the earth in its entirety.

In a previous book, *The Living Energy Universe: A Fundamental Discovery That Transforms Science and Medicine,* Linda Russek and I explained how contemporary science is leading to the conclusion that everything in the universe is eternal, alive, and evolving.

Now I describe how Linda and I continued along that earlier path and explain how contemporary science is investigating the hypothesis of survival of consciousness after physical death—the possibility that the soul, or spirit, or call it what you will, continues eternally. This work will show you how science is experimentally addressing the hypothesis of a living spiritual reality—from the immortality of consciousness to the dynamic, evolving, and enduring nature of the universe itself.

This book is written for people who long to find scientific research that bears on what they hold most dear—that love matters, that love evolves, and that love continues forever. Discovering the existence of the living soul may be one of humankind's greatest gifts.

All of this is documented here for the first time.

## THE FRAUD OF "COLD READINGS"

In these pages I bring to life the chronology of our research as it unfolded, going well beyond the confined details presented in our technical papers that appear in scientific journals.

You will read actual transcripts and be a witness to what no scientists have had the privilege of experiencing before: apparent contact with the beyond, under increasingly controlled experimental conditions in the laboratory.

Most attempts to contact the dead are made through people who earn a livelihood by manufacturing hope for the bereaved—which perhaps is not entirely dishonorable, since it makes people feel better, but nonetheless relies on trickery.

These charlatans, known in the business as "cold readers," like to say things to every "sitter" (the person having the reading) such as, "They're telling me you know someone, living or dead, whose name is Charles. Do you know a Charles?"

Almost everybody knows a Charles or Charlie. But if this gets no reaction, the medium will continue with a stream of other information, something like: "I'm seeing a gray-haired person having some trouble walking, and a woman dressed in white . . . I'm getting a woman with an M in her name, an L . . . there's a younger person who's crossed over, a son or a brother . . . a dog has just entered the room, an old dog. . . ."

Who hasn't had a gray-haired grandmother or grandfather, old enough that they had trouble walking, and maybe spent time in a hospital or nursing home where they were helped by a woman dressed in white? But if not, the medium keeps right on talking with a string of clues, meanwhile watching closely for a telltale reaction—even the subtlest of indications such as a sudden blink, an intake of breath, a tensing of the body, a twitch. As soon as a sign like that occurs, the medium will start following up on whatever he just said, not *leading* the exchange but *following* the clues about statements that are correct, or nearly so.

The medium keeps talking, ignoring the statements that didn't get a response as if they had never even been said. "A woman with an M in her name, an L . . ." is typical. No reaction to the M? Not a problem; just try another letter.

At the end of the session, the sitter may be in tears, convinced she has heard information the medium couldn't possibly have known, certain of having been in contact with departed loved ones—when in fact all along she was unconsciously signaling which statements were meaningful to her.

That's the technique of cold reading—and it is, frankly, what many people who call themselves mediums are doing. And it is what the skeptics assume is *always* going on.

Yet, in our scientific experiments in the laboratory, we have been working with a group of top mediums who have consistently received messages, supposedly from the dead, that are impossible to explain as cold reading or any kind of recognizable trickery. We have received help from professional magicians, oversight from other scientists, videotaped scrutiny by professional documentarians. In our later, more carefully conducted experiments, no one who has witnessed the work or examined the data has been able to point out any flaw in our procedures or produce a rational explanation that would suggest how the mediums could conceivably be cheating.

## A Typical Reading in the Laboratory

If cold readings are easy to spot by anyone familiar with the techniques, the kinds of readings we have been getting in our laboratory are quite different in character. Not that they're error-free, but they do indeed present a very high percentage of correct information, and much of the information is very specific.

Here's a sample, so you can see for yourself. These are excerpts from a reading presented more fully later in these pages, where it comes complete with an unexpected ending that you will, I think, find amusing and surprising.

The medium had no way of knowing anything about the sitter—not the name, not even the sex, age bracket, background, city of residence, or any other details. And the sitter was placed in a chair directly behind the medium, who therefore could not gain clues from the physical appearance nor from any reactions of the sitter to the medium's statements. To make the conditions even more challenging, in the first part of the reading the sitter was instructed to give no responses and make no sounds.

Professional cold readers tell us that they are incapable of conducting a successful reading in this way.

After a brief explanation to the sitter about how he conducts readings, the medium began:

> *The first thing being shown to me is a male figure that I would say as being above, that would be to me some type of father image. . . . Showing me the month of May. . . . They're telling me to talk about the Big H—um, the H connection. To me this is an H with an N sound. So what they are talking about is Henna, Henry, but there's an HN connection.*

Could this have been simple guessing? Would these facts be broad enough to fit most sitters? Do they fit anyone you know?

The sitter in this case immediately recognized the "Big H" as an apt phrase for describing the father of the family, a man deeply respected by his professional colleagues and affectionately referred to as the "gentle giant." HN: his name was Henry; his mother's name was Henrietta. He died in the month of May. The probability of getting just this pattern of hits is on the order of a million to one.

No other person in the sitter's family fit the cluster of facts "father image, Big H, Henry, month of May" except her late husband, Henry.

The medium also spoke of this man's connections to literature and education.

> *Very strong symbolism of teaching and books. . . .*
> *The books come up where there may be something published.*

The sitter's late husband had been a distinguished scientist who published two hundred papers, edited seven books, and was a well-known educator. A clear hit.

After moving into the part of the session when the medium was allowed to ask Yes/No questions, the tempo picked up.

> *An out-of-state tie . . . They're talking about the Gemini or the sign of the twin, so whenever I'm shown this, they want me to talk about actual twins, like they're in the family, or they want me to talk about someone who is now the sign for Gemini. . . .*

The sitter's daughter lives out of state, has twins, and was born under the sign of Gemini.

> *Are you the twin?*

> No.

A clear miss.

> *There're telling me to bring the Big S. Also that comes up around Henry or the H. There's a big S that comes up—they're making me feel that it's important that I acknowledge this. . . .*

The couple's daughter and mother of the twins is named Shelley.

> *They show me lab-related stuff, so whether there's someone who works in the health care field or they're in some kind of lab-related function, but they're coming from a lab background.*

Shelley has a Ph.D. in molecular biology and psychopharmacology, and runs a laboratory at Boston University Medical School. More hits.

> *But I need to tease you from the H, tied up to the going to the beach and having something funny happen at the beach. . . .*
>
> *This is going back, this is not a recent thing, but I feel it's a funny thing that I have to like memorialize or kind of bring up. . . . Going back, and I'm feeling that you have pictures or were reminiscing about it but there's that kind of connection.*

The sitter, who had been a professional singer, had been a beautiful young woman but had thought her legs were not perfect enough and was very shy about them. During her courting days, she went to the beach with the young physician whom she would eventually marry, and didn't want to take off the cover-up over her bathing suit because it would reveal her legs. He was left wondering whether she was scarred or was the victim of some disfiguring ailment. When she finally overcame her reluctance, he told her, "Your legs are beautiful." It was a story the sitter's daughter had heard repeatedly through her childhood.

> *"And enjoy the tea" . . . I have no idea what that means, "enjoy the tea"—like I feel like, I'm having tea but "enjoy it." Like "drink" . . . I have no idea what this is but I feel it's kind of inside humor, "Enjoy the tea."*

The sitter had never liked tea when her husband was alive, but since his death had begun to drink tea regularly.

How many of the medium's statements would apply to you? They were approximately 70 percent correct for the sitter over the course of the entire reading.

Some people still insist that all we have been seeing in our laboratory experiments is examples of cold-reading technique that any professional stage mentalist can duplicate. But in fact, cold readers blanch when we challenge them to produce information this accurate and this unusual with a sitter unknown to them. And skeptics who claim that this is some kind of fraud the mediums are working on us have nonetheless been unable to point out any error in our experimental technique to account for the results.

The mediums have provided information that is sometimes chilling, sometimes painful, sometimes shocking, sometimes unknown even to the sitter, but later verified as correct.

But sometimes it has been just plain funny, as when a medium said of a sitter's grandmother, "She's definitely a pistol; she must have had false teeth, because she's taking them in and out, in and out. And she's not supposed to do that in front of everybody." For the sitter, this was a stunning moment because so accurate, and stunning for the experimenters as well because so very, very different in character from anything a cold reader—a medium who relies on guesswork—could possibly ever do. Yet the more experiments we did, the more we discovered many remarkable statements like this.

But does all this mean the mediums are actually getting information from the departed? It seems unlikely—it contradicts accepted science. Yet we have been unable to find any other convincing explanation for the totality of the findings. And as you will discover, many of the readings in these pages had an accuracy rate as high as 90 percent.

You will see how throughout the process we insisted on science first, continuously devising more rigorous and more carefully controlled experiments. You will become aware of how each experiment brought new surprises and revelations, and how even our skeptical beliefs were consistently and cautiously revised over time. You will take this journey of discovery along with us as we are carried forward by the scientific evidence.

## Searching for Truth in a Sea of Skepticism

Though the totality of the findings are surprisingly consistent with the concept of life after death and what we call the "living soul hypothesis," the data—as in all areas of science—are open to alternative interpretations. For example, are the messages being received from the mind of the sitter or the mind of the deceased? Are the leading people we have worked with engaged in highly sophisticated deception, or are they really doing something extraordinary? Paraphrasing the late Carl Sagan, our laboratory follows the philosophy, "Extraordinary claims require extraordinary data."

We are exceptionally aware of the need to conduct responsible and creative research with absolute integrity. Our essential guideline can be expressed in a single word, which is the motto of my alma mater, Harvard. The word is *veritas:* truth.

One of our overriding concerns turns on the issue of fraud and deception. Over and over we have asked ourselves and continue to ask, "Is the wool being pulled over our eyes?" Even worse, "Are we pulling the wool over our *own* eyes?" Because the more striking the findings, the greater is the temptation to say, "This can't be true. There must be a mistake!"

As the research evolved, Linda and I designed the experiments to be ever more fraud-proof. Reading these pages, you will witness the conceptual and emotional struggles as I was tempted time after time to accept as truth what I was seeing with my own eyes—that something extraordinary and wonderful was indeed going on.

Scientists and nonscientists alike are experiencing a test of faith—in this case, whether we can put our belief in the scientific method itself. Because if we are to put our faith in the scientific method, and trust what the data reveal, we are led to the hypothesis that the universe is more wondrous than imagined in our wildest flights of fancy.

How can you make this science relevant in your personal life? The answer is that what you absorb in this book can be polished and developed, and your own skills in this area can be nurtured. You can become more open and aware of your interconnections with others, both in this life and after this life—both here and there.

One fair warning: Be prepared for surprises. In this unique area of science, surprises are the rule, not the exception. You may find your jaw dropping every now and again. We have all shared your experience and know that extreme surprises and great wonder come with the territory.

Is love eternal?

Is there life after life?

If we truly have evidence that this is so, then we are indeed at a turning point in the history of human consciousness and the evolution of the human soul.

Is this mankind's ultimate lesson on earth?

You be the judge.

# PART I

# You Don't Find a Mission—a Mission Finds You

# · 1 ·

# The Journey Begins

It has been said that truth is stranger than fiction and that God works in mysterious ways. Gifts can appear at the strangest times in the most unexpected places. Sometimes a gift is in the form of a question. Sometimes a gift is fleeting. And sometimes a gift stays with us forever.

In the spring of 1993, at a conference of the American Psychosomatic Society, I met a clinical psychologist, Linda Russek, Ph.D.

Following the conference, I spent some time visiting this new acquaintance. At the end of our visit, at 4 o'clock in the morning, Linda was driving me to the Fort Lauderdale airport so I could catch an early morning flight back to the University of Arizona in Tucson. For me, what happened then was entirely unexpected—though I suppose she had been waiting for just the right moment. I now know that Linda offered me a special gift by asking a question unlike anything anyone had ever asked me before: "Do you think it's possible that my father is still alive?"

Fatigued yet intrigued, I wondered why Linda was asking me such a deeply personal and important question.

"I'm not sure," I replied. "Would it matter if I told you that I thought it was possible?"

Her gaze became intense. "Yes," she said.

"Why would it make a difference what I think?"

"Because you're a serious scientist, and if you think it's possible, you probably have a good reason."

Without fully knowing why, I felt compelled to share a secret I'd shared with no one else. "Years ago, when I was a professor at Yale, I stumbled on a hypothesis about how systems store information." I told her that it had led me—in fact, forced me—to recognize the possibility that consciousness might survive after death. "But I've never before shared the hypothesis with anyone because it's so painfully controversial."

Excited, she immediately wanted to know more. But the answers would have to wait until I could return to Florida.

Two weeks later, I was back. Walking with Linda on the beach in Boca Raton, I explained: "All systems, in the process of becoming and remaining whole, store information dynamically. Systems are composed of component parts that share information and energy—from atoms and chemicals, through cells and organisms, to planets, galaxies, and the universe as a whole.

"Mathematical logic," I said, "leads to the conclusion not only that all systems are 'alive' to various degrees, but also that this information continues as a living, evolving energy system after the physical structure has ceased to exist."

Following the logical line of reasoning, everything I knew about physics and psychology forced me to entertain the hypothesis of "living info-energy systems." To put it in a more familiar yet more controversial way, I used the words *living souls*. (Appendix A offers more on the living soul hypothesis.)

When I first presented these ideas to Linda, I found her skepticism just as strong as my own. Her eyebrows came together in an expression I would soon love and respect, as she intensely searched for flaws in my reasoning. I waited, and watched her try. At that moment, at least, she could find none. Instead, she challenged me about the possible impact of my hypothesis. "Do you realize the implications of what you're describing?"

"I'm aware of some of the implications," I said nervously, "and I'm frankly quite afraid of them."

I soon learned that Linda was driven to pursue this for a very personal reason, the one that had launched the conversation in the first place. She had a longing to know whether it might be possible to communicate with her father. Dr. Henry I. Russek had been a distinguished cardiologist and scientist, beloved by his colleagues, patients, and family. When he passed in 1990, Linda began a quest to discover scientifically whether her father, who had been her mentor, colleague, and best friend, was still with her.

So it wasn't surprising that she coaxed me to pursue the possibility. She urged, "For the sake of my father and my family, we must test your hypothesis. Will you help me?"

Put yourself in my shoes.

You've just confessed a potential scientific bombshell to a caring and beautiful person you hardly know. You're well aware that many of your colleagues at the University of Arizona and psychology professors everywhere would ridicule you and even attempt to destroy your academic career, if they knew that you were actually considering doing research in this area.

But there I was, having fallen in love with Linda's love for her father. I was faced with her dream to know scientifically, one way or the other, whether her father's consciousness still existed.

I looked into her searching eyes and could not resist her pleas that I begin this dreaded research. "Yes," I agreed.

"But only if we don't tell anyone!"

## THE RESEARCH BEGINS ... IN SECRET

For the next two years, in our spare time, we struggled to define ways of experimentally exploring the living soul hypothesis. Our research was done very quietly in Boca Raton. Some experiments were conducted in the medical office of Linda's late father. Others were conducted in Linda's condominium, and one in her mother's condominium.

Over a period of two years, we did some twenty different experiments. In one series, for example, using complex Hewlett-Packard spectrum analyzers and Lexicor 24-channel brain wave machines, I measured Linda's vital signs and brain activity during two periods: first while she simply thought about her father, and then while she attempted to communicate with him.

We collected a substantial amount of intriguing data appearing to support the hypothesis that Linda and her father could communicate. But these first exploratory efforts were far from conclusive. We began to wonder whether we could design scientific protocols that involved Henry as an active participant in the research—participating in a role we would come to term a departed hypothesized co-investigator.

"Hypothesized." The skepticism and scientific caution that would underlie all of our work in this suspect field demanded a label that took nothing for granted. Linda and I committed ourselves to a program of systematic research.

I'll say about our experiments in this period only that they produced no publishable science but led to some baffling pieces. One in particular still has us scratching our heads: after an attempt to contact Linda's father in which the spectrum analyzer and brain wave data seemed to suggest that something unaccountable had indeed taken place, Linda mentioned that her watch, which her father had given her, wasn't keeping time.

When I took her watch to a jeweler to have the battery replaced, he discovered to his amazement that her Seiko digital watch was running *backward;* he and several other jewelers I contacted at the time said they had never heard of such a thing. I'm not claiming that there was a connection with the experiment; it's just one of those ripe anomalies seemingly so abundant in this field that leave you unsure whether to groan or laugh.

## TWO LIVES

At the time of this secret research project, my "day job" was at the University of Arizona as a professor of psychology, medicine, neurology, and psychiatry. To some of my peers, it must have seemed an unexpected place for me, after the more highly esteemed institutions in my background. But there were good reasons. My academic career had not followed a very likely path. As a freshmen in electrical engineering at Cornell, I had realized after only two weeks that I had chosen badly; shifting gears, I graduated four years later from the Arts and Sciences College in the premedical field, with a major in psychology and a minor in chemistry. (My mother would probably want me to add that I was Phi Beta Kappa.)

Starting graduate school, I made another mistake—choosing the University of Wisconsin because professors in its departments of psychology, psychiatry, and medicine had a focus on an area of interest to me: the fields of psychophysiology and psychosomatic medicine, which is the study of how the mind affects the body. Once again I shifted gears, transferring to Harvard, where I earned my master's degree in clinical psychology and my Ph.D. in personality psychology, and was then recruited to stay on as an assistant professor.

Three years later I was recruited by Yale. At the age of thirty-two, I became one of the youngest tenured associate professors on campus, and was quickly promoted to professor of psychology and psychiatry. My research efforts during the Harvard and Yale years were focused at the forefront of mainstream science in psychology and medicine, in the then-new areas of biofeedback and relaxation (I was an early president of the Biofeedback Research Society as well as founder and early president of the Division of Health Psychology of the American Psychological Association), and in the areas of repression and the relationship between emotions, personality, and health.

I also played a leading role in creating the interdisciplinary field of behavioral medicine. Over the years I've had more than four hundred articles published in peer-reviewed scientific journals and have presented over six hundred papers at scientific meetings.

My move to the University of Arizona in 1988 came about partly because their psychology department and the school of medicine offered a unique opportunity to do work in evolving interdisciplinary areas of interest to me (and, to be honest, because I was inspired by the culture and environment of the Southwest). And that's where I was, teaching undergraduate courses and guiding graduate students through their masters' and doctoral work, when Linda and I met and began our secret research.

## Some Things are Forever

The first step in the new direction my life has taken actually began back while I was a professor at Yale, on a trip to Vancouver, Canada, to deliver an invited lecture.

During one sleepless night on that trip, as I stood at my hotel window looking out at the stars and the light coming from other windows in my view, the thought came to me that starlight, traveling in space forever, could be interpreted as an expression of immortality. At the time I was reading a book about quantum physics and the nature of light. The book explained that long after stars have "died," photons of their energy—i.e., their light—continue to exist.

Suddenly I realized that the moonlit glow illuminating my body was also traveling into space, albeit as tiny electromagnetic waves. Though the energy of my reflected waves was tiny compared with the moon's, those waves carried a history of my essence. A being out in space, with a sufficiently sensitive instrument of the right design, could clearly detect my photons as they whizzed past.

I asked myself, "What kind of God would allow the starlight from distant stars to continue forever, even after the star has 'died'—a fundamental premise of contemporary astrophysics—yet would not provide the same opportunity for our personal biophotons?"

Contemporary astrophysics has advanced to the point of documenting that 12-plus-billion-year-old photons, supposedly from the time of the so-called Big Bang, continue to exist in our present universe. If these cosmically ancient "info-energy packets" persist in the universe today, why can't our info-energy packets persist as well? It has been said that humans are made of the same stuff as stars—and we share the same energies.

The philosopher-scientist in me wondered, "If there really was a 'Grand Organizing Designer,' and this G.O.D. created eternal starlight, why wouldn't she/he/it/they have allowed our own personal electromagnetic waves—our information and energy—to be eternal as well?"

This realization was accompanied by a deep personal revelation, in which I experienced myself as an extended energy being, continuously reflecting visible and invisible light into space. I came to know firsthand how our individually patterned energy is like all energy—that it extends into space at the speed of light throughout our physical life and beyond.

While the theory stimulates many novel ideas that have challenging and sometimes complex consequences for life and society, it is really quite simple in its core. What I've done is to take a few well-accepted ideas in science and integrate them for the first time. In this sense, the theory doesn't require that we imagine a totally new universe, but only—as Marcel Proust said—that we "see it with new eyes." (For the curious, see Appendices A and B for a more extended discussion of the scientific reasoning underlying our research.)

## BUT SOME THINGS ARE DIFFICULT TO PROVE

Some years after that memorable trip to Vancouver, when I set out to help Linda conduct research about the possibility of contacting her father, we were undertaking an exploration that is suspect to most scientists but is, for creative people, a subject of intense fascination. One exploration of the topic lives vividly in my memory. The movie *Contact*, based on the book by Carl Sagan, provokes the mind as it pulls on the heart. One scene in particular expresses the challenge of documenting scientifically the existence of the seemingly ineffable. And it speaks to the challenge of envisioning and researching the existence of what can be called living energy souls—or, more simply, living souls.

Midway through the movie we see a scientist, Dr. Ellie Arroway, explaining to the spiritual scholar Palmer Joss, a man of faith, that she requires scientific evidence in order to believe. Dr. Arroway is especially adamant about the necessity of compelling evidence when it comes to belief in the existence of God.

I understood the Dr. Arroway character well because I was trained to look at the world as an intellectual, a scientist. In science we hypothesize; we do not believe. And science ultimately does not establish "proof" so much as provide evidence for or against a hypothesis. I learned the philosophy and methods of science effectively and have taught them for years, so I empathized with Dr. Arroway's position.

As the scene progresses the spiritual scholar asks Dr. Arroway, "Did you love your father?"

Arroway pauses, and then answers, "Yes."

Palmer Joss tosses a challenge, simple and to the point: "Prove it."

Dr. Arroway is speechless. How can she document her love with scientific evidence? Does she need scientific data to prove it to herself? And how can she convince the scientific community that what she knows in the deepest recesses of her heart, through direct personal experience, is in fact true—that her love for her father is real?

Think about it.

How can you *prove* to anyone that you love your husband or wife, a child, a friend, a pet? Not by what you say—people often lie to protect themselves or others. Not by what you do—we all do some things because they're expected of us rather than because we truly want to do them.

What Reverend Joss was teaching Dr. Arroway was that there

is no substitute for having the experience of love—or, for that matter, any other experience. One must ultimately have the experience for oneself. Everything else is indirect—a process of inference, of interpretation.

But the deep question arises, how do we know whether the *interpretation* of our personal experiences is genuine?

Just as it's difficult to determine whether what we interpret to be love is actually love, it's even more difficult to establish that what we may believe are afterlife communications are, indeed, afterlife communications.

Fortunately, just because something is difficult doesn't make it impossible. Linda and I were setting out on a journey of discovery not only about human experiences of love and the afterlife but about the process of using the methods of science to discover the reality of these experiences and their correct interpretation.

Scientific exploration begins by forming a hypothesis, and then gathering evidence that will support it or will prove it false.

We started with the hypothesis, the working assumption, that science can establish that love exists, that consciousness exists, and that survival of consciousness exists, in the same way that science has established that gravity exists, that electrons exist, and that photons from "deceased" stars continue to exist.

Let me repeat this because it's so important. We were proposing that in the same way science establishes that gravity, electrons, and photons from long-dead stars exist, it's possible for science to establish that love, consciousness, and survival of consciousness exist.

Physics teaches us that it's scientifically appropriate to infer the existence of invisible processes through careful observation in repeated experiments. Just as we scientifically infer the existence of an invisible force termed gravity through the systematic and careful observations of objects falling to the ground, our hypothesis said that one can scientifically infer the existence of invisible living info-energy systems—living souls and spirits—through systematic and careful experimentation.

All the research that lay before us as Linda and I set out on this journey would be based on two special gifts that science provides.

*The First Gift:* Science gives us the capacity to infer the existence of things we cannot see directly through the systematic observation of what we can see. Again, gravity is a prime example.

*The Second Gift:* Science gives us the capacity to evaluate alternative interpretations of a given observation.

These two gifts from science enable us to cherish all the more our capacity to have personal experiences. Science enables us to go beyond our personal experiences (the first gift) as well as help us interpret all of it, both the visible and the invisible (the second gift).

## HARNESSING THE POWER OF SCIENCE AND THE HUMAN MIND

Though science is clearly very powerful, it is only as powerful as the human mind that brings it into being. And the potential power of the human mind is vast.

The history of science reminds us that for thousands of years, humans believed the earth was flat. This belief was held by nonscientists and scientists alike. History is replete with common-sense observations that were later revised through the creative courage of women and men of frontier science.

The research I describe in the following pages examines the possibility that our current commonsense idea of death will ultimately turn out to be as "flat" as our past commonsense idea of a flat earth. It also predicts that our appreciation of the "yet unseen" will grow as we research and experience the invisible living energy universe.

## FOR BELIEVERS, AGNOSTICS, AND NONBELIEVERS: DO YOU WANNA TAKE A RIDE?

For those of you who already believe, taking the journey with us will confirm your beliefs. It will give you, as one physician put it after reading our earlier book, "a scientific reason to believe what we already know in our hearts to be true."

For those of you who do not know what to believe, taking the journey with us will help you make a decision about this most fundamental of questions.

And for those of you who do not believe and are in fact convinced that it is "ashes to ashes, dust to dust—period," taking the journey with us may lead you to reconsider your position.

The truth is that if the results of these studies continue to be positive, humankind will experience a watershed in our understanding of the universe and our role in it.

Having been there myself, I know what it's like to feel that "this simply can't be true." I know what it's like to literally see things with my own eyes in the laboratory and discount them because of prior learning, ignorance, or fear. I have experienced, firsthand, the feeling that "these are the kinds of data I wouldn't believe, even if they are true!" I know intense skepticism first hand.

However, the data appear to be real. If there is a fundamental flaw in the totality of the research presented in these pages, the flaw has managed to escape the many experienced scientists who have carefully examined the work to date.

Our approach is simple: let the data speak. And it's worth remembering, to paraphrase, that "data can be stranger than fiction." Are you ready for the data? As Carl Sagan wrote in *Contact,* "Do you wanna take a ride?"

# Bringing Soul Science into the University

Only a few major universities have, or ever have had, programs investigating paranormal phenomena or exploring other nontraditional aspects in this area.

Perhaps best known is the work by the late J. B. Rhine at Duke University. Rhine has been called the father of modern parapsychology, and in fact he coined the term, to distinguish the work from mainstream psychology. In thirty-three experiments of precognition, involving nearly a million trials, he was able to present statistically significant evidence in support of this phenomenon. (His experiments, and work in other labs by independent researchers replicating his studies, produced a cumulative probability of $10^{-24}$, or only one chance of error in a trillion trillion.)

The University of Virginia has a long-established research effort, still ongoing, to study near-death experiences and reincarnation, based largely on data from India. Since the 1970s, researchers at Princeton have been conducting research in their Anomalies Laboratory, which is attached to the university's electrical engineering department. That sounds curious until you understand that their goal is to "pursue rigorous scientific study of the interaction of human consciousness with sensitive physical devices, systems, and processes common to contemporary engineering practice"—in other words, the mind/machine connection.

In Scotland, researchers at the University of Edinburgh have been running a parapsychology centre (as they spell it) since the 1980s. Other work is being done today at universities in Gothenborg (Sweden), London and Northampton (U.K.) and Adelaide (Australia).

And there are more programs at other universities—but not many.

Yet, no major university has a formal research program investigating the possibility of survival of consciousness after death. It will come as little surprise, I'm sure, that on most campuses the idea of performing such research would receive the same kind of welcome Galileo received when he suggested that the earth was not the center of the universe.

So how did an extremely controversial research program such as ours come to be officially accepted at the University of Arizona?

Our earliest work on this subject was a moonlighting effort we had begun while working together on a more mainstream subject: a follow-up to a Harvard study that had been launched years before, continuing in the footsteps of work that Linda and her father had pursued even before I came on the scene.

## LESSONS OF LOVE IN A HARVARD STUDY

The Harvard Mastery of Stress Study was originally conducted in the early 1950s with 126 healthy male Harvard undergraduate students. Each student received a physical and psychiatric exam, and filled out an inch-thick stack of pencil-and-paper tests. They also experienced several laboratory stressors, including painful electric shocks, while various physiological measures were simultaneously recorded.

A 1957 book, *The Mastery of Stress,* authored by the three primary investigators of the stress study (Funkenstein, King, and Drolette), described the psychophysiology of coping with stress.

Twenty years later, Linda and her physician father decided it would be valuable to conduct follow-up interviews with the original participants and collect their medical records along with other psychosocial data to determine whether stress perceived in college was a predictor of long-term physical heath. Stanley King, a psychologist at the Harvard Student Health Service who was one of the study's original researchers, accepted the proposal and appointed Linda to be director of the follow-up study.

Over the course of a decade, Linda had flown around the country, managing to personally interview 116 of the original 126 men. Her devotion to this research was matched by those of the Harvard men, whose love for their university and their desire to contribute to knowledge made this research possible.

Each year the men mailed their medical records to Linda's father, who evaluated them and confirmed the medical diagnoses. Thirty-five years after the original study was conducted, the hard work of Linda and her father yielded a landmark paper on the effects of stress in college as a predictor of long-term health. Just before Dr. Russek passed away, their paper—a collaboration of Linda and her father, along with Stanley King and Linda's sister, Shelley Russek, a psychopharmacologist—appeared in the journal *Psychosomatic Medicine*.

## First Causes

By the time Linda was engaged in this study, I had left Harvard for Yale. The fact that I ended up on university campuses of such distinction was something I could never have predicted—a nearly missed stroke of good fortune, one of those happenstances that change our lives.

I had grown up on Long Island, in one of those families of high talent but low success, with a mother who was a classical pianist turned grade-school teacher, and a father who, I later learned, had been unfairly denied the Ph.D. he had earned in chemical engineering from Columbia University during World War II. Instead he became a pharmacist, a job he thoroughly disliked, which kept him working absurdly long hours in return for a very modest income. I grew up seeing little of him, and not much more of my mother.

Encouraged to use my mind and to explore, but left to entertain myself, I developed a passion for science (creating chemistry, biology, and electronics labs in our basement), for animals (gathering a myriad of pets, including turtles, hamsters, and snakes), and for music.

Music became a particular passion—no surprise, since I turned out to have an uncanny talent for it. By the age of twelve I had managed to learn how to play a dozen different instruments. Mastering the guitar, instrument number thirteen, came easily and just in time for me to be recruited by a band, in those early days of rock and roll.

On a local scale, the band was a great success. I managed to keep up my status as an honor student in math and science while helping to contribute to my family finances. It seemed such an easy way to make a good income (and bring people joy in the process) that my decision wasn't hard to make: I would quit school and become a professional musician. It seemed a no-brainer—I was already studying guitar in New York with the jazz great Sal Salvador and playing in the prestigious NBC Youth Orchestra.

That's where the happenstance came in. En route to my new life, I packed my guitar and stopped off to say goodbye to my high-school girlfriend. Her father heard my plans to quit high school and sat me down for a lengthy talk. Somehow I was willing to listen, and he managed to convince me that I could always pursue the music career but should get my degree first.

That one conversation shaped the course of my future life. I will be forever grateful for the push in the right direction from a wise person who cared, which got me started on the path I still pursue today. (Mr. Scoca, whether you're in this world or the next, I send my grateful thanks to you.)

## THE LOVE-HEALTH CONNECTION:
## A PERSONAL SCIENTIFIC GOAL

After my undergraduate work at Cornell and my years at Harvard and Yale, I came to the University of Arizona in 1988 with the intent that one of my primary goals would be to conduct research on the relationship between love and health. I had wanted for many years to investigate the love-health connection, both bioelectromagnetically and psychophysiologically. In fact, when people asked me why I had left my tenured professorship at Yale and moved to the University of Arizona, I explain that it was first and foremost a move of the heart—that love for the Southwest, its people and beauty I've already alluded to.

However, I soon discovered that my personal enthusiasm for investigating the love-health connection wasn't shared by national funding agencies. When I wrote a letter in 1989 to more than eighty private foundations requesting possible funding, seventy-nine of them responded with a polite letter indicating either that my interests didn't fit within their topical areas or that maybe they would entertain a proposal sometime in the future.

Only one individual, the late Brendan O'Regan, then the director of research at the Institute of Noetic Sciences (*noetic* meaning "pertaining to the intellect"), contacted me to discuss the possibility that his organization might fund some research in this area. Unfortunately, before our respective schedules permitted us to have a meeting, he unexpectedly died. In light of this seemingly definitive disappointment, I all but gave up the dream of ever addressing the love-health connection scientifically . . . until I met Linda.

In 1992, the International Society for the Study of Subtle Energy and Energy Medicine scheduled a special symposium on the topic of love and its relationship to health and healing. When I learned that this topic was to be discussed at a scientific society, albeit a strange one, I decided that I had to attend.

I was sufficiently nervous about being present at this unorthodox meeting that I didn't tell my academic colleagues I was going. I paid my own way (extremely rare for me; historically I have been blessed either to be an invited guest speaker at scientific meetings or to present papers funded by grants and foundations) and sat quietly in the audience in Boulder, Colorado. I even opted not to wear a name tag so I could remain for the most part anonymous.

It turned out that the symposium on love and health was remarkable. Following the formal presentations, there was a general discussion period when a long line of people from the audience waited their turn to approach the microphone so they could ask questions or make comments.

I, too, felt moved to speak. When it was my turn, I told the presenters their work had touched me so closely that I felt inspired to share with them and the audience a verse from the haunting James Taylor song "Secret O' Life." It was the first and only time I've ever been moved to break into song at a scientific gathering. (A musician I may be, but I am *not* a singer.)

The audience, as they say, went wild.

Scanning the room on that high well known to singers, musicians, and actors, I noticed a well-dressed black-haired woman who returned my gaze.

Nine months later, while I was attending one of my regular, conservative, scientific meetings—the American Psychosomatic Society—I noticed the same black-haired woman. When she recognized who I was and remembered my moment of musical playfulness at the energy medicine meeting, she came over and introduced herself. It wasn't long before we shared our mutual secret interests in love and health—initially scientific, and for a while, romantic. My personal attachment with Linda Russek began with our professional discussion about the love-health experiment she was preparing to conduct, which led to that 4 A.M. question of whether I believed in the possibility of survival of consciousness after death.

In 1993, in addition to beginning our secret pilot research that examined the living soul hypothesis, we also began to conduct more mainstream research on the love-health connection through that Harvard Mastery of Stress Study.

## Analyzing the Data from the Harvard Health Follow-up

When Linda and I began analyzing the data and carefully reviewing the thousands of questions the men had answered when they were in college, we discovered that Stanley King had included fourteen questions that rated the men's perceptions of their mothers' love and caring, and fourteen that rated the men's perceptions of their fathers' love and caring, based on criteria such as how loving, fair, just, and kind the parents had been during the men's childhood and adolescence.

Could these simple ratings of perceived parental love obtained in college serve as a predictor of their long-term health thirty-five and forty-two years later?

When we calculated the scores and entered them in the computer, the results were clear cut—and startling. The findings indicated that perceptions of parental love in college did indeed predict long-term physical health in later life.

We created four possible subgroups based on their college ratings: (1) father and mother both rated high; (2) father rated high, mother rated low; (3) father rated low, mother rated high; and (4) father and mother both rated low.

For those men who rated both their parents high in love and caring while they were in college, about 25 percent had a confirmed diagnosis of physical disease thirty-five years later. The diseases included cancer, heart problems, high blood pressure, arthritis, and asthma.

However, for those men who had rated both of their parents low in love and caring, 87 percent had a diagnosed disease thirty-five years later.

Not surprisingly, of men who rated one of their parents high and the other low, approximately half had a diagnosed disease in midlife.

The higher their perception of parental love, the healthier their lives. And we found that these patterns were independent of family and genetic history of disease, death, and divorce history of parents, as well as the smoking and marital histories of the men themselves. None of these familiar, well-established risk factors could explain the findings obtained.

What did these strong data suggest?

Since the men who perceived themselves as coming from the most loving parents had the lowest rates of physical disease, this implied that *love might be acting as a buffer, protecting a person from the deleterious health consequences of risk factors—even such significant factors as genetic predisposition, divorce, and cigarette smoking.* (The results of this study were reported by us in a 1997 article in the journal *Psychosomatic Medicine.*)

The question arises, how could love serve as a buffer for stress and a protector for disease? Linda suggested a follow-up experiment, and a very novel hypothesis emerged.

## A NEW ENERGY CARDIOLOGY STUDY

In 1994 Linda and I began to collect psychological and physiological data on forty of the Harvard men who had participated in the original study, using a portable laboratory featuring two brain wave/electrocardiographic systems. Her intention was that we record the electrical signals not only from the men's hearts and brains but from hers as well. To reach as many subjects as possible, we did a three-city tour on the East Coast: in New York City, Boston, and Boca Raton. During a two-month period, it was possible to collect data from forty subjects of the original sample.

In collecting this data, Linda sat directly across from the subject, both of them wired to record brain waves and heartbeats. Was it possible that Linda's heartbeat signals were being "received" by the man facing her a few feet away?

Each time Linda's heart beat, it sent out an electromagnetic signal, just as mine does, and yours. Physics predicts that within microseconds, the electromagnetic signal from Linda's heart would reach the gentlemen sitting opposite her. He would also be sending his heart info-energy back to Linda. This would theoretically create a systemic feedback process between the two people.

Theoretically, circulating energetic memories should be formed between Linda and each of the subjects. Of course, neither person would be aware this was happening, any more than they were conscious that they had electrocardiograms in the first place.

Using sophisticated computer software that I developed specifically for this purpose, we were indeed able to detect the presence of Linda's electrocardiogram in the brain waves of the men, and conversely, detect the men's electrocardiograms in Linda's brain waves.

Linda had offered a truly innovative prediction. She reasoned that the men who had perceived their parents to be high in love and caring would register a loving cardiac info-energy signal more strongly than the men who rated their parents low in love and caring. Linda hypothesized that people who experienced their parents as loving would be more open to receiving loving energy from other people, including her.

When we analyzed the brain wave and electrocardiographic data, we discovered that Linda's prediction was confirmed. The men who rated their parents high in love and caring in college registered Linda's heartbeats in their brains more strongly.

Linda's vision and persistence led to the creation of "energy cardiology," which examines the sharing of heart-brain information and energy between individuals. The experiment established a link between parental love and the registration of other people's heart energy. If Linda's further reasoning is correct, there may well be a bioelectromagnetic cardiac bond between people that is related in a fundamental way to one's openness to love or loving energy. If the systemic memory hypothesis is correct, these interpersonal cardiac info-energy memories will not be forgotten. Cardiac info-energy patterns may even continue to exist after the body has decomposed. Is it possible that cardiac energy provides a loving bond that not only exists in the physical realm but continues as info-energy after physical life has ceased?

So it turns out that the theory of energy cardiology does more than just offer a potential explanation of how love contributes to health. It potentially explains how loving energy can continue after death and enable us to remain connected to the living souls of our loved ones. (For more on the energy of love, see Appendix B.)

## INTRODUCTION TO A JOURNALIST'S "GREAT EXPERIMENT"

The focus of our research took a sudden shift in January 1995 as a result of a meeting with one unusual elderly woman, so out of the ordinary that I never imagined, in my wildest dreams, such a person could exist.

But surprise is the rule, not the exception, in this field. We were to become accustomed to an abundance of surprises.

The adventure is about to begin. The date is January 1995, and Linda has decided to move from Boca Raton to be near me in Tucson. I feel like a college student again. I'm driving a twenty-four-foot moving truck across the country, towing Linda's 1987 red Chrysler convertible that had been a gift from her father, which I know means she will drive it forever. Sitting with Linda and me, on a pillow on the front seat, is Freudy, Linda's ailing West Highland terrier.

We reach my Tucson town house and receive an overly effusive greeting from my two Cardigan Welsh corgis. When I check the stack of mail waiting for me, resting on top of the pile is an envelope from Dr. Richard Lane, a dear friend and colleague in the Department of Psychiatry at the University of Arizona.

He has sent a copy of a newspaper article describing a woman named Susy Smith, aged eighty-five, who, while preparing to die, was also planning what the reporter termed a "Great Experiment." The article described how for more than four decades, as a layperson and journalist, Susy had been attempting to do research on the possibility of survival of consciousness after death.

After several years of writing for the *Salt Lake Tribune* and the *Deseret News*, among other publications, she had written twenty-nine nonfiction books published by major houses, six of which had been translated into foreign languages and one into Braille.

The article reported that Susy's research had led to a most remarkable development: her purported ability to communicate with her deceased mother for the past forty years. In addition, Susy also claimed to have received after-death communication from a man who, when they were first in contact, humbly announced himself simply as "your guide, James."

The piece went on to describe how, after a number of "visits" with Susy, he formally identified himself as Professor William James—the eminent nineteenth-century physician and professor of psychology at Harvard University. I learned that Ms. Smith had published two books about the experience—*The Book of James* and *Ghost Writers in the Sky: More Conversations with James*—and claimed that both books had been written in collaboration with him.

So there I was, corgis yapping at my heels and a lot of unpacking waiting to be done, scanning the article and starting to laugh. Those extravagant newspaper claims were not what I needed at that point in time. My brain began a fight with my emotions while the scientist within me disappeared for the moment.

However, having received my Ph.D. in none other than William James Hall at Harvard University, and holding deep admiration and respect for James, one of the most progressive intellects of his century, I tried to resist the temptation to make a quick judgment.

Considered to be the father of psychology in America, William James was not only open to the possibility of survival of consciousness but had actually studied some of the greatest mediums of his day. I saw the obvious connection here to the secret research that Linda and I had been conducting. And the coincidence of Susy Smith living in Tucson was compelling.

With some trepidation, I showed the article to Linda. Her response was immediate and to the point. "We have to talk to Susy Smith. Please call right now and find out if we can take her out to dinner!"

We hadn't even begun unpacking the car. The rental trailer was taking up two spaces in front of my house. Now Linda enthusiastically suggested taking a complete stranger to dinner.

I discovered there was a Susy Smith listed in the phone book. The rest is history.

Working secretly on survival of consciousness in Florida opened our minds to the possibility of working with Susy in Arizona.

Working with Susy would open our minds to everything that was to follow.

## MAKING CONTACT

Over dinner the next night, Susy told us of her personal history, including the illnesses that had kept her in a wheelchair and housebound for many years. She told us of her personal research, her many books, her private foundation, and her publicized challenge that offered a $10,000 reward to the first person who successfully received the "secret message" she would attempt to communicate after she died. This message, if received correctly, would decipher a code left in a bank vault in Florida and, more recently, secreted on her web site, www.afterlifecodes.com.

As clinical psychologists, and ever suspicious, Linda and I both observed closely for any evidence that Susy might have a thought disorder or a mental illness such as delusions, paranoia, or schizophrenia. She seemed as logical and sane as could be.

The problem was, she said she talked to dead people—people she knew well, such as her mother, and even people she had never met in the flesh, such as William James. Moreover, she said she had been collecting scientific evidence over the years to convince herself and others that her experiences with Professor James were more than just her creative imagination.

We ended the evening assuring Susy that we were interested in her research and would be in touch. But first we had to get Linda settled in; mourn the death of one of our dogs; finish, edit, and publish scientific papers in our more mainstream mind-body and energy medicine research; and attend to all those other necessities that take time away from what we really want to be doing.

Somehow, more than a year went by without further contact with Susy.

Then, one day in 1996—around the time that Linda and I were establishing our research facility, the Human Energy Systems Laboratory, under the auspices of the university—a message arrived on our answering machine: "Have you guys died or something?" Click.

No "Hello," no "This is Susy, please call," no "I hope to hear from you soon." Just "Have you guys died or something?"

It turned out that this was quintessential Susy Smith. After more than seven decades in journalism, she didn't mince words.

We called immediately and were sobered to learn that she was quite ill, preparing to die, hoping to be with her mother and William James, and simultaneously planning to continue her research in the afterlife. Susy told us she wanted only to live through the summer so she could witness just one more Olympics.

## CREATING THE SUSY SMITH PROJECT: THE GIFT OF WORKING IN A SUPPORTIVE UNIVERSITY ENVIRONMENT

Realist that she was, Susy knew she would die with her life's work neither known nor acknowledged by the scientific community. Linda and I were now eager to help bring her research to the attention of the scientific world.

Susy, no scientist, had created a simplistic afterlife code experiment that—no surprise—was not scientifically designed. Did we stand a chance to help ensure her work would be taken seriously? We made the decision to assist.

First we designed a more definitive experiment incorporating additional codes—one known to all three of us, one known only to Linda and me, and so on. This way, after Susy's death, if someone came forward with the correct solution to the code known to Linda and me, it would appear to be telepathy—reading our minds—and not a message from the beyond. Admittedly, this was not very sophisticated, but it might be sufficient to establish the kind of control acceptable to scientists. The test would be whether we could get an article published in a reputable journal describing Suzy's efforts and our new design.

## THE NEXT STEP

In May 1997, that article was published in the *Journal of Scientific Exploration* under the title "Testing the Survival of Consciousness Hypothesis: The Goal of the Codes."

Once Linda and I had seen to the publishing of the details of Susy's experiment, we knew that our secret (and safe) research days had come to an end. At that point Linda, ever bold, challenged me: "Gary, I want you to find a way to bring Susy's experiment into the university."

It's one thing to publish a single paper in a scientific journal, quite another to bring this research into a university as a formal project.

Though I was admittedly hesitant, I knew that what Linda was proposing made sense and should be done. I wondered how I could present to the head of my department and the dean of my college a project I knew they would find outlandish and perhaps even unprofessional.

I had been hard at work preparing to teach a new course, called "The Psychology of Religion and Spirituality." Students yearn for a reason to believe in a larger spiritual reality, and the course was intended to provide a discussion opportunity in a scientific framework. The content had been approved by Lynn Nadel, the head of my department. A distinguished professor of psychology and neuroscience, Lynn is also a wise and caring person—a man whose philosophy of science I much admire—and I'm honored to be in his department.

Scheduling a meeting with him, I could raise the possibility of creating a Susy Smith Project. But how could I present the subject?

I didn't want him to laugh or throw me out of his office—or worse, begin to question my judgment as a professor and scientist. Not an easy challenge.

Still, I would have the advantage of arguing that the subject wasn't new on campus. Systematic research on the survival of consciousness hypothesis had begun over a hundred years earlier at Cambridge University and at Harvard, and continued as parapsychological research at major institutions such as Yale, Duke, and Stanford.

In addition, substantial research exists in the broad area of religion and spirituality. Yet, even so, only a handful of laboratory studies had ever been published on the topic of survival of consciousness after death.

A few days later, sitting in Lynn's office surrounded by the many books and papers piled there, I launched hesitantly into the approach I had settled on. If it was valid for the Department of Psychology to offer a course that discussed other universities' research in religion and spirituality, then the department should also be brave enough to allow its faculty to conduct studies on topics of their own choosing, even when those topics seemed highly controversial.

I told Lynn about Susy Smith's professional history, her many books, her experiments, and the events that led to the research article on her planned experiment using coded communication from the afterlife. I even confessed that Linda and I had quietly begun our own research on the living soul hypothesis, though I thought it the better part of valor not to share any details just yet.

Lynn said he agreed that all questions important to humanity should be legitimate areas of exploration in a university, so long as the research adheres to the standard canons of scientific reasoning, caution, and integrity. This, we both knew, is the established foundation of what is termed academic freedom.

So I had won his approval to do research within the university and the department on this avant-garde, eyebrow-raising topic. Fine. That proved easier than I had feared—so easy that perhaps I could try for one additional request I had been thinking about.

I told Lynn of the plan to create two advisory boards for the Susy Smith Project—not just a local one but a national one as well. And then my request: "Lynn . . . would you be willing to serve on the University advisory committee?"

He tried to duck by saying he didn't know enough about the subject to be of value. "I'm no expert," he protested.

I said, "Lynn, for all practical purposes, there *are* no experts. What this work needs more than anything are open-minded scientists willing to entertain the hypothesis and critique the experimental designs as they emerge." And I reminded him of the wise statement that "extraordinary claims require extraordinary evidence."

Lynn pondered for a long moment and then said, "Gary, life is short and you only live once . . . maybe." And, yes, he would serve on the local advisory committee.

The formal mission statement for the project was issued to Holly Smith, dean of the College of Social and Behavioral Science, on January 11, 1997. The statement to the dean gave the purpose of the project as continuing Suzy's forty-year effort to "conduct responsible scholarly and scientific research on the challenging question of the possibility of survival of consciousness after death." It went on to acknowledge that "this controversial hypothesis forms the foundation for most of the major religions of the world and receives scholarly consideration in universities and colleges."

The conclusion of the statement noted that "the Susy Smith Project . . . is designed to bring careful and systematic scientific research to bear on this fundamental question."

Since the inauguration of our program, Dean Smith has taken the further step of approving our proposal to create the Soul Science Research Campaign to raise funds for expanding this research into areas that include investigating children who appear to receive spirit communication, and addressing the possible health consequences of life-after-death communication. We were highly fortunate to have a head of college like Dean Holly Smith (no relationship to Susy), who is deeply committed to fostering the dialogue between science and spirituality.

With open-minded people like Dean Smith and Professor Nadel willing to place confidence in our integrity and dedication to science, we had managed to successfully open the doors of academe to our unusual research endeavors.

Now, how would we take advantage of those open doors? A chance meeting was about to move us another step in our probing of that question.

· 3 ·

# Five Words That Changed My Life

## A Turning Point

Susy's personal life story was an excessively strange one. But learning how to listen to Susy with an open mind turned out to be necessary training for us to learn how to listen to the next person to appear on stage in this saga, who would make Susy's history seem mundane by comparison.

In the fall of 1997, I was invited to give a keynote address to the Biofeedback Society of California. The meeting was being held south of Los Angeles in Irvine, near the home of a friend, psychiatrist Dr. Donald Watson. Don had told me about a woman he had met who, he said, seemed to have the powers of a medium—a person who claims to be able to receive information from individuals who have died—and had been remarkably accurate in receiving communications about his deceased son.

Of course I was curious. So Don took me to visit Laurie Campbell. No sooner had we met than she said to me, matter-of-factly, "I sense your mother is here." She then described my mother's loud and loving personality and her large physique: a verbal portrait of a woman remarkably like my strong-willed, devoted, heavyset mother, Shirley Schwartz.

I wondered how Laurie could even know that my mother was dead. Had Don Watson told her enough in advance to have given her the time to do research about me? Did she somehow get detailed information about my past in some other way? Was Laurie reading my mind telepathically? Or was something else going on here?

I had come to meet Laurie as a scientific observer, and steered the conversation away from anything personal. But within minutes, Laurie said she felt compelled to share an urgent message from my mother. She said, "Your mother wants you to call your brother—he needs to talk to you." She correctly described him as living on the East Coast and also talked about his children. She then spoke of a short, quiet male standing behind my mother. Her detailed description resembled my deceased father, Howard Schwartz, both in personality and appearance.

With information getting too close for comfort, I decided to redirect the session by informally testing Laurie. Wanting her to describe someone she might have had less time to gather information about, I challenged her to receive any information from a man named Henry—thinking of Linda's father.

Laurie entered a state of concentration and began reporting the presence of a deceased physician, showing a large heart and roses, who was overflowing with love for his daughter. She related statements, purportedly from Henry, such as "I've been waiting for years to communicate with my daughter" and "I've been following your research with my daughter."

Laurie's tone of voice and style of communication was deeply loving, intense, animated, mature, firm yet gentle, and—was it my imagination?—sounding as if the speaker was relieved at finally being able to say things he had been wanting to say for years. The combination of voice and manner is difficult to describe, but it was completely different from how Laurie spoke when she related the bold comments purportedly made by my forthright mother and the gentle comments purportedly made by my mild father. Suddenly it seemed that a new third personality, very different from either of the other two, was being introduced, and the personality seemed quite similar to Linda's description of her father.

If this was a show, an act put on for my benefit, it was a performance worthy of an Oscar nomination.

Laurie confessed that she actually felt embarrassed by the enormous amount of love this man was expressing for his daughter and family, claiming she had never emotionally observed so much love from someone on "the other side."

At this point I decided it was time to try an even bolder test of Laurie's purported mediumship. Remembering Susy Smith, I braced myself and asked, "Can you receive any information from a man named William James?"

"Who is William James?"

Given that Laurie's formal education had ended with little beyond a high school diploma, it wasn't surprising that she was unfamiliar with the long-dead professor.

"He's a friend of a friend," I answered quietly, "and he's deceased."

Laurie literally changed her persona before my eyes, beginning to speak in a deep voice that bellowed and lectured with great distinction. I sat transfixed as I experienced firsthand my first "trance mediumship" session.

She reported seeing a distinguished man in a nineteenth-century setting, surrounded by books. The man began to lecture about the psychology of consciousness, the importance of doing research on the afterlife, and the need for integrating science and spirituality. For almost fifteen minutes, this simple woman with little advanced education delivered a polished lecture on philosophy and soul science.

I did not interrupt, did not say a single word. I did not reveal to Laurie that her lecture sounded in content and style remarkably like the renowned Harvard scientist.

Laurie, I noted, did not mix up the personalities of the three men—my father, reserved and soft-spoken; Linda's father, strong, loving, and verbal; and William James, erudite and professorial. All the voices remained in character for the personalities even though, as far as I knew, Laurie did not have any knowledge or information about any of these men. She did not see Henry Russek giving a lecture on consciousness, or William James speaking about a father's love. And her accuracy in describing my mother was, in a word, compelling.

Given that I could confirm the information about Shirley, Howard, Henry, and William, what was I to do about the information that I could not immediately confirm? For example, Laurie's claims that she had been working for the past five years with the late eminent Scottish scientist Sir James Clerk Maxwell, whom she said originally introduced himself simply as "Max"? And who, she claimed, had said he was grooming her for a career as a medium scientist working in *my* research laboratory?

Susy Smith had claimed that Professor William James had introduced himself to her simply as "your guide, James." First Susy, and now Laurie—both purportedly communicating with distinguished dead scientists who introduced themselves to strangers on a first-name or nickname basis. Give me a break!

Laurie then said that when Max ultimately revealed who he was, she didn't believe it, and went to various mediums to ask whether they could confirm anything about her experience. Laurie claimed that she had told these mediums nothing about her conversations with a famous deceased scientist. Yet, according to her account, at least four separate mediums reported hearing the name Max or Maxwell, seeing a well-known scientist from the 1800s, and so forth.

Of course, while there have been many such claims, none have ever been verified or even explored scientifically. Still, I was intrigued enough to want an opinion from my enthusiastic but skeptical research partner, Linda. I telephoned her on the spot.

What happened next proved to be a turning point.

## THE FIVE WORDS THAT CHANGED MY LIFE

When Linda answered, I told her something "interesting" was taking place and asked her not to say anything, just to listen. I then handed the phone to Laurie, who immediately said, "I'm receiving communication from your father. He wants me to tell you, 'Thank you for the music.' "

"Thank you for the music?" I said to myself. "What could that possibly mean?"

I later learned that at the moment Linda heard these words, she collapsed into the chair. Those five words echoed in her heart and throughout her entire being. Simply put, she was shocked to the core.

Upon my return home, the enormous meaning of "Thank you for the music" was explained.

This is Linda's story: In May 1990, her father had been on a ventilator in a hospital intensive care unit. Though the doctors were certain he was unconscious of his surroundings, Linda was determined to do anything that might help. She brought in a pillow speaker and tape recorder, and softly played specially recorded tape cassettes for her father. Only the friend who prepared the tapes, Linda's mother and sisters, the doctors, and a few nurses knew that Linda played him this music during the last five weeks of her father's life.

So the words "Thank you for the music" had a dramatic impact on Linda. No longer just a scientist on a quest, she had been reminded that she was her father's daughter, and this was where her quest had begun. With just those five simple words, Laurie had brought Linda back to the most painful time in her life, when her father lay dying.

So, how had Laurie been able to provide this specific information?

Did she somehow find this out ahead of time? If my psychiatrist friend had told Laurie who he was bringing over to meet her, she might have looked up some information about me and perhaps even about Linda. But to have found out in a short time about the connection between music and Linda's father seemed unlikely—so few people had ever been aware of it. Obtaining that information by trickery appeared next to impossible.

Had Laurie read my mind? That was clearly impossible, too, because I didn't hear the story of the music until I returned home.

Had she read Linda's mind, a thousand miles away, immediately upon receiving the phone? If you believe in mind-reading, that might seem plausible . . . except that Linda assured me the music connection to her father was not part of any conscious thought. She had not been thinking about this unique aspect of her past history.

Perhaps it was just a lucky guess. In theory, that's possible. But is it likely? Of all the millions of guesses Laurie might have made, the odds of a stab-in-the-dark striking home about something this unusual were clearly stacked against her.

The experience suggested numerous intriguing possibilities.

Laurie deeply cared about science and was willing to collaborate in any kind of serious research on mediumship. The ball was in our court—or, more precisely, in our laboratory.

Could we devise a way to test whether or not Laurie was for real? Could we establish whether or not she was knowingly or unknowingly cheating?

In the process, could we also figure out a way to test whether Susy Smith had earned the right to be believed?

The human mind works along curious and unexpected avenues; this is the nature of all creativity. As Linda and I discussed how to proceed, an experiment suggested itself. The probability that it would succeed, however, seemed slim at best.

We would work with both Susy and Laurie, and each of them independently would attempt to contact the same dead people. If such a thing as contacting the dead were really possible, then the experiment would also require that the deceased people be willing to participate.

Here we were, still at the very beginning of research into this strange field, and already we seemed to be departing from anything that almost any established scientist would consider worthy of investigating.

The experiment we devised would be like a three-legged stool: one leg each for Susy, Laurie, and the dead people.

If any one leg of the experiment was in error, the stool would topple and the experiment would fail. The only way the stool could remain standing was if all three legs were in place and strong. The stool might wobble, but it must remain standing.

This was clearly a high-risk experiment, one that might damage our reputations in science if it were to become widely known. Yet we had to give it a try.

# · 4 ·

# Here-to-There-and-Back-Again

Our three-legged stool experiment was conducted a few months later, on a Saturday and Sunday in February 1998.

In advance, Susy had attempted to establish contact with four deceased people and make them aware of our interest in having them participate. The four were Susy's mother, Betty Smith; Linda's father, Henry Russek; my father, Howard Schwartz; and Professor William James. Susy asked each of the four departed people to suggest a picture that she could draw for them. She then drew four separate pictures with colored pencils, supposedly representing the preferences of each of the four people. And she also drew one additional picture, as a control.

She then placed the five pictures in an envelope, which she sealed. At this point, Susy alone knew the subject of the paintings and which of the departed was associated with each.

Laurie had flown to Tucson accompanied by Don Watson, the psychiatrist and neuroscientist who had originally introduced her to us. In our home, Laurie sat on a couch facing Linda and me, with a videotape camera recording her throughout the session. The experiment began about 1:30 in the afternoon. In two videotaped sessions, Laurie attempted to contact each of the deceased individuals and receive specific information about the pictures that Susy had drawn for them, and also attempted to get information about the control picture that Susy had drawn for herself. She wrote down what she received, and I also recorded notes about the form and color of each picture, based on the information she was receiving, though of course I had no idea whether any of it was accurate.

I couldn't help wondering whether she was getting good information. But I would have to be patient.

If Laurie correctly identified the control picture, this might imply that she was receiving the information through "remote viewing" of Susy's apartment, reading Susy's mind long distance, or some other extraordinary paranormal process (sometimes called super psi).

## Picturing the Results

After the sessions, Susy was brought to our home to join the rest of the participants, and the two mediums met in person for the very first time.

In the presence of two video cameras, Susy opened the sealed envelope and showed us the five pictures. We then individually attempted to guess which picture we reasonably thought Susy might have drawn for each of the people, and which for herself. This step was to provide a control; since none of us knew which of Laurie's answers were right and which wrong, we all took part, including Laurie.

Then we went through the pictures a second time, each of us individually using the summary information I had prepared of Laurie's readings. This was the key step, intended to evaluate whether Laurie had been in any degree successful in describing the pictures Susy had drawn, and associating them with the correct person.

In the control reading, Laurie, relying only on her own reasoning and guesswork, got one out of five correct—exactly what the laws of probability predict: given five pictures and five names, statistically there is a one in five chance of guessing one picture correctly. Don, Linda, and I, on the average, got the same result. I got one correct, Linda got zero, and Don got two. Clearly, using our own reasoning, we could not guess above chance the identity of the person who had requested a specific picture be drawn.

In the second evaluation, in which we matched pictures with people based on the information Laurie provided from her readings, the results were startlingly different.

Laurie herself got all five right. So did Linda. So did Don. So did I.

The combined probability of getting five out of five in four tries is less than one in a thousand.

As impressive as the raw numbers are, they do not convey the stunning quality of the content that Laurie received during these sessions. Laurie "saw in her mind" Susy's control picture clearly and vividly as "purple, and green, many circles and shapes, possibly a vase of flowers, a 'rainbow' of flowers."

It turned out that only one painting was a striking, colorful bouquet of multishaped flowers in a purple vase. This was the picture Susy drew for herself. Even Laurie was shocked by the clarity of her vision of the control picture.

Now, if Laurie *was* in contact with the dead, it clearly wasn't the only thing going on. I was struck by what Laurie experienced when she tried to connect with Susy to get the information about her picture. She reported seeing a living room with a couch, and a wall opposite it with paintings, and a chair to the left, and something that drew Susy's attention to the right.

It turned out that the layout of the furniture "seen" remotely by Laurie precisely matched the actual layout of Susy's apartment; the item drawing attention on the right was a television set. (Could she have gotten the layout of Susy's apartment telepathically by reading Linda's mind or mine? Yes . . . but neither of us was consciously aware of the paintings Laurie accurately described on Susy's walls.)

## ANOTHER EXPLANATION?

The question then arises: Can *all* the data of this experiment be explained by remote viewing, or by telepathy with the living? Was Laurie just being psychic, or was she also being a medium and talking to dead people as well?

It was intriguing to me that Laurie's attempts to receive information we wanted from the dead had been complicated by a flood of information that we had *not* requested. Moreover, the personalities and intentions of the dead people seemed to interfere with Laurie's ability to get the pertinent information about the pictures.

We were frankly not interested at the time in hearing from Betty, Susy's mother, about how much she loved her daughter. And we did not ask for images about where Susy grew up as a child. However, Laurie reported seeing a farmlike house with a cow in the back yard, plus a flower and vegetable garden.

Still, some of this extraneous information proved highly interesting. When the experiment was completed, and Laurie and Susy had a chance to talk, Susy told us that she had not lived in a farmhouse, but there had been a cow in her back yard at one time, and her mother did have a flower and vegetable garden.

Though trying to concentrate on images for her pictures, Laurie reported that she had been flooded with other information, wildly diverse and varied. Among the pieces: My mother insisting on coming along as an "uninvited guest" and expressing concern that my brother was pondering a major change in his life (news to me, but confirmed when I called him). Linda's father expressing concern that his wife was depressed and secretly crying in their bedroom in Boca Raton (information later confirmed.)

The dramatically emotional scenes this created in my mind would remain with me as one of the most vivid in the entire series of experiments.

Something more than remote viewing or telepathy seemed to be going on. Not only was Laurie accurate about each of the respective pictures, but she also appeared to have received selective, meaningful, and unrequested information from each of the deceased, some of which we were able to verify as correct.

Certainly there are magicians who engage in fake mediumship, and there are mediums who use cold reading.

Could any of that have been going on here?

Absolutely. Frauds with any skill at all could pull the wool over our eyes, probably without half trying. Within months of this reading, we would create an informal Magicians' Advisory Committee so that we could have professionals in the field examine our experimental design and conduct of the research to uncover possible sources of cheating or deception—from the mediums, from the sitters, or even, inadvertently, from us, the experimenters.

Without scientific integrity, all of this is worthless. It's that simple. Even though this was a carefully designed double-blind experiment (both Laurie, the medium, and we, the experimenters, were blind to the content and identity of the pictures), the possibility of clever fraud needed to be considered and ruled out.

## WHERE DOES THE INFORMATION COME FROM?

One issue this experiment confirmed is the difficulty of distinguishing exactly where all this fascinating information is coming from.

If it's reasonable to conjecture that communicating with the dead is possible, then it must also be reasonable to conjecture that mind-reading is possible. Perhaps mediums like Laurie are doing nothing more than reading minds, retrieving memories from the physically living. Or reading the mind of the deceased. Or some combination of the two.

Though this question is difficult to address scientifically, it's not impossible to bring into the laboratory. Linda and I designed another experiment with Laurie to pursue the question.

It worked like this: I, as the experimenter, created a list of twelve names—six deceased people and six living—and wrote each name on an index card. Some of the people I knew personally (for example, my mother and father), and some I had never met (for example, Linda's father and William James). Laurie was not told ahead of time whose names had been selected, and Linda, as well, was "blind" to the names. This is called a single-blind experiment: the information was kept secret from the medium and everyone else but was known to the experimenter.

When all was ready, I randomly picked one card, looked at the name, and then imagined the person, who might be one of the living or one of the deceased. For example, when I pulled the card for Linda's father, I focused my thoughts on the loving qualities that Linda had told me about Henry.

After imagining the person for a few minutes, I would ask Laurie to tell me if the person I was imagining was male or female, young or old, living or dead. Laurie's task was to try to "read my mind" and get this specific information.

Without giving any indication of whether her responses were correct, I would then silently invite the person to attempt to communicate with Laurie, and she would write down whatever impressions she received.

We hypothesized that the living subjects would not be aware of Laurie's attempts to communicate with them, and therefore they would be unlikely to "communicate" with her. So we expected she would receive more information from the deceased people than from the living.

I also assumed that Laurie would do poorly on the telepathy part, attempting to determine the sex, and so forth. As usual, I was wrong.

In the telepathy attempts, Laurie was 100 percent accurate for sensing the sex, living status, and age category (young, middle-aged, or old) of the twelve people. A perfect score, not a single error. Dazzling.

This is the kind of data so prized by skeptics: binary data, meaning that each answer is either entirely right or entirely wrong; there are no shades of gray, no judgements involved in assessing the degree of correctness. Although the controls were less precise than we would use in later experiments, I still thought this result impressive and significant.

Some of the information Laurie received when attempting to communicate with the dead was, if you'll excuse the expression, dead on target. One example: when I came to the card bearing the name of Linda's father, in the communications period, she said, "This person feels very close to you, like a member of your family." Moments later, she went on with, "He's correcting me, not a member of your family. He's telling me he's not your father, he's Linda's father."

After the session had ended, I asked Laurie if she had ever been corrected by a dead person before. The response was unexpected: "It happens a lot," she said.

## A FIELD FRAUGHT WITH FRAUD

Stories reached us from several sources about a young Asian-American girl, living in Los Angeles, who had the ability to discern what was written on a folded, sealed piece of paper. Studies over seven years, beginning when the child was only nine years old, had led to reports in various journals in mainland China confirming her abilities. Other studies, including one from medium-skeptic James Randi, had cast doubts on the claims.

In early 2000, Linda and I were to have an opportunity of running tests on the young woman, then aged seventeen, in front of a group of scientists from Taiwan, Beijing, San Francisco, and Toronto. The procedure called for writing a group of random alphabet letters and numbers from 0 to 100 on a piece of paper, folding the paper several times to insure that the writing could not be seen, and then enclosing the paper inside an opaque cloth bag. We had agreed to follow the procedure used with her in experiments in Taiwan, in which the bag is tied to her elbow and she is allowed to feel the paper inside the bag with her other hand.

Our first set of experiments appeared to confirm the claims. But there were a few aspects of the tests that raised doubts about what was really going on. We designed a new protocol with more rigorous protections, and tried again.

That second set of tests was never finished. We cancelled the experiment part way through, after Lonnie Nelson, one of my Ph.D. students, discovered traces of blue lint under the Scotch tape used to seal the papers, showing that the tapes had been lifted to permit the paper to be opened inside the bag, and then the tapes re-sealed. Careful examination of the videotapes confirmed our suspicions: the young woman had developed skillfully deceptive techniques that allowed her to steal a glimpse of the paper.

We advised the girl and her mother that we would be interested in conducting further experiments with her, but only under conditions that we would dictate—in particular, that the girl's hands would have to remain in full sight at all times, and that a barrier would be used to prevent her from seeing her hands or the paper. Those conditions were apparently unacceptable, and we never conducted further experiments with the girl.

I later provided written documentation of our findings to James Randi's attorney for his use in defending Randi in a lawsuit filed by the young woman's family. I have not often agreed with Randi, but when he's right, I have and will continue to speak up for him. Yet this occasion would, so far, prove to be one of the few times we found ourselves in the same camp.

## Next Steps

That fraud-detection work with the purported Chinese child psychic would remind us—if we needed reminding—of the need to remain skeptical and suspicious and to be cautious about accepting "evidence" from other people, regardless of their credentials.

All of that was still in our future. In 1998, following the apparent success of the experiments with Susy and Laurie, we were faced with accepting that the results, though impressive, didn't prove very much scientifically. The arrangements were informal, and there was no screen between Laurie and me, so she could have been reading my facial expressions or watching, even unconsciously, for other similar clues. Though we remained alert for any deception, it was, from a scientific viewpoint, not very rigorous in its controls.

Yet, taken all together, our experiments to this point had revealed surprising data that were consistent with the hypothesis of survival of consciousness after death.

We now knew that it was possible, in principle, to conduct systematic laboratory research on this subject that fascinated us. We were intrigued and tantalized, eager for what would come next. But we had yet to conceive an experiment that would truly move us forward.

An answer was not long in coming.

# PART II

# The HBO Dream-Team Experiment

# · 5 ·

# What a Difference a Dinner Can Make

<br>

When Professor William James wrote that "In order to disprove the law that all crows are black, it is enough to find one white crow," he set a guideline for researchers through the ages.

In our studies so far, Laurie seemed to be a significant white crow, and it looked as if Susy was a white crow, as well—albeit an elderly one.

Following James, we reasoned that if there were two white crows, there probably were at least a few more. We needed to find some. Given Susy's advanced age and ill health, her ability to participate in laboratory research would be limited. How could we find mediums with integrity who would be willing to collaborate on research in a serious university laboratory? Place an ad in the employment section of the newspaper?

We didn't have long to wait for an answer. It dropped into our laps not much later, quite unexpectedly. What it represented was like a quantum leap in our research, as if we had by great good fortune leapfrogged past a year or two of methodically evolving our experiments and suddenly, dramatically, landed on the verge of an experiment that, the day before, we couldn't even have imagined.

It all began with a phone call from a television producer named Lisa Jackson, of Lucky Duck Productions. Sounds like a joke, but it really is the name of a prominent television production company, started by award-winning former network journalist Linda Ellerbee.

I was curious but suspicious, hopeful that there might be a real interest in doing a serious documentary on our subject, and reassured by hearing of the documentaries on other sensitive topics that Lucky Duck had been doing.

The company's initial research had led it to Patricia Kubis, who had written on communicating with the dead. Patricia knew of our work through our friend and hers, psychiatrist Don Watson, and had passed our names along to Lucky Duck.

Lisa flew in to meet with us and discuss the project she had in mind, over dinner at the elegant Ventana Canyon Resort. With a striking view of Tucson and the nearby mountains as background, Lisa explained that Lucky Duck was planning to do a serious documentary for HBO on the survival of consciousness question.

Following a meeting in Phoenix with Dr. Elisabeth Kubler-Ross (best known as the author of the bestseller *Death and Dying*), who agreed to be interviewed for the program, Lisa had come directly on to Tucson. And she had already spoken with various well-known mediums, including George Anderson, John Edward, Rev. Anne Gehman, Suzane Northrop, and James Van Praagh, about participating in the show. John, Suzane, and James were particularly reluctant to participate.

Mediums have been burned often by the press, and all five on her list had experienced the heat intimately. As a group, they know that the press tends to be every bit as skeptical about what they do as reputable scientists are. Could these mediums be convinced that our experiments would be fair and unbiased? Could they trust Lisa to present their stories fairly? Could they trust that if they succeeded in giving highly successful readings, the experimenters or the television producers would not make it look as if they had instead been engaged in stage magic or outright fraud?

I was concerned, as well. If the mediums were dismissed as

charlatans, then, by inference, our research would be considered stage magic instead of science. We had to find a way to prevent the worst of all possible worlds: conducting an experiment that achieved highly accurate readings but being treated as outright frauds.

To prevent this from happening, which would create a roadblock to all our future research in this area, Linda and I shaped a plan on the spot and offered it to Lisa over the dinner table. I asked, "If you're really interested in exploring the science, and you have access to superstar mediums, why don't you invite them to come to the University of Arizona. We'll set up a multimedium/multisitter research experiment." I pointed out that it would be a first-time-ever event.

Lisa agreed. Linda and I would invite the mediums to participate in a genuine scientific experiment in our laboratory and would assure them of our remaining open to the possibility that what they were doing was real. To overcome resistance as a result of any bad experiences with the media, skeptics, or other research attempts, we would invite them to help design the experiment with us. That way they could be reassured we were seriously taking their perceptions and experiences into account.

The entire experiment, from beginning to end, would be professionally filmed and available for viewing by the scientific community, the press, and the public. In a word, we proposed that Lisa and the Human Energy Systems Laboratory should "let the data speak, whatever it says."

Linda and I felt personally ready to telephone these superstar mediums and invite them to collaborate in the scientific process. Though Lisa had access to these mediums, and HBO had the funds to bring them to Tucson, it would be up to Linda and me to convince them to take part.

Our dinner that night was another turning point in our research.

Ever since, I've thought of Lisa's company affectionately as "White Crows Productions."

## ROUNDING UP SOME RELUCTANT MEDIUMS

As a rule, mediums—especially famous ones—do not trust scientists any more than they trust the people in the media. They imagine scientists, as a group, to be closed-minded disbelievers who are motivated to show that all mediums are fakes, frauds, or worse.

Of course, that's not surprising. History reminds us that mediumship does not have a solid reputation for integrity, so the doubts shared by virtually all scientists have a strong grounding. Linda and I were raised to believe that mediums were oftentimes unsavory characters and that we should be very careful. We vividly experienced the fear of fraud.

But we had become convinced both Susy and Laurie were doing things that were not fraud, not faked. Here was a potential opportunity to explore the authenticity of famous mediums . . . *if* we could overcome their mistrust and convince them to cooperate.

We prepared a formal proposal for a mediumship experiment, shared our philosophy of research with HBO, and then, with fingers crossed, started contacting the five prominent mediums on the HBO list.

Despite three attempts to reach James Van Praagh by phone, he refused to speak with us about the research. His attitude was understandable yet regrettable, since he was then the best known medium in the United States. But considering his past experiences with unfavorable press coverage, we appreciated his dilemma. Reluctantly, we crossed him off the list. (Later he was to become understanding and supportive of our work.)

George Anderson and Rev. Anne Gehman read the materials we prepared, spoke with Lisa, and agreed to take part.

John Edward and Suzane Northrop were very nervous about HBO, Lucky Duck Productions (I'm sure that name didn't help convince them that the project was serious research and on the level), and even the Human Energy Systems Laboratory. Linda and I spent hours on the phone with each of them, explaining who we were, what convinced us that this particular scientific research would be fair, the history of our research with Susy and Laurie, and provisions in our contract with Lucky Duck that gave us confidence they would live up to our expectations.

We explained that the portion of the documentary that presented the science—our laboratory—would have to be previewed and approved by us for accuracy and clarity. This procedure is rarely allowed in video journalism, but Lisa complied, partly because we otherwise would not have taken part, and partly because she really wanted to present the facts accurately and fairly. (In the end, the science segment of the documentary would be revised three times by Linda and me, yielding a final version that was an honest representation of the findings.)

We also explained to the mediums that the raw data of the actual mediumship sessions would become the property of the University of Arizona, not of Lucky Duck or HBO. The videotapes would capture the raw data, collected first and foremost for scientific reasons. And the raw data had to be available for concise scoring. It also had to be available for anyone to see.

These assurances, though essential, were not sufficient to convince John and Suzane to join the team and the documentary. They wanted to know if we would listen to them, respect them, and work with them as experienced professionals. Were we going to treat them like weird mice in a maze, and design unfair research that would end up throwing out the mice with the bathwater? Or would we invite their active collaboration and be willing to change our minds based on their suggestions?

So we shared with them our favorite way of describing our expectations from mediums.

## CONVINCING THE MEDIUMS WITH OUR MICHAEL JORDAN METAPHOR

Following a sports metaphor we had learned from Dean Radin's seminal book *The Conscious Universe,* we explained to John and Suzane that superstar mediums can be likened to the superstar basketball player Michael Jordan, considered by many to be the best basketball player ever to grace the game.

"Can you guess," we asked the mediums, "how accurate Michael Jordan was, on the average, in making shots from the floor?" Many people suppose his success rate was somewhere around 90 percent. In fact, Jordan's accuracy was only about 45 percent. In a great game, he might put 60 to 70 percent of his shots in the basket, but on many a bad night, he got 20 percent or less.

So how can someone who, on average, misses more than half of his shots, be a superstar? The answer is very simple. He need only be better than everyone else.

The same logic, we proposed to John and Suzane, applies to what Linda and I think of as the Michael Jordans of mediumship. Mediums need not be perfect. Quite the opposite. They can even miss more than 50 percent of their shots. Like Michael Jordan, they can have great success on some tries, and do poorly on others. They can have good days and bad days. To qualify as a superstar, all they need to do is, on the average, be statistically more accurate than guesswork, and better than everyone else.

This metaphor revealed to John and Suzane that we were not expecting them to be perfect. Quite the contrary. We understood, both theoretically and practically, how difficult the "game" of mediumship is—that if they are indeed communicating with the dead, there might well be all kinds of interference, weak signals, and perhaps difficulties we cannot even imagine in receiving the messages. We understood that superstars don't always perform at their best, and may from time to time have a string of hits and then a string of misses. It comes with the territory. Even superstar models have bad hair days.

Another thing—fans know that Michael Jordan produces "dazzle shots" every now and again. He will be at half court, falling down, and with his left hand, through a sea of arms, somehow connect and make the seemingly impossible shot.

We recognized that the same thing might be true with the stars of mediumship—every now and again they just might dazzle us by making seemingly impossible connections, just as we had already seen Laurie do.

John and Suzane liked the Michael Jordan metaphor. However, being tough New Yorkers, they were interested in more than just philosophy. They wanted to see whether we would practice what we preached, whether we would walk the talk.

We spoke with them several more times. Finally they offered to figuratively shake hands. We had a deal.

## THE PERPLEXING SEARCH FOR A SITTER

A few weeks before the filming was scheduled, Lisa Jackson called to say that they had found a subject for the experiment—what we term a sitter. The person's identity would remain known only to the production company until the time of the experiment, as a protection against any possible fraud. We would not be in a position to sneak the information to the mediums.

Of course, the same concern was at play in the opposite direction: we needed to be absolutely sure we could rule out with assurance any sort of collusion between Lucky Duck and the mediums, certain they were not slipping the sitter's name to the mediums behind our backs. So I insisted on another sitter, as well—someone who would be known only to Linda and me, not revealed to Lucky Duck and certainly not revealed to the mediums. If Lucky Duck wanted to be certain there was no collusion taking place, we, as scientists—whose reputations were on the line—were at least as eager. They had one production to contend with; we, on the other hand, knew that if the science was not reported accurately, our peers around the country would think we had lost all perspective, and our careers would be at stake.

So we were all carefully monitoring the situation and one another.

Now our problem was how to go about finding a sitter who met the profile Linda and I had agreed on with the mediums—someone who had had very close relationships with people now dead. Somewhat arbitrarily, we set the requirement of at least six deaths of closely related people within the last ten years. And the candidate would have to be willing not only to take part in the experiment but also to keep it secret from everyone, including the media.

Again we laughed at the idea of placing an ad in the newspaper. "People with six deceased loved ones wanted for an experiment on mediumship to be aired on national television." Hardly.

A week before the experiment, we still hadn't figured out how to find somebody who fit this difficult profile.

While we were pondering the last possible avenues to somehow locate this missing someone, Linda sent me on an errand to buy a piece of equipment for the laboratory—not some exotic item of scientific paraphernalia, but merely a washer/dryer.

At the store, as I talked wash cycles and load capacities with the saleswoman, she spontaneously shared with me that she was feeling sad because she had just returned from visiting her mother's grave in Phoenix.

As I do whenever possible, even with strangers, I listened to her story. It wasn't long before she moved on to talk about several other people in her life who had died. When the number reached four, I began listening with rapt attention, practically holding my breath. When she started telling about number six, I took a deep breath and broached the subject.

Though she had never considered seeing a medium, she turned out to be curious about the upcoming research and willing to take part, as long as we could arrange a schedule that wouldn't conflict with her working hours.

So less than one week before the filming, an appliance saleswoman named Ronnie Nathanson had sold a washer/dryer, and we had gained our sitter.

We were now ready for the experiment.

## ARRANGEMENTS

The complex integration of research and filming began the day before the mediums were to arrive. We made sure that everything was in its place in our new laboratory space, a recently acquired small house that had been tenderly landscaped, painted, and refurbished, the funds coming from nationally famous Canyon Ranch spa and resort and from an anonymous donor.

But the careful and peaceful design of our laboratory turned out not to matter once HBO's five-person team arrived: producer Lisa Jackson, two camera operators, a soundman, and a production assistant. As, I guess, movie and TV crews do everywhere they go, these folks rapidly altered the space to fit their needs. Cables, lamps, cameras, amplifiers, microphones, stands, and tripods were placed in various rooms of the laboratory, with our furniture rearranged to suit their requirements. Though everything looked organized and matter-of-fact when the documentary aired, the setting was neither neat nor peaceful when the research was actually being performed.

Through our many phone conversations with John Edward and Suzane Northrop, we knew they were tough New Yorkers who genuinely cared about their profession and recognized the essential role science could play in validating their work. We were told that George Anderson was an unusually sensitive person who often avoided social situations. We knew almost nothing about Anne Gehman, save for the fact that she was mature and sophisticated, and a minister. While we had come to know Laurie Campbell well through our prior research, we had to soothe her fears about working alongside these superstar mediums who might well view her as just an unknown housewife.

We expected some personality clashes. Unfortunately, those expectations were met. The mediums were often competitive with one another. But we were determined to foster a successful working relationship among these five very talented people—putting them together at meals and other occasions, hoping they would get to know and respect each other. We wanted to create an environment that would allow them to leave their egos at the door, so to speak, so that they could bridge their personal differences and become, as Lisa Jackson called them, the Dream Team.

## THE SITTERS PROVIDE DETAILS OF THEIR DEAD LOVED ONES

February 19, 1999, the day before filming. That morning, with the mediums en route to Tucson, the two sitters came to the lab for instructions. Joining our local sitter was Lisa Jackson's choice, Patricia Price, a schoolteacher who lived about two hours' drive from Tuscon.

Although we would later become more rigorous in our precautions, at this early stage of the work we were willing to accept the earnest assurances from Patricia and Ronnie that neither had ever had any contact with our selected mediums—had never communicated with them or been contacted by them. They gave their assurances, appeared sincere and truthful, and we accepted them at face value. In retrospect, the trust was well placed; we never encountered any evidence to contradict their assertions. Even so, as scientists, we would add appropriate safeguards to later experiments.

I met with the sitters one at a time and gave them instructions on filling out a detailed questionnaire we had prepared, asking for exact information on the history and death of each person they expected or hoped might "visit" during the experiment. These were sealed and stored safely.

For obvious reasons, none of us—not Linda or me, not any of our staff people, not any of the film crew, and certainly not the mediums—was allowed access to these documents.

## THE NIGHT BEFORE

The night before the HBO experiment was anything but restful.

Linda and I had never been as nervous in the face of an upcoming experiment as we were then. The only thing we knew with certainty, beyond our efforts to create a well-designed and fair study, was that whatever the results were, our lives would not ever be the same again.

The stakes were high, regardless of what the data showed. We weighed the various possible outcomes.

If the results proved to be negative, my conservative scientific colleagues would be smug and reassured, and my academic career would be secure. But then we'd have to deal with unhappy mediums (to put it mildly), an HBO production company with a stack of bills and a truckload of useless footage, and a large contingent of disappointed enthusiasts. Linda and I knew we could handle their pain. Both trained in clinical psychology, we had plenty of experience dealing with emotionally distressed people—though we had ordinarily encountered them walking through the door as patients, not as angry, disappointed participants in an experiment!

As for our own disappointment, we reminded each other of a favorite quote we shared. In his 1998 book *Skeptics and True Believers,* Chet Raymo, a physicist, wrote that one must "choose truth rather than peace of mind"—which, if the experiment turned sour, would be an excellent motto for Linda and me.

On the other hand, if the results turned out to be positive, I knew that some of my scientific colleagues would be suspicious and quick to question my intelligence and integrity. I feared that some of them would make my academic life difficult if not precarious.

Would that be enough to balance a group of happy mediums who would finally feel vindicated, the people of Lucky Duck Productions and HBO who would have the makings of the show they had envisioned, and, hopefully, an enthusiastic public when the show aired?

A lot of uncertainties, a lot of ways we could be disappointed, or worse. Yet, we went to bed knowing that we would wake up in a few hours to face the most exciting experiment of our lives.

## Setting the Stage

Saturday, February 20. We arrived at the lab about 8 A.M. to find the HBO crew already setting up.

As the mediums arrived they were escorted to the fenced-in back courtyard of the lab. This would keep them separated from the two sitters at all times, save for the readings. They would also be under constant observation by Linda and another staff member, Carolyn, to insure that there was no exchange of information between them.

The sitters had two places where they could relax between sessions: the lab's living room at the front of the house, or our private "laboratory on wheels," a thirty-six-foot research motor home parked in the driveway.

Before each session, the sitter was prepared in a separate research room for the electroencephalogram with an electrode cap and for the electrocardiogram with arm electrodes, so we could monitor for the same kind of heartbeat-to-brain wave effects we had observed in those earlier energy cardiology studies.

When the testing was to begin, the first sitter, Patricia, was escorted into the experimental room, where she was seated in a chair behind a large white opaque cloth screen. The other chair would soon be occupied by the medium. I then connected the lines from Pat's electrodes to the computers that would record her brain waves and electrocardiogram.

Meanwhile the first medium, Suzane Northrop, was being brought from the courtyard into the separate room, where she received the same hookups. Then she was brought into the experimental room, seated in the medium's chair, and her leads also attached to the computer. At this point, the medium and the sitter were essentially sitting side by side in front of HBO's cameras, but unable to see each other because of the screen between them.

The medium was allowed to offer a brief verbal welcome, but the sitter was instructed to give no response beyond a simple "Hello" or the like. Then we instructed both subjects to sit quietly with their eyes closed for two minutes, which allowed me to collect what is called a resting baseline on the brain wave and electrocardiogram readings.

Sitting at the side of the room, I was monitoring the two computers, one recording the brain and heart of the medium as well as the sitter's heart, the other recording the opposite: the sitter's brain and heart and the medium's heart. And having given myself the job of monitoring the computers, I was about to have the opportunity of witnessing firsthand what no scientist had ever witnessed before: sequential readings made by purported superstar mediums of two separate research sitters.

I was impatient for the first session to get rolling.

# Mediums Read While Cameras Roll: The Patricia Readings

---

## WITH SUZANE NORTHROP

Medium Suzane and sitter Pat were comfortably seated, adjustments were made to the lighting, and water was placed nearby. And the cameras began to roll. After the two-minute resting baseline, the medium and sitter opened their eyes, ready to begin. During the next ten to twenty minutes, the medium was instructed to conduct a typical reading but with two exceptions: that no eye contact would be possible, because of the screen placed between them, and that only yes/no questions and responses would be allowed, to reduce the possibility of the kind of guesswork and feedback that psychic magicians rely on in their cold reading sessions.

Suzane's reading began simply enough. She asked Pat, matter-of-factly:

> *Have you ever done this before?*
> Pat answered, "No."

After a few basic instructions, what happened next happened very fast, and Pat and I were both dazzled. Suzane asked a simple question—one of only five questions she asked during the entire reading.

*I have to tell you just very, very, very fast here,
I'm getting a couple of people around you very, very
strong. Your papa's gone, please? Your papa?*

Yes.

*You and your papa were very, very, very close.
He shows me a watch, it is passed down, must have
been passed down to a brother because he keeps giving me brother. . . .*

*Father's been gone some time, they tell me, Pa-
tricia. And I don't know why, but your father gave
you your name, 'cause he says, "I gave her my
name, I gave her my name." Or "I gave her a
name connected to me." Feels like he's been gone a
long time, feels like your father passed very very
fast.*

*Your father also wore hats. He's got a hat on
today. He's actually quite a cute man, and your father smoked. I don't know if that's what he passed
from, but he shows me the center of his chest.*

As I sat there hearing this uninterrupted barrage of information, I asked myself if these could be guesses. Would they apply
equally as well to others? Certainly not to me; I estimated that
maybe 20 percent of the information applied to my family. My father was long deceased, true, but nothing else fit.

However, for Pat, virtually all the information, I would
learn, was accurate. Especially important and specific to her was
that her father had given her his name, he wore hats, and he
smoked.

*I want to quickly ask you this, please. He's telling
me something. Did he meet your husband, may I
ask, Patricia?*

I thought the question was obvious, almost pointless. Yes, in most families, the bride's father certainly meets the man she marries. But Patricia's wordless reaction showed that the answer was not a simple Yes or No; to her, it had a very poignant significance.

After the reading, she described a scene at her wedding: "Even though he had passed in 1960 and I was married in 1969, my father appeared when I was walking down the aisle." So—did her father meet her husband? She believes he did . . . but not in life.

*Is your mama still here, please?*

No.

*Okay. The woman had cancer. She shows me cancer. She shows it to me in the female area of her, would you understand this? And there's somebody connected to her with an M name, I don't know if that's her or her side of the family. 'Cause it sounds like I didn't know what, Mark or Merrit or something to that effect. They also give me an A name. I don't know if it's first or middle. But that's how they gave it to me.*

*Now I have to ask you this, please. Three. There must have been three children, or something. She's showing me three children, very, very strong. I don't know if you're one of three, but that's what she's giving me. . . .*

Later scoring would show that this information, too, was about 80 percent accurate.

*When I sat down with you, I heard a couple of their names, I didn't honestly quite know what to do with them. I heard a male with a D name. I want to say something more like Donald and Danny, but it*

*had decent N's in it. And I also heard an L name; it
really sounded like Lin or Linda. Very, very strong.*

Many people have difficulty thinking that our pets might be with
us after death, but mentions of pets show up repeatedly in the
readings.

> *There now is a dog who walked into the room. Oh,
> it was Mother's and Papa's dog. They gave me the
> dog that walked into the room. And dog was very,
> very connected to them, that's what they give me. . . .*
> *I have to ask this, please, did mama lose a sister,
> please?*

> Yes.

> *When you sat down, there also was a young boy
> who passed. The young boy who passed was a
> tremendous upset in the family, tremendous upset in
> the family.*
> *It feels like it's a long time ago, Patricia, I almost
> want to say I don't think it's your son, I have to say
> it feels like it's connected somehow to your mother.
> So I don't know if that's your brother or it's her
> brother, but it was a younger man, it was a tremen-
> dous, tremendous upset in the family.*

That part would prove wrong; not anyone's brother, but Pat's
deceased son.

> *He had a quick passing, it was some kind of a
> freak accident, a freak accident they tell me.*
> *And they said to me that this was a tremendous
> disturbance, and I get a splitting in the family from
> this passing. They show me a splitting of the family.*

The mentions of "quick passing" and "tremendous upset in the family" would come to have a powerful meaning for me in the hours ahead.

> *And somebody, I don't know why on that side, either liked to go to the dances or they had the dances. But this is like, not modern dance, this is more like rural dances. I don't know if they did square or something, but she says to me, "We like that on that side of the family," she tells me quite, quite strong.*
>
> *I have to tell you something. I think that this is her mother, she's definitely a pistol, she must have had false teeth, because she's taking them in and out, in and out. And she's not supposed to do that in front of everybody. . . .*

This was something I missed during the barrage of facts and discovered later in the transcripts. It turned out to be one of my favorite pieces of information obtained by any medium.

Psychic magicians don't like to tell a sitter such peculiar, specific behavior as, "Your grandmother is a pistol, and she's taking her false teeth in and out in public," even though "she's not supposed to do that." I couldn't help laughing at the image. And Pat later acknowledged that, indeed, the description fit her maternal grandmother perfectly.

The first reading was over, but Pat didn't want the session to end quite yet. She had some reactions she wanted to share on camera:

> *Can I say something? Is it okay? They're strong [meaning the statements by the medium] on my mother's side, very, extremely.*
>
> *The dog that you're inquiring to is a little dog by the name of Pee Wee, was a little Chihuahua, lived to*

*be twenty years old and I had to put him to sleep last year . . . The man, his name is Danny. And he, actually, it's Nelson Daniel, but everybody called him Danny . . . The dancing that you're referring to was my mother and her—I learned 'cause of the, my ethnic background, which is Czechoslovakian. She's very dead-on with everything that she said so far.*

Pat was drained, and I was impressed. Yet this was just the beginning. We had a long way to go before the HBO videotaping would finish.

## With John Edward

Though the mediums were being kept under observation so they could not compare notes after their sessions, we were struck by the amount of identical information they came up with—names, personalities, and so on—especially so for John Edward. A medium whose abilities were recognized very early, John as a child continually stunned his family by his knowledge of family history and events that had taken place before he was born.

John's reading proved remarkable. He began simply enough:

*Okay, what's going to happen is they'll be a series of impressions, pictures and words and things that make no sense to me come through in my mind. What I'm going to direct to you in statement form is a question. I'm going to tell you what I'm seeing, hearing, and feeling, and basically ask you to confirm and verify it simply by yes's and no's. Please don't say anything, don't give out any names or anything. Don't elaborate.*

*If I refer to somebody being above you, then I'm talking about somebody who's older, like a parental figure—to me, a father, father-in-law, your grand-*

*father, your uncle, your best friend's father. I'm going to see that as your dad.*

*To your side, that to me would be like a husband or wife, a brother, a sister, husband, or a friend. A brother-in-law, half brother, stepbrother, I'm going to see that as being a male figure to your side. And below you would be children, nieces, nephews, and grandchildren. So think about a family tree. People who are above you are older. People to your side, around the same age, and people below you as younger.*

*Anybody can come through, even people that you don't think might show up. Friends of friends, your friend's relatives, if they see this as an opportunity, they'll take it. I just need you to confirm what you can understand, and what you don't understand, write it down so that we can try to document this for them later. Do you understand that?*

Yes.

And then the information began to flow.

*Okay, the first thing that's coming through is they're telling me to talk about a male figure to your side. A male figure to your side would be a husband or a brother who has crossed over. Do you understand that?*

Yes.

Pat must have been confused, nervous, or overly determined to be cooperative, because she had just suggested her husband was dead, when he was not only very much alive but sitting in a nearby room.

*Okay. Actually, there's two, there's three. There's three. They're showing me . . . one seems to be like a husband figure to you. Do you understand that?*

Yes.

*Okay. And there's like a brother figure to you, and I think either his brother, which would be your brother-in-law. . . . But there's that person that comes through. Do you understand that?*

Yeah.

*Okay. They're telling me to talk about a happy birthday in October, or a celebration around the tenth of a month. Do you understand that?*

Yeah.

*Okay. They're telling me, because I'm seeing a white flower, and a white flower means that. They're telling me to also indicate that, this is your husband that's coming through, I believe, and I be-lieve that there's a mother figure with him who's there. Okay? Do you understand that?*

Yes.

*Okay. Now he's making me feel either his mother passed very young in his life, or that he was absent or distant from her in life, that there might have been some type of emotional disconnect some-how. And I feel like on the other side they were able to reconnect that. Okay? That's what's being shown. Do you understand that?*

Yeah.

*Okay. He's telling me to tell you that he is okay, this is very very important. He's talking about some blackness to the chest, which to me would indicate either lung cancer or emphysema, some type of heavy respiratory problem, filling up with fluids that's connected to one of these people. Do you understand that?*

Yes.

*Okay. He wants me to also confirm to you that he has made a visit to you, and what I classify as being a visit is where somebody comes through to you without a psychic and he's telling me to confirm for you where he came to you, where he was standing in what looks like to me to be the bedroom, where there was a closet door that's open and you had just been smelling his clothes or you were smelling something that connected to him. Does that make sense?*

Oh, yes.

Yes after yes after yes. Whereas Suzane asked only five questions, John asked many questions. However, the number of affirmative answers appeared well above 80 percent. And much of the information was very specific.

John continued talking about what he thought was a deceased male. Yet, apparently without realizing it, he was no longer talking about Patricia's husband, but about her son; these statements made more sense because the son had indeed passed over.

*He's showing me a bouquet of pink roses. Pink roses is their way of expressing their love to you, and he wants me to bring this to you. Now, you do not have the opportunity to talk to him in the way that you wanted to talk to him prior to his passing, correct?*

Right.

*He's telling me it's okay. He wants you to know that it's okay. He's making me feel like that's why he's made it so important for you to know that he's here. Okay? Who's got the D . . . there's a D-N sounding name, like Dennis, Diane, or Dan. Do you understand that?*

Yes.

*Okay. Is that person still here?*

No.

*Okay. That's my mistake. That's their way of acknowledging, like I said earlier, who's coming through. There's a younger male figure also connected to your husband who's crossed over, which either means it's his brother or there's a son who's crossed. But there's a younger male figure. Do you understand that?*

Yeah.

*Okay. And somebody passes that I feel is being like Boom! They go out Boom! There's like a big explosion or there's some type of big boom that happens. Does that make sense?*

Yes.

At the time, I did not understand the significance of "somebody passes . . . like Boom . . . an explosion." It would all become clear soon enough.

John had received names, causes of death, and many other specific facts but never recognized his mistake in thinking Pat's husband was dead. John was confused; Pat was cagey. We would in time discover a possible explanation, but that was still some four months in the future.

## WITH GEORGE ANDERSON

After a short break, Pat began the third session, this time with medium George Anderson. Like John Edward, George had begun to recognize his psychic abilities while still a young child, in this case following an attack of encephalitis at age six. Reserved in manner, he nevertheless is firm in style when doing a reading.

George's instructions were a bit different:

*Whatever I say to you, just acknowledge with Yes, No, or that you understand only. Don't go into the type of details, whatever. Please don't ask me about anyone. Please don't say, "Yes, that's my dad," or anything like that. Just leave it as a simple Yes. Let me do all the talking.*

*Also, who you least expect may show up along with who you hope will. Doesn't matter how close you were to them, how long ago they passed on, or whatever. . . . I just don't want you to make the mistake a lot of people make—for example, I get the name Matilda, and you had a great-aunt Matilda, and you think, "Well, I never really knew her, why would she be here?" And say No to me. That's the worst thing to do. Let it be acknowledged and keep going.*

*Okay, well, first of all a male presence comes around you. Two, as a matter of fact. And it feels like two different generations. Somebody's older, somebody's younger.*

*Now, again, I don't know if they mean this by age or by generation, but they talk about the younger male that passed. Does that make sense to you?*

Yes.

*He states he's family, that's correct?*

Correct.

*This I don't understand. If you do, say Yes, you understand, but don't explain. He speaks about his dad, does that make sense?*

Yes.

*I don't know why yet. I don't know if he's trying to tell me his dad is there or if he's calling to his dad. So don't say anything, I want them to say it.*

*Also, another male presence comes forward to you and says, Dad is here. Is it correct your dad is passed?*

Correct.

*Your dad speaks about the loss of a child. That makes sense?*

Yes.

*Twice?*

Yes.

*'Cause your father says twice. Wait a minute, now he says thrice. He's saying three times. Does that make sense?*

That's correct.

*'Cause your father said, "Once, twice, thrice."*

That's correct.

*It . . . there's talk of the son that passed on. That is correct?*

Yes.

*Okay, he's claiming to be the first male who came in the room. That would make sense?*

Yes.

*Okay. So him and his grandfather are together. Now your son's dad is still on the earth, I take it, yes?*

Yes.

*Wait a minute now. There's talk of loss of another son, is that correct? Wait a minute now. Wait a minute, don't answer yet. Your father speaks about a miscarriage. Is it correct, you did have one?*

Yes.

Later, Pat confessed that not she but her daughter had had a miscarriage, a female child; this fact had been kept secret from her husband at the time.

*There's also talk of loss of a daughter, too. Does that make sense? Possibly another miscarriage?*

No.

*"No." They're saying "Yes." No, he argues with me that it's right. I'm going to leave it go. There's talk of loss of a daughter, but prior to birth. So, I'm leaving it with you that it's either you or somebody immediately close to you. But they insist they're correct, I'm not going to argue with them. We don't have the time, so I'll just leave it with you.*
*Your son claims he passes tragically, yes?*

Yes.

*He also says beyond his control. Do you understand?*

No.

I thought to myself that George was finally making some errors.

*Now, let me leave it with you. He says beyond his control, let me leave it with you, 'cause I don't [know] what he means by it yet. He also claims he's come in dreams; is this true?*

Yes.

*He doesn't like to be challenged, so I'm just gonna say Yes. He also thanks for the memorial. Does that make sense?*

Yes.

A bit later, George again brought up the death of the son.

*It's not your fault.*

Yeah.

*He states, "You have not failed me as a mother, or as a person." So that does make sense. Correct?*

Yeah.

*He tells me he contributes to his passing. Make sense?*

Yes.

*He does take his own life, correct?*

Correct.

A chill ran through my body at this stunning, awful revelation.

*That's why he's apologizing. But he was never really happy being here to begin with, true?*

Very true.

Suzane had spoken of a "quick passing" and a "tremendous upset in the family." John had talked of "a younger male figure" and "some type of big boom," an "explosion." And now George is even more specific.

After the readings, Pat acknowledged that her son had committed suicide by shooting himself in the head. Even this long after the event, recalling that painful moment of Pat's personal revelation sends another shiver through me.

## WITH ANNE GEHMAN

Suzane, John, and George are New Yorkers with a direct and forthright communication style. Anne Gehman is a minister who has lived in the Washington, D.C., area for more than forty years. Her style of communication is warm and descriptive, though her comments in this particular reading were general and often vague. Yet some of her hits were impressive.

She began with no instructions, just a single request:

*Let me just hear your voice.*

Hi, Anne. How are you?

*Fine, thank you.*

*Okay, all right. As I'm tuning myself with you now and I'm beginning to feel the touch of spirit, I see many people around you. I'm particularly conscious of a woman who stands about average height, rather round, full figure as I see her. She has particularly pretty eyes, rather large, wide-set eyes. Highly arched brows. She has a very sweet, very warm smile.*

*Her hair is gray, and it's a little bit wavy around her face, as I see it. A rather soft hairstyle, and I have the impression that she's very close to you from the world of spirit and has been for many years. So I sense that she's been gone for a long time.*

*My sense is that she passed over, having had some problems related to heart and circulation, although I believe there were some other complications sur-rounding her physical condition as well. All right. She's showing me a stroke just at the very end of her life, and I can sense a partial paralysis to her body. But I'm not sure that that was ever determined be-*

*cause it feels as though it was just before she passed over. Can you recognize her?*

Yeah.

With so many "either this or that" statements, and things like a stroke that might not have been recognized, it sounded more like guessing than what I had been hearing from the others. This impression was about to change.

Soon Anne came up with statements that Patricia later described as "deeply meaningful."

*They tell me to tell you that you are never alone. You never walk alone, that they are with you. And the same entity is responsible for the light that often flickers in your house. Is there a light that goes off and on?*

Yes.

I wasn't sure I had heard that correctly. A light that goes on and off?

*Okay, because this same person is responsible for this, this flickering of the lights. And that's one way of getting your attention. And there also occasionally would be a little tapping sound on the wall?*

Yeah.

Lights flickering and tapping on the wall? This was beginning to sound like something out of a grade B parapsychology movie, or maybe a remake of *Gaslight.*

*They want you to feel the reality of that other world and the reality that we are spiritual beings here now, that we're still temporarily in this physi-*

*cal body and no matter how we pass to the other world, in one way it's all the same. We simply leave the physical body and go on to another dimension, where we continue to grow and to unfold. . . .*

*I see a beautiful girl in the spirit world also. And she has, I'm not sure really the color of her hair, but I just see a beautiful golden light that just surrounds her. So beautifully, and it's as though it's also golden around her hair and around her face. And she's just very radiant, very beautiful, very happy to connect with you here in this way today. And she tells me, all right, oh, something about a dog. Something about a dog. Would you understand?*

Yeah.

And I remembered Suzane had also made reference to a dog.

*All right. And I'm not sure what that is, I'm not getting that clearly. But you, as long as you understand, that's all that matters. And tell me, is there, why do I feel drawn to your fingernails? Your fingers, for some . . . ? Your fingers. Okay, your fingers, not your nails. Your fingers. I sense a little irritation in the joints recently. You understand?*

Yes.

Anne had picked up on one of Pat's health issues.

*I see a woman, and she doesn't like for me to call her elderly, although she was well up in years. She's, okay, her mind was always clear and bright and very up with the times, always. She didn't miss a thing in the world around her.*

*And to describe what her physical appearance was, I would say a little taller than average. Later in life, rather full through the abdominal area and the hip area, as if she carried quite a bit of weight here, which contributed somewhat to problems with the lower extremities.*

*And I feel that toward the end of her life there was a weakness in the joints and I don't think she was totally immobile, but I feel there was a stiffness and a painfulness through there with her. But she also had a cough, a lot of coughing. She comes near me, I feel the irritation to the throat and the bronchial area. Can you recognize her from that description?*

Yes.

Pat's mother had died of lung cancer caused by smoking cigarettes.

Four different mediums, four different styles—from the gentle toughness of Suzane to the spiritual softness of Anne. Of greatest interest was the information that overlapped—in particular, the dog, and the tragic death of a son.

## WITH LAURIE CAMPBELL

It was now time for Laurie to do her reading. Realistically considering herself an amateur in this esteemed company, she was on edge. How would her accuracy rank when contrasted with the results of these seasoned, well-established professionals?

After brief preliminaries, Laurie quickly got into the swing.

*Do you have a grandfather in spirit?*

Yes.

*Okay. I will tell you that this person is a very, very strong man. He comes through with a lot of zest, a lot of energy, very strong, started coming through the minute I walked in this room, if that can bring you any comfort, because he's very, very loving, very, very kind person watching over you.*

*I also want to tell you the other thing I got was a dog. I think there's a dog, and I want to tell you that I feel like the dog has wire hair. Does this make sense to you? Yes or no.*

Yes.

Obviously, the information about the grandfather being deceased and loving was pretty general. But the dog coming in again? This was getting very interesting.

*Okay. And I get the feeling it's some type of terrier or terrier mix and I just feel like there's so much love, if I can tell you that, from this dog surrounding you. And he feels like he was, had so much energy when he was here. Is that a . . . do I get a yes on that?*

Yes.

The specific breed was wrong, but the size and personality were accurate.

*Is your mother also passed over?*

Yes.

*Okay, your mother's coming in beautifully. And I'm really thanking these people. . . . Normally it kind of doesn't work this way with me, so I'm very grateful to your family members for coming in. Your mother gives you a lot of love. Was her hair going kind of whitish when she passed over?*

Yes.

*Okay, was it somewhat full? Okay, wait, please don't say anything for a second. She gives me a feeling of a real softness to her hair, that it, it looks full, it doesn't look real, real thin. And so does this description fit?*

Yes.

In fact, the answer was misleading: Pat's mother had full hair when younger, but lost hair toward the end of her life.

*I guess I'm jumping through here really quick but they're just coming in so fast for you with so much love and . . . I also have . . . I want to say . . . do you have a son that passed?*

Yeah.

*. . . I want to slow down a little bit here. I know there's a great deal of emotion from you, and there's a great deal of emotion from him. There's, he wants to say, "Mom, there's so much. . . ." Can I have a tissue? Thank you. There's, wow, so much emotion from your son to you, you must have been just a really, really spectacular mom because he shows. . . . The dog's with him. He wants you to know that the dog's with him. Was he tall?*

Yes.

*And thin?*

Yes.

*Okay. 'Cause I'm getting that [inaudible]. He just keeps saying, "Mom, I love you."*

After more apologies about rushing through things, and about the dog being "rambunctious," she turned to another topic.

*Do you have a very close friend who's passed over recently? A woman with dark hair?*

Yes.

*Was she from the East Coast? From back . . . ? Because it doesn't feel like . . . oh, that's her [inaudible]. It feels more like from the East Coast. Was she from back there, like Florida or somewhere? Back that way? 'Cause she keeps giving a warmth, you know. Yes or no.*

Yes.

*Okay. 'Cause she keeps giving the feeling of, she says you know, of warmth and stuff. And, but she's quite chatty, she's quite chatty. Is it that you talked on the phone a lot?*

Yes.

*Okay, 'cause it feels like that there's distance between the two of you, but still she knows how much you loved her. She's like a sister to you?*

Yes.

*Yeah, 'cause that's what she says. She said you're like her kid sister.*

Yeah.

*Yeah. Oh God, there's so much love, so much love for you. Oh, that's so, so important. She came here to visit? It could be maybe just in spirit, but she gives the thing of visiting so. Mostly she shows me with you on the phone, talking just about daily life. Did she have two sons?*

Yeah.

*Yeah. She sends them love. Lots and lots of love to them.*

Like the other mediums, Laurie made mistakes. Later in the reading, she saw the two boys on the East Coast, though they had moved. She saw Pat's son dying from some kind of what she identified as a "blood disease . . . [a] problem of circulation," but did not figure out that it was suicide by gunshot.

However, like the other mediums before her, she received a pattern of information that most certainly fit Pat. And just as certainly, the information did not fit me, or any of the camera people or the producer.

Would the mediums be able to do as well with our second sitter?

## · 7 ·

# The Ronnie Readings

With her available time growing short, we called on the sitter I had found, saleslady Ronnie Nathanson. She declined to wear a jelled electrode cap, explaining that she didn't want to show up at Sears looking as though she had just gone through a washing machine. I couldn't blame her. (In any case, the brain wave and heart data would turn out to be inconclusive, except to suggest that the mediums were not receiving information by means of telepathy with the sitter.)

But the process of attaching the brain wave and heart electrodes to sitters and mediums was taking longer than I had anticipated. We were way behind schedule, Ronnie would have to leave for work before long, and there was time for only two of the mediums, George Anderson and Suzane Northrop, to work with her. Nonetheless, the results were well worth the effort.

### WITH GEORGE ANDERSON

Except for the introductory comments, this reading is presented in its entirety as an illustration of what can happen when a medium is, so to speak, "in the zone."

*First of all, a female presence comes around you,
and a male. Excuse me, and another female. She
seems to be hanging around you, but doesn't come
forward yet. And another male presence comes
around you. Interesting. There's another male presence, too, that seems to come through, but he seems
to be staying in the background. Somebody . . . somebody just stated, "Dad is here." Does that make
sense?*

Yes.

*Okay. Is it . . . it is correct your dad is passed on?*

Yes.

*Okay, 'cause he claims he's here. He also speaks
of his folks passing on. I'm sure they've passed on,
yes?*

Yes.

*I was gonna say, unless they're 150. So more than
likely they're with him. Just keeps speaking about
his folks being with him. I don't know why, but
your father blesses you for being good to him prior
to his passing. Does that make sense?*

Yes.

Ronnie had taken care of her father before he passed, so this
was a good guess or a solid hit.

*Okay. He knows that you love him and he loves
you. And I don't know why he says that, and it's*

*not my business to. Also, there's talk of a younger male presence around you, that makes sense? I'm gonna say Yes, because he seems to be around your dad, and it seems he's been over there awhile.*

Uh.

*Don't deny, or don't say anything. Just leave it alone. I want them to explain it. Also, a female presence comes up to you and embraces you with love.*

Yes.

*She is family, she states, yes?*

Yes.

*Actually, there's two of them, because another one just did it.*

Yes.

*Okay, 'cause, now don't respond to this yet. Somebody says to me, "Mom is here." Do you understand?*

Yes.

*But I heard it twice, and that's what . . . all right, let's just leave it alone. That's what's confusing me, because I heard it twice. Somebody states, "Mom is here." It is correct your mom is passed on?*

Yes.

*Okay, because she's one of the females that embraces you with love. Your mom draws very close to you, so I take it you and she were close.*

Yes.

*Because mom and daughter, but also good pals.*

Yes.

Ronnie and her mother were truly best friends in life. George appeared to be sensing the depth of their relationship.

*Your mother states she's walking fine. That could either mean she had trouble with the legs or she's back to her old self. So I'll leave it with you. I hope you understand. If she didn't have trouble with the legs, it means she's back to her old self. Your mother also thanks you for being good to her prior to her passing. And then she states you took care of her. Make sense?*

Yes.

At this point, the conditional probabilities were adding up in my head. Father dead, mother dead, best friends, taking care of her before she died. The string of shots continued.

*And she says, "You did not let me down." Because she knows you still have a little bit of guilt thinking you didn't do enough for her. And your mother seems to have a nice sense of humor. She jokes that it's post-transition, we call death-guilt. But it's not true.*

*Your mother didn't have the easiest life on the earth, but she had a fulfilling life. Correct?*

Yes.

I would later find out that Ronnie's mother had had a remarkable sense of humor, and also had been no stranger to using guilt.

*And she jokes that in the hereafter, she's on the vacation she never really had. Or hadn't had in a while. Her and your dad are together, which is something you might have wondered about.*

Yes.

*Your mother is also a woman of faith.*

Yes.

*Because I see Christ appear in front of you. So I take it she was of a Christian sect.*

No.

An error. At this point, it was almost comforting to hear George get something wrong.

*But why does Christ appear . . . does it make sense?*

No.

*I'm going to have to leave it with you. He appears in front of you. Then I'm going to have to take the appearance as a spiritual one, if not a religious one.*

Okay.

It seemed a clear mistake, yet the subject would be brought up later and take on a very different character.

*Your mom also speaks another language.*

Yes.

I knew very little about Ronnie's family history. I had no idea where this might be going.

*Or can I say has knowledge of it?*

Yes.

*Okay. She was not a religious woman, but she was spiritual, correct?*

Yes.

*Okay. I think that's why, again this has nothing to do with organized religion, I think it's for my benefit. I see Christ appear in front of you to signify spirituality. Funny, your father didn't believe in the hereafter. Make sense?*

Yeah.

*It's kind of like, "We'll find out when I'm dead."*

Yes.

*It's not like he, like I was brought up to believe in one. His attitude is like, "We'll find out when I'm dead."*

Yes.

*It sounds like your mother speaks some sort of German-like language; is that true?*

Yes.

*Okay. I'm not saying it's German. Is that correct? But it's German-like?*

Yes.

*So it has to be like German or Slavic-like. It sounds like that to me; I'm not a linguist, so that's the best I can do, that it sounds like that to me. Also, hearing the name Rose. Make sense?*

Yes.

The name was actually Rosie, an aunt of Ronnie's mother.

*But passed on?*

Yes.

*Cause your mother says, "Rose is here with me." So they would know each other, yes?*

Yes.

The statistical probabilities were now way off the chart. I was thinking again, "This is more than cold reading." The statements were incredibly specific.

*And I think it's somebody you didn't expect to show up today.*

Yes.

*It's a surprise. That's why I said who you least expect can show up. And also Sam. Does that make sense?*

Yes.

*He's family, yes?*

Yes.

*I keep seeing the American Uncle Sam in front of me. Is it correct he's an uncle? Or that could be my clue for the name Sam, so all right, don't answer. If he was an uncle you would have said Yes, so let's just leave it alone. But your mother knows him.*

Yes.

It was only after reading the transcripts carefully that I saw the complexity of George's questions. It was as if he could sense when he was sure of something, and when it might be a metaphor. This level of information retrieval deserves careful scientific analysis in the future.

*'Cause your mother keeps saying, "Sam is here with us." Wait a minute, sounds like somebody's speaking Yiddish. Is that correct?*

Yes.

Could this be trickery? After being wrong about the Christ image, perhaps he took a guess at Ronnie being Jewish and reasoned that, in this case, her mother might have spoken Yiddish—especially since he had already said he wasn't good at identifying languages.

> *Oh, that's the German-like language. Okay. Now, I also see the Star of David in front of me. So the people were basically Jewish, correct?*

Yes.

George was smiling.

> *Okay. Well, when you think about it, Christ was a Jew, too.*

Yes.

> *So, one Jew to another. It's funny, though. Your mother's a very good, living person when she's on the earth.*

Yes.

> *That's why Christ appeared. She was not a Christian obviously, but she would have . . . how do I put this without sounding like religion? . . . she wouldn't have believed in his teachings, but would have believed in what he stood for, like being good to people and so forth.*

Yes.

> *That's what I'm getting at. That's why I think Christ appeared in front of you as a spiritual sym-*

*bol, not as a religious one. Your mother would have
admired what he would have done, in regards to
how we all should live, like trying to create heaven
on earth.*

Yes.

This could simply have been a way of covering up the apparent
mistake about the Christ image. Yet Ronnie later explained that she
had always thought of her mother as Christlike because of her
love, caring, and devotion.

*Also, Max?*

Yes.

*Passed on?*

Yes.

Max had been a friend of Ronnie's parents. First Rose, then
Sam, now Max. What was the probability of guessing three names
by chance, all of people known to the sitter, all of whom had
passed?

*'Cause he's in the room and he says he's family,
and he says you also didn't expect to hear from him.
But surprise again. Also, somebody back there spoke
Russian.*

Yes.

*Because I hear another language, Slavic, and
that's, I see the, I see the Czar Nicholas in front of
me, so I assume they're trying to tell me he spoke*

*Russian. I mean, they spoke Russian, or whoever it was.*

*Your father does admit he could have been closer to you, that true?*

Yes.

Yes, this could apply to lots of people. It could certainly apply to me. However, at this point, less than 20 percent of what George had said applied to me. The statement, I would later learn, fit Ronnie's relationship with her father like a glove.

*He just wants you to know that he always loved you and still does, even though he might have had a strange way of showing it or not showing it. His heart's in the right place but he feels in many ways he was there and he wasn't there. Definitely your mother was the heart and soul of the home.*

Yes.

*And you're mommy's girl.*

Yup.

*That has not changed. It doesn't matter if you're five or 105, your mother tells me you're still mommy's girl. And she says as long as you know that, it makes you feel 100 percent better.*

Yes.

Ronnie kept looking at me and nodding; I was glad the screen kept George from seeing this giveaway affirmation of his accuracy.

*You know, because you have your ups and downs about a life hereafter, and it's not like it's an issue to you, but the thing is as your mother states you certainly want to see her again someday. And you will, when your time comes to pass on to the next stage, when there's essence of fulfillment. 'Cause your mother believed in living for here and now, and she's got the right attitude. We're here to fulfill, so let's not worry about what's to come. Let's focus on where we are.*

*Also, the name Ruth?*

Yes.

Ruth had been a friend of Ronnie's mother.

*. . . Passed on too, yes?*

No.

*No, your mother says, Yes. So I'm going to challenge you before you even hesitate. Because your mother says, "Ruth is here." And she said in the hereafter so I'm going to leave it go. And Lillian also.*

*These seem to be almost . . . I feel friendship. These might have been people your mom knew.*

Oh yes, yes.

Lillian had been an elderly friend of the family. George had now given five names, some of them not very common (Rose, Max, Lillian), and had been correct on every one.

I could think of only two explanations: either George had somehow learned the identify of the appliance saleswoman we

planned to use, and then done some research into her family . . . or
something extraordinary was taking place before my eyes.

*Because your mother's arguing with me that she's
right. And I have to be honest with you, one thing
about your mother, if she argues she's right, she's right.*

Yes.

Ronnie's mother is correcting her daughter from the afterlife as
she did in this life? Could I believe this?

*She's a no-nonsense woman. And as she states,
but she's got a heart of gold. That's the difference,
correct?*

Yes.

*As she states, she's a no-nonsense woman, so
when you said No, you hesitated, she's like, "No,
no, I'm right." Don't even argue with her, you
know, because I know what I'm talking about. And
she states that they are all there with her.*
*She also brings up a brother. Is it correct she lost a
brother?*

No.

*. . . or a brother-in-law?*

Yes.

I thought to myself that George was not perfect, or the detective he employed was not perfect, or he was deliberately missing
shots to make it look like he was not perfect.

Or else he was the real thing, and I was witnessing it, hit after hit after hit.

*Oh, 'cause she argued with me again that she was right. Okay, Ma, as long as you clear it up, that's what I'm looking for. 'Cause she said, "Brother is here with me." You said, No, and she said, "No, I'm right." She said, "Brother, but through marriage. Brother-in-law."*

Yes.

*Who's there with her? I'm not trying to make you sound like a mama's girl, but in many ways your mother was your world. 'Cause she keeps surrounding you so closely with love. It's apparently somebody you do miss.*

Oh, yes.

*That's what I mean. Like, in many ways, it's not that you couldn't live without her, but you know, she's your world because it is somebody that you do miss.*

Right.

*Also, in many ways she does feel she could have been closer to you, yes?*

Yes.

I was hearing vague comments again, comments that could apply to me, or anyone. In fact, the statements were approaching

30 percent accuracy in describing the history of the deceased in *my* family.

> *Because she does admit she was a little on the tough-to-get-along-with side? At times. 'Cause I see a nutcracker in front of you, and that's a symbol at the time she might have been a tough nut to crack.*

Yes.

> *She also shows me the play* The Glass Menagerie. *So maybe at times she might have been a little on the domineering side.*

Yes.

> *And she does apologize for that. Her heart was in the right place, but in many ways she was an insecure woman. And her insecurity made her a bit on the domineering-controlling side.*

Yes.

Ronnie later told us that this fit her mother perfectly.

> *She jokes at me that in many ways she fits the stereotype of a Jewish mother.*

Yes.

> *And your mother is not the type of woman who admits she was wrong too easily. So she's admitting she was wrong and just wants you to know that she*

*always loved you and still does even if at times she was a little too overbearing about it. 'Cause she admits that in many ways it was kind of either her way or no way.*

Yes.

*There was no gray area. It's either black or white. You know? And Mom's way is the right way. She wanted the best for her children or for you, but her way of going about it sometimes might have seemed too demanding. But again, I still feel her heart was in the right place.*
*Also, the name Gertrude?*

No.

I must confess that at this point, I was again secretly praying for misses. But this apparent miss only lasted for a moment.

*Are you sure? Your mother said Gerty or Gertrude.*

Yes.

"Gertrude" had not originally registered because Ronnie had always called the woman "Aunt Gerty"—a great-aunt on her father's side.

*Okay, 'cause your mother argued again. She's right. I don't want to get into an argument with this woman, so think. 'Cause she said Nope, she's right. "Gertrude, yes," she calls. Gertrude has passed on?*

Yes.

*'Cause she keeps saying, "Gertrude is here with me," so she must be passed on. Now wait a minute; again she calls, "Ruth." From what you gave me the impression before, there is a Ruth on the earth.*

Yes.

*She must be calling to her. Maybe that's my mistake, because she brings the name up again, and I know from the way you stammered before that more than likely there is a Ruth on the earth. So I'm not trying to be a wise guy. You don't have to be too psychic to figure it out, but your mom says, "Please tell Ruth you've heard from me." Does that makes sense?*

Yes, yes.

But this was old content, I thought to myself.

*And she also congratulates her. Make sense?*

Yes.

Sounded as if it could have been a guess, but Ronnie found it especially meaningful.

*So, 'cause your mother extends white roses to Ruth, and congratulates her, saying that she's hearing of happy news.*

Yes.

Happy news? Ronnie later told us that Ruth was their hairdresser who had become a dear friend through the years.

Before her mother died, Ruth had suffered two separate bouts of stomach cancer but outlived the doctor's predictions. Since her mother's death four years earlier, Ruth's cancer had returned, but surprisingly she had beat it again recently.

*So Ruth must be . . . yeah, there's reason to celebrate around her.*

Yes.

*So there's white lace all around you. Reason of celebration. And I see . . . and this is specific celebration. Correct?*

Yes.

*This is not just bull. Why does your mother speak about a lack of communication with a brother? Does that make sense? With you? Or . . . do you understand?*

Yes.

*Okay. 'Cause your mother is speaking about a lack of communication with a brother, and then she kind of joked like business as usual.*

Yes.

*So it must have always been the way it is, but she wishes that loose ends could be tied up. But I don't think they will be in this world. Meaning on the earth. Does that make sense?*

Yes.

*Okay. As long as you understand. And I think your mother kind of buries it, so maybe she's trying to tell you to put it at rest?*

Yeah.

*Makes sense?*

Yes.

We almost always have some loose ends with someone who has died. By itself, not an impressive piece of information.

*Okay. Also, I heard the name Helen, too. Make sense?*

Mmmm . . .

Finally, a name Ronnie could not connect with.

*Your mother's saying Yes, so I'm not even going to . . . I'm going to leave it with you even if you don't remember right now, because I'm not even going to get into an argument with her about it. She says, Yes. Yeah, it's either Helen or Ellen. But I think it's more Helen. 'Cause your mother knew a lot of people.*

Yes.

I thought to myself that most people know a Helen or Ellen. I am a well-trained skeptic, I reminded myself; I can calculate the odds.

*'Cause she jokes that "I know everybody and everybody knows me."*

Yes.

*But she says here in the hereafter, she's like a universal "bubba" type, she says. Does that make sense?*

No.

*She says Yes, so I'm going to leave it go. In the hereafter.*

Oh.

*It's like everybody . . . she's like a universal mother type. She's a bubba type. She does claim to work with children in the hereafter. Would that seem, well, I shouldn't even ask you. That's what she's telling me. Yeah, your mother's a woman of fact. You know, this is the way it is. No questions asked.*
*So that's why when I start to try to think, "Oh, gee, could that be possible?" she's like, "Well, that's the way it is, so why do you have to explain it? That's what it is." But she claims she works with children in the hereafter and, again, she says, "I'm like a universal bubba type over there."*

At that point, the session ended so that there would be at least a few minutes for the second medium before Ronnie had to leave for work. But as I went to unhook George from the recording equipment, he continued.

*'Cause your mom is, just let me quickly sign off, 'cause your mother embraces you with love along with your dad. And wait a minute, why does your mother bring up a sister? Make sense?*

Yes.

One last parting hit. Ronnie appeared dumbfounded.

Most of the reading had been almost too accurate, clearly above and beyond mere generalized guesses. The conditional probabilities for getting names, personality characteristics, and other descriptions was off the scale. However, when the next medium was brought in, the picture changed dramatically. It proved to be something we would all remember.

## WITH SUZANE NORTHROP

It was clear, right from the outset, that Ronnie and Suzane were not on the same wavelength. As the young people used to say, the vibes were not good. I shouldn't have been surprised—we all know from personal experience that when we introduce two people we like to each other, they don't always click. Just because Suzane's earlier session had gone well didn't mean that would necessarily be the case all day long.

From early in the session I could tell that Ronnie was not reacting well and that Suzane appeared to be getting more things wrong than right. The experience would ultimately prove to me how wrong at-the-moment impressions can be in this work.

As I listened, Suzane really did seem to be misconnecting. Examples:

> *You've got one parent here and one parent gone, please, may I ask?*

No.

> *. . . I don't know why I want to say this; I'm getting double marriage, double marriage. So I have to assume somebody must have remarried or something after that point that they're telling me.*

No.

*. . . And I am also going to ask you this, please, did Mama move after Papa passed, please?*

No.

*Were you not with Mama when she passed, please?*

I was.

*. . . Your father also had a sister, I have to tell you. There must have been a connection between the both of them. I think she went after him.*

Right about the father having a sister. Wrong about the sister dying after him.

*I don't know if she had the M name or it's somebody else that's connected to her. [If] I didn't know better, it sounds like Mary, Marie, it's an M-A-R sounding name. I want to say really, really strong.*

Close—the name was Martha.

*They're also telling me there's a sister passes, a sister passed. . . . When I hear sister, I hear distinctly cancer. I hear it much more, I wanna say, in the female area than in the other part of the body.*

No cancer—in the female area or anywhere else—because the sitter never had a sister.

*And mother also tells me this very very strong, and I quite honestly do not [know] who she speaks about, but there was a passing of somebody, I think age six-*

*teen, at the age of sixteen, she tells me. . . . She says,
"I'm with the person of the age of sixteen, Ronnie,
and you need to know that because it's extremely extremely extremely important."*

Ronnie did not recognize this description. The closest she
could identify was her mother's mother, who married young and
died at eighteen. But what could be so "extremely important"
about that?

*. . . Papa's side . . . He keeps showing me the rail-
road tracks. . . . And the noise, I hear the noise in
the railroad tracks. Something. So I assume he must
have lived with it.*

Her father had no connection with a railroad nor railroad tracks.
Another complete miss. And they continued coming.

*. . . Are you not married now?*

No.

*Okay. Were you, please?*

Yes.

*I'm distant with this man. This man's not spirit, is
he?*

No.

*Okay, because [inaudible]. They say, "Pain in the
ass, you know? Pain in the ass, you know?" You
know what? Mother never liked him. You didn't—
you married him even though—she didn't want you*

*to marry him, but you would have done anyway. . . .*

Entirely wrong—the sitter's mother had no objection to her choice of a husband.

Yet Suzane managed to be very much on target with certain sets of information, confirming some of the details that the previous medium had obtained, and adding some pieces, as well.

> *Your mother keeps showing me, "At the end, breathing, I couldn't breathe, I couldn't breathe, I couldn't breathe. My air was cut off, Ronnie, my air was cut off. They had me hooked to the machines. I'm so glad I'm not on those machines anymore. I don't want to be on those machines any more."*
>
> *She says, "You did right by me, you did right by me."*

According to Ronnie, this was a very accurate description of her mother's last days—she had indeed been hooked up to machines and had trouble with her breathing. And Ronnie had been with her at the last, a possible interpretation of "You did right by me."

> *This is a woman that is very into taking care. Very much into taking care here. And I also have to tell you this, please. I don't know why; she talks again about this fairness. And she says you did take an awful lot of it on, but she says, "You need to know of our connection. You need to know our connection."*

About the statement "You need to know of our connection," Ronnie offered a possible explanation I found intriguing. Her mother's birth mother had died when Ronnie's mother was very young. Her grandfather's new wife, presumably insecure, insisted that knowledge of his first marriage be kept secret. Ronnie was an adult before she learned her grandmother was not her blood relative. Perhaps her mother now wanted to be sure the truth was known and Ronnie would remember it.

Or was this simple stretching to find a favorable interpretation for what Suzane had said? Despite my earnest intention to maintain a scientist's critical detachment, was I unwittingly playing the game that magician mediums count on—so eager to believe that I was finding "facts" where they didn't really exist, in order to bolster the belief?

Another series of statements began badly, then took a stunning turn.

*Father went before your mother.*

No.

Wrong.

*There was a long time between their passing.*

No.

*One of them passed and I want to say in the winter months, December or January, unless it was a birthday.*
*One went very fast; one was a long-term illness.*

Ronnie's mother was ill for fourteen months before she passed; her father did, indeed, pass much more quickly.

And then the stunner:

*She died in the house. . . . They both died in the same room ten months apart, ten months apart. . . . In the same room.*

Ronnie had somehow missed this during the reading. Later, when it was read back to her, she was floored, asking repeatedly, "She said that!? She said that!?"

How she had failed to grasp it the first time was bewildering to her. Every part of this brief statement was, for Ronnie, astonishingly on target. Yes, her mother had died in the house. Yes, her parents had both died in the same room. Yes, they had died ten months and some days apart.

And despite the impression we both had at the time of the sitting that Suzane had done poorly, when the scoring was completed, the data showed that she had in fact obtained a remarkably high percentage of accurate facts.

We were probably misled by the many misses in conveying opinions—only 30 percent of the opinion statements were correct.

But overall, the experience illustrates how the unique selectivity of our memories can sometimes complicate and even confound this research. It shows why it was so important to have research sitters carefully examine the transcripts of a given experiment, item by item, word by word, which is what we did after this experiment and would do in all subsequent ones.

We believe that selective memory may also affect viewers observing readings on television. If the viewer is negatively biased—for example, if the viewer is a strong skeptic or disbeliever—he or she may selectively *under*-remember the actual success. And certainly, as we've said from the beginning, it's possible for sitters to over-remember, based on one or two facts that struck deeply home.

Selective remembering applies to all of us—believers, agnostics, and disbelievers alike. That's precisely why we make sure that the scientific data we report are based on careful scoring of the actual transcripts, not a person's selective memory of the sessions.

## WRAPPING UP

We had been in the lab since 8 A.M., and filming for seven hours. Though we had not completed all the sessions that had been planned, we were thoroughly washed out and frankly glad for the excuse to wrap up.

By the end of that very long Saturday, I had witnessed these two remarkable women who courageously sat with the mediums and allowed their personal histories to be revealed under laboratory conditions. Time after time, they looked at me with tears in their eyes as each of the mediums shared intimate details about their families—from names, initials, and historical facts to information so personal that it literally raised the hairs on their arms and on mine.

It was as if each medium told a given chapter of the sitter's story. Each subsequent reading revealed facts that seemed to interlace with the information brought from the previous sessions.

Right at the start, Suzane Northrop had begun talking virtually nonstop, reminding me, as I've said, of some New York City cabbies who talk as fast as they drive. Only momentarily did she pause to ask a question, a total of five questions during more than twelve minutes of constant communication. The raw video footage shows Suzane mostly ignoring Pat sitting on the other side of the screen as she waved her hands and spoke seemingly into thin air. While this was going on, there was Pat, nodding her head yes, yes, yes, in disbelief.

Then there was John Edward, exhibiting extreme caution to ensure he disclosed precise, particular facts in an often dry, matter-of-fact voice. He remained as cool as Suzane was hot. And again Pat was continually nodding or saying yes.

Next, George Anderson, a seemingly devout person wearing a cross and thanking the spirits for the opportunity to speak with them that day. His discussion brought tears to everyone's eyes—the sitter, the film crew, even mine—as he shared information that even Pat's husband didn't know, so accurate yet so painful.

Anne Gehman, in her beautiful soft voice, amid descriptions of relatives and fond family pictures, remaining absolutely dignified and providing some eerily uncanny hits like the lights flickering and the tapping on walls.

She was followed by our much-admired Laurie Campbell, who had been so nervous about how her performance would compare with those of the other mediums. Yet she managed with her own style of love and enthusiasm to introduce some new and totally unexpected information, like the friend from the East Coast who had recently died.

In the past, skeptics have insisted that a medium's single session of lucky guessing could not be duplicated a second time with another medium. But right in front of my eyes, I had watched as the five mediums continually replicated key information that paralleled and complemented the information evoked by their predecessors. I was personally surprised not so much by the mediums' replication of specific facts as with the way little details progressively unfolded during the day, such as filling in the portrait of a son's suicide and a frisky little dog.

## THE END OF THE DAY

Throughout the day, sitter Pat's husband, Mike, had remained in the living room of our laboratory. To give him something to do, I had asked him in the morning if he might be interested in reading the first few draft chapters of the book Linda and I were then working on, *The Living Energy Universe*. To my surprise, he said yes. He had sat there all day—a man who not only drove Harley Davidson motorcycles but actually rebuilt them, sitting peacefully in the background of the comings and goings of the researchers, mediums, and film crew, quietly reading the draft of a book that proposed that everything in the universe was eternal and alive, and remembers. As I watched him read a chapter titled "The Reluctant Believer," which began with the question about whether Linda's father is still alive, I had the impression he was thinking about his own family.

The day after the experiment was completed, as Patricia and Mike were readying to leave Tucson, he stopped by the university to tell me, much to my surprise, that he was leaving the lab a believer. I asked if he would write down for me the story of what led to the dramatic transformation of his feelings and beliefs, which he agreed to do.

I could not know at the time that Mike himself would figure in the history of our research, in a heart-breaking way.

Meanwhile there was still work to do. About an hour after the readings, all gathered in the living room of the lab and, with the cameras rolling again, I stood alongside a computer monitor, ready to create a plot that would graphically depict a preliminary rating of how successful the readings had been.

Pat had initially listed six people she thought might come through, and reported that all six had shown up with at least one medium. Impressively, three of these were independently observed by all five mediums.

All five had also independently reported information about a deceased son. This is like flipping a coin and getting five heads in a row. None reported receiving any information about a deceased daughter. Again, correct: there was no deceased daughter—three daughters, but all living. So, again, the equivalent of getting five more heads.

The probability of getting just this single string of 10 hits (five mediums reporting a dead son and none of them reporting a dead daughter) is approximately one in a thousand by chance. This is calculated by multiplying 2 times 2 times 2 times 2 times 2 times 2 times 2 times 2 times 2 times 2—where 2 refers to heads or tails and is multiplied 10 times, representing the 10 flips; the result of the multiplication is 1,024.

(To demonstrate that this result cannot be achieved by guessing, we later asked sixty-eight control subjects to guess whether Pat had a deceased son. The results were almost exactly as predicted by the law of averages: approximately 50 percent guessed that she did and 50 percent guessed that she didn't. When they were asked to guess "Does Pat have a deceased daughter," the results were essentially the same, almost 50/50.)

But this is just the beginning. Now add that three of the mediums mentioned the initial "M" for Pat's son's name. None reported any other initial.

If we conservatively estimate that at least sixteen possible initials can reflect common first names of males, the probability of three mediums getting the same correct initial is 16 times 16 times 16 ( = 4,096) which is less than one in four thousand by chance.

Now, how do we estimate the conditional or combined probability of just these two sets of findings?

The probability of all five mediums getting a deceased son and none making the mistake of guessing a deceased daughter, combined with the probability of three mediums getting the same initial, M (which was correct), and none getting a wrong initial (one in four thousand by chance) would be estimated as 1,024 times 4,096: slightly over four million—that is, less than one in four million by chance.

Concerning the son, three of the mediums saw much blood, one said he "went out with a boom," and one said he shot himself. Pat's son killed himself with a gun. None of the mediums said leukemia, drug overdose, car accident, or other cause.

Our control group's rate of actually guessing his cause of death correctly was less than 10 percent. If we go by the data we collected, the combined probability would now be 1,024 times 4,096 times 3 times 10: 125,829,120.

This is less than one in 125 million.

These are the initial estimates of probability, just for Pat's deceased son.

Note that we were able to calculate these probabilities because our experiment involved multiple mediums—important, because information that is obtained by two or more mediums provides replication, meaning that it's obtained from more than one source or in more than one way. And only when data can be replicated will serious scientists (and skeptics) begin to take the experiment seriously.

Detailed unexpected information, obtained immediately after the readings, was even more interesting. Beside the six people on Pat's list, nine other deceased individuals not on the list were also identified by Pat from the readings.

My favorite example was the deceased little dog known to Pat's family as PeeWee. Four of the five mediums independently reported seeing a dog who was beloved by Pat's deceased son, and all four saw the dog as little. When color was spontaneously reported, it was perceived as black and tan, or at least dark. One medium described the hair as short.

PeeWee was a small, black and tan, short-haired chihuahua mix. No one said a spotted dalmatian, or a medium-sized blue merle long-haired mutt, or a large black poodle. In only a single instance was the dog incorrectly described as having "wire hair."

How do we calculate getting this combination of information—dog, small, black and tan, short-haired? One in ten would be quite conservative.

Now combine the deceased dog with the deceased son—for two of the mediums, the son and dog came through together.

We take the 1,024 times 4,096 times 3 times 10 and multiply this by 10. The combined probability is less than one in two and a half billion.

Proof of survival of consciousness? Of course not.

Evidence that *something* was going on? The probability numbers were compelling.

Given these initial observations, the raw data deserved to be looked at more closely. This was easy in principle but hard in practice.

We would have to have the entire set of raw tapes transcribed. Then each individual item would have to be identified, categorized, and entered into a database. Finally, the sitters would face the task of scoring each and every item.

Meanwhile, it was rather like walking out of a crucial exam in college, thinking you had done well but knowing you would have to live with uncertainty until the results were posted. From what I had seen and heard, I was convinced the experiment would prove to be a resounding success, but that feeling was based on entirely subjective impressions. And maybe it represented more of what I wanted than what had really happened. The uncertainty was like a throbbing headache that won't go away.

But I would have to live with that headache for quite a while. As it turned out, the scoring would not happen for months, not until late the following summer.

# • I N T E R L U D E •

## A Case of Precognition?

The Sunday morning after the HBO experiment, we were to pick up Laurie and Anne at their hotel, and bumped into Suzane Northrop and John Edward. As they were departing, John remarked, "While I was in the gift shop earlier, I spotted an item that I thought symbolized the HBO experience." Mischievously, he suggested that we might like to look for it . . . without telling us what "it" was. The only clue he offered was that when we saw it, we would "know it psychically." And with those words, he hurried off.

Linda and I headed straight for the gift shop. On the right-hand side of a counter near the door sat a cuddly stuffed dog resembling a chihuahua. Despite John's suggestion that we would know it only "psychically," no psychic talents were required to see the connection. The store had two, and we bought them both.

We had no sooner arrived at the lab than Pat called to ask whether she and Mike could drop over to say goodbye. We wrapped up one of the toys as a gift for her.

When she opened the package and became aware of its contents, Pat exclaimed, "Now I understand!" Anne had said in the reading that Pat would be receiving a little stuffed animal gift with personal meaning.

Had Anne Gehman seen into the future and predicted this gift?

Later that afternoon, when we dropped Laurie and Anne at the airport, for the second time that day we bumped into John Edward and Suzane Northrop.

I proceeded to share the details of Anne's prophetic statement in her reading with Pat the day before, followed by Pat's chance visit to the laboratory that morning, and reminded John that it had all been sparked by his request that Linda and I go into the store and "psychically" find what turned out to be PeeWee II.

"Look at this," John said as he held out his arm to show that all the hair on his arm was standing straight up. "That's really weird," he said.

His reaction both startled me and made me smile. Even mediums, I discovered, can be surprised by what they themselves, and other mediums, are able to do.

# · 8 ·

# HBO Results

---

Several months went by while I was busy teaching, doing other research, writing journal articles, and attending to all the tasks of daily life. Finally we had time to take the two hundred pages of stenographic transcripts from the videotapes of the HBO shooting and have them scored. Pat Price came back in the summer of 1999 to tackle the time-consuming, laborious, and detailed job.

We classified each item into one of six categories: Initials, Names, Historical facts, Personal descriptions, Temperaments, and Opinions, which also served as a catch-all basket for anything that didn't fit into another category.

The categories were straightforward. If a medium said, "I'm seeing a dead son," this would be classified as a historical fact: a son had died. "I'm hearing the letter 'M'" or "He's telling me his name is Michael" obviously belonged in Initials or Names. "I see a thin man" was Personal description. "He appears to be shy" was Temperament.

It's worth noting that most of the categories—Initials, Names, Historical Facts, Personal Descriptions, and Temperaments— could be confirmed by the sitter's living relatives and friends.

However, if the medium said, "Your son wants me to tell you he doesn't blame you for his death," this would fall in the Opinion/Other category. Though this kind of information is often the most meaningful to a sitter, it's the least convincing from a scientific point of view.

For each item, the sitter was asked to assign a rating on a hit-or-miss scale, in the range of –3 to +3, with the minus numbers representing a complete miss (–3), a probable miss (–2), or a possible miss (–1), and the plus numbers representing a possible hit (+1) to a definite hit (+3). If the sitter did not know, she was instructed to assign no rating. Along with rating each statement, the sitter was required to justify her answer and to tell us if information other than Opinion could not be verified by another living person.

We continually reminded the sitters that whenever they were uncertain about the appropriate rating, they were to assign the more conservative value so as not to unintentionally improve the results.

The scoring, unfortunately, took an average of a minute per item. Pat Price had to score over six hundred items, which took some ten hours.

Although everyone's impression at the time of the experiment was of quite high accuracy, we anticipated that the detailed scoring process and the passage of time would lead to severely reduced scores.

Our predictions were wrong.

## RESULTS FOR PATRICIA PRICE

Across all the categories, the results for Pat showed that the mediums ranged from 77 percent to 95 percent accuracy. Their average for +3 hits—that is, a statement rated by the sitter as completely accurate—was an extraordinary 83 percent.

Our first thought as scientists was "maybe anyone can guess like this." We later arranged to test this with a control group of students, giving sixty-eight students at the University of Arizona the challenge to see whether they could guess as well as the mediums did.

The students were shown a picture of Patricia Price (an extra item of information, since the mediums had done their readings screened from the sitters), and they were told that she had lost at least six close relatives or friends in a ten-year period. We then gave them a list of yes/no questions, including these: Is her husband dead? Is her son dead? Is her daughter dead? Is her cat dead?

We then asked a set of specific questions, including these: Who loved to dance? Who raised roses? Who was a "pistol"? Who did not meet her husband before the wedding? What was the cause of the sitter's child's death?

This control group achieved hits ranging from 20 percent to 54 percent, with an overall average of 36 percent—much below even the least accurate of the mediums (Chart 8-1).

Chart 8-1. Comparison of Guessing Performance of Control Group with Results of Individual Mediums

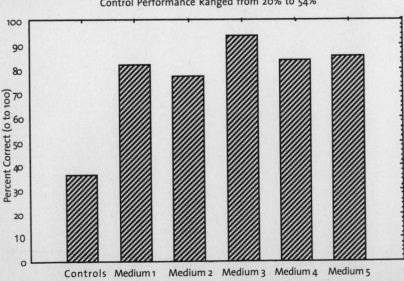

Comparison of Guessing Performance of Controls (n=68) with Each Medium
Control Performance Ranged from 20% to 54%

When the 83 percent for the mediums was compared with the 36 percent for the control group of students, the statistical probability of this difference occurring by chance alone was less than one in ten million.

We also looked at the results for the six categories separately, combining the five mediums (Chart 8-2).

The accuracy for names was above 65 percent for the five mediums combined. Remarkable.

And I know from experience that when something appears to be too good to be true, it usually is. Hence we were immediately skeptical of the results. Was Pat mistaken in her ratings? Had she secretly been in contact with the mediums? Did the mediums obtain facts ahead of time about her, making the session a well-practiced charade? If she asked her friends, neighbors, and family whether any strangers had been trying to chat with them about her, would she find people had been snooping through her past? Were some of what we scored as hits actually based on the sitter's

Chart 8-2. Average Percent of +3 Hits per Category for All Five Mediums

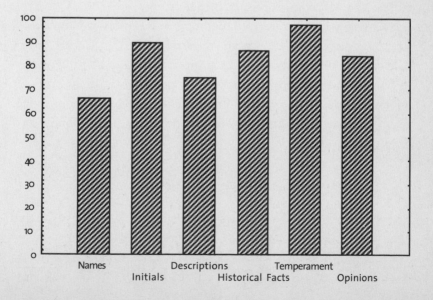

previous answers? Had the mediums somehow passed information from one to another in between the readings? Had the mediums engaged in cold reading or some other form of magician's trickery?

We had many questions in mind, and wondered what we would find when our other sitter was available.

## RESULTS FOR RONNIE NATHANSON

Ronnie, who became available a few weeks later to score the data from her aborted session, was convinced that George Anderson had done really well. She was just as certain that Suzane Northrup had done quite poorly.

There were over two hundred specific items for Ronnie to evaluate. And her assumptions proved correct . . . but only in part.

George scored 90 percent accurate, which is astounding. Suzane scored only 64 percent.

Perhaps by comparison, 64 percent sounds like a rotten score. Yet it was well above the average guessing rate of 36 percent achieved by the control subjects. Looked at objectively, it has to be ranked as a very impressive performance.

When the data for the two mediums were combined and the +3 accuracy scores were plotted separately for the six categories (Chart 8-3), one surprising fact popped out. In two categories—Initials and Personal descriptions—the mediums were 100 percent accurate. Even Suzane, who Ronnie was so sure had not done well, achieved perfect results in these two categories, by Ronnie's own scoring of the data.

## A RETHINKING

And yet . . . Siegfried and Roy, the magicians in Las Vegas, make tigers appear apparently out of thin air; magician David Copperfield, on television, has made jumbo jet aircraft and even the Statue of Liberty seem to vanish. Our rational minds tell us that these

Chart 8-3. Percent +3 Hits per Category Averaged over Two Mediums

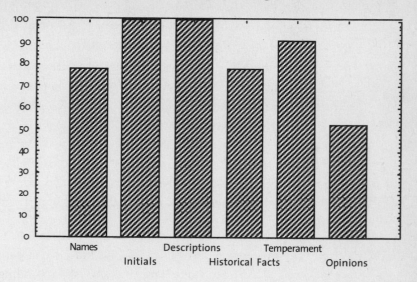

things haven't truly happened, but we're convinced we have seen them with our own eyes.

We delight in having professional magicians fool us. They have mastered the tricks for deceiving our senses—tricks developed over many, many years.

How could I truly be sure I was not being fooled by these mediums in a similar way?

It seemed highly unlikely. Surely one of the sitters would have heard about strangers asking neighbors or associates at work about them, and told us. On the other hand, some people are desperate to believe, and might suppress information that could cast the work of the mediums into doubt.

How many other techniques of illusion or misdirection might the mediums have used that no one but a professional in their field could begin to recognize?

Other scientists would demand incontrovertible proof before even beginning to accept what we thought we had witnessed. As a scientist myself, I had a nagging certainty I could not yet answer all the challenges that might be thrown at me.

Were there ways to make the experimental procedure even more fraud-proof? There must be. We would have to figure out how, and plan much more rigorous experiments.

Yet for the time being, I could hardly help but feel elated. In this territory so unknown to us, we had planned and carried out a significant experiment with fairly elaborate safeguards. The results were decidedly impressive, certainly enough to give us confidence and the strong desire to continue.

And if it all went well, Linda and I would in time know the excitement of having the experience of the experiment seen and shared by millions of viewers over HBO. By then, I hoped, we would have conceived and carried out one or two more efforts in this eye-opening field.

# PART III

# The Miraval Silent-Sitter Experiment

# • 9 •

# Seeking a New Design

To do successful research in an area outside mainstream science, one has to be ready for other scientists and ardent skeptics to throw barbs at the work and at the people involved, so a thick skin is one of the first requirements.

Another qualification, I believe, is that one needs the fortitude to constantly step aside from the research and ask, "What are the doubters going to find in this experiment that allows them to deny the results and label the work as invalid because the procedures and controls weren't sufficiently rigid?"

After the HBO experiment, Linda and I didn't even wait for the doubters to attack. We started conceiving a new experiment.

As we've noted, it's a standard ploy of the street-corner psychic to make a series of statements that are no more than stabs in the dark, and see which of them you respond to. "I see a woman in uniform whose name seems to begin with a B or an M; she's helping an older man with gray hair and a nice smile who may be having some trouble walking." Could be your great-aunt Beatrice, who volunteered at the hospital, or grandma Maude, who was in the WAVES in World War Two, or an older uncle who broke his hip and spent time in a nursing home, or . . .

So you smile, or nod, or say yes, yes, somewhere along the line. The medium, who has been waiting for any kind of signal of recognition, immediately picks up on that bit of lucky guessing and begins scurrying down the line to wherever it might lead.

You get the idea.

A close reading of our HBO transcripts showed places where it was possible to suspect that one medium or another might have been trying to use a stunt like that. Certainly any skeptic looking at the transcripts might use such a claim as a point of attack.

What's more, there was the possibility that the mediums had managed to pick up nonverbal clues from the sitter's responses. The emotional states of both sitters caused their tone of voice to alter at various times during the readings. It could be that a highly skilled person might be able to use the subtle (and sometimes not so subtle) signs of a sitter's breathing, voice patterns, and who knows what other indicators to formulate high-probability guesses: the kinds of cues that psychic magicians use in cold reading.

While we were pondering a new design, the mediums also began pressing us for another experiment—and they wanted it soon. John Edward and Suzane Northrop, in particular, were concerned that the public might think the HBO experiment had just been a publicity stunt. They leaned on us heavily to design a second experiment—and to collect the data in early June, well before the scheduled October showing of the HBO documentary. They wanted everyone, especially the press, to know that all people involved were deeply concerned about the quality of the research. Even more, they wanted the research to convincingly rule out fraud and deception as a possible explanation for the findings.

Laurie Campbell accepted the role of coordinating our work with the mediums and agreed to serve as chairperson of the mediums' group, which we were now calling the Mediumship Research Committee.

Meanwhile Linda and I, stimulated by the openness and commitment of the mediums, agreed to design a more sophisticated experiment. A few weeks after the HBO videotaping, we held an auspicious meeting at our home. Included were members of another group we had organized, which we called—with just a little tongue in cheek—the Friendly Devil's Advocates committee. It was an august assemblage of skeptics and doubters from the University of Arizona who were, nonetheless, willing to work with us. (But there was a catch: to protect their own reputations, these folks insisted on remaining anonymous.)

Linda was struck with a clever idea. If these mediums were actually picking up information from the spirit world, then theoretically they should be able to obtain accurate information even if they didn't have any verbal communication with the sitter.

That line of thought led to the next experiment, which we arranged for June 1999. To me, the design was a brilliant improvement. This time there would be ten sitters, not just two. The medium would never know which of the ten was the subject of the particular session. And during an initial period, the sitter would remain *entirely silent,* so the medium would get no clues to sex, age, or personality from hearing the voice or any responses.

I would come to call Linda's silent-sitter test the Russek Protocol, in honor of her deceased father. It became the cornerstone of this experiment and the next one, as well. We had no idea whether the mediums could function this way, nor did they. However, after much discussion to overcome their initial reluctance, all the mediums agreed to give it their best shot. (I thought this alone was evidence of their confidence in their own abilities.)

As a compromise designed to give the mediums a sense of assurance that they would not completely fail, we agreed that each reading would consist of two parts: the silent-sitter period, during which the mediums would attempt a reading with no responses from the sitter, and then a period during which they would be allowed standard yes/no responses.

This is also good science: you repeat a procedure that has worked in the past (replicate), and you add a new aspect that you want to explore (extend). This is a regular part of "doing science," and we follow the concept of "replicate and extend, replicate and extend" regularly in our own laboratory, as one of our research mantras.

Also, the sitters would be carefully selected to vary in age, sex, history of departed loved ones, professions, and belief in the possibility of survival. They would also be selected from different geographic areas; in the end, the group included people from New York, Florida, Minnesota, Arizona, and Hawaii.

As another factor deliberately complicating the challenge for the mediums, we varied whether or not the sitters were previously known to the experimenters, even to the point of including one sitter related to an experimenter.

We reasoned that by using ten sitters, it would be impossible for any prior knowledge of a particular sitter to help the mediums during the silent periods. Since they did not know who was sitting behind them at any given time, prior knowledge of the sitters somehow obtained through detectives, by web searches, or from the other mediums would be virtually worthless.

## PREPARATIONS

Four of our five original mediums were able to juggle their busy schedules to return to Tucson for this new experiment. Only George Anderson could not manage to be with us.

This time, not one but two nationally famous resorts in the Tucson area generously supported the project, with Canyon Ranch providing room and board for the mediums and the Miraval Resort providing buildings for holding the sessions, with four separate rooms for the readings plus a fifth room where the sitters would be sequestered.

It wasn't any big surprise that we were contacted by many people who had heard of the effort and were clamoring to take part as sitters. We decided to give the opportunity to people we already knew—some colleagues, a few friends, one relative, and some students. The majority of the sitters asked to remain anonymous out of concern that their reputations might be damaged by taking part in this kind of research. Their requests seemed reasonable, and we agreed to honor them.

Linda and I chuckled over the idea of slipping ourselves into the lineup of sitters. We imagined walking into a medium's room supposedly escorting the next sitter, and then settling unseen into the sitter's chair as the medium began the silent-reading period.

But of course, as soon as the yes/no period began, the medium would immediately recognize Linda's voice or mine. The rest of the session would be invalid for scientific purposes because the mediums all knew too much personal information about us. Very tempting, but a bad idea. Still, it seemed a bit like cooking a grand banquet and not getting to taste the food. Or designing the world's greatest roller coaster and never getting to ride on it.

## Shocking News

It was a Saturday morning in early June 1999, and I was at the University of New Mexico in Albuquerque to present the preliminary findings of the HBO study at the annual meetings of the Society for Scientific Exploration. The Miraval experiment was scheduled to be conducted the following week.

When I called Linda, she had shocking news. "I'm sorry to have to tell you this," she said. "Michael is dead."

Michael—Pat Price's husband, the motorcycle buff who favored Harley-Davidson T-shirts—had died behind the wheel of his truck, the victim of a heart attack followed by crashing into a tree. I would remember Michael fondly and regretted losing him in my life. Despite our very short contact, I felt he had made me a better and more accepting person, and I would be forever grateful for having met him.

Linda and I had been expecting a visit from Michael in just a few days, and after that Linda and I were to pay him and his wife a return visit. He wanted to share with me how his beliefs had dramatically changed since the HBO experiment. Now he was dead.

Pat and her family were doing as well as could be expected so soon after the accident, Linda assured me. She then asked a question that momentarily stunned me. "Gary, do you think we should invite Pat to be a sitter in the Miraval experiment?"

In the midst of Pat's time of grieving, Linda's suggestion could seem either heartless . . . or inspired. She was absolutely convinced that Pat would be soothed by the experience and would welcome the invitation as a special opportunity—a gift better than flowers.

Selfishly, we both realized that if Pat, the new widow, agreed to be a sitter again, this would be a set of readings unlike any in the history of research on survival. We fully expected that the mediums would figure out who Pat was during the yes/no periods, but during the initial silent period, it would provide the opportunity to determine whether they could obtain new information about Pat's loss. If so, it would offer valuable replication.

Linda was right: Pat quickly accepted. We all agreed to tell no one that Pat would be a sitter. Nor would we tell them that Michael had died.

## SETTING UP

Our experiment participants arrived on a sunny, hot Friday a week later. Linda and I, with two of our staff people, would serve as the experimenters—each working with a given sitter, shepherding him or her from medium to medium. At any given time, four readings would be taking place.

We were able to round up five video cameras, including two from friends and a new Sony digital camera received as a gift from an anonymous benefactor just before we started the experiment. As backup, an audio tape recorder would also capture each session.

The decision to include backup audio tape recorders turned out to be fortuitous. For some unfathomable reason, we ended up having difficulty with four of the video cameras and were able to record only a few of the readings using the new digital unit. The audio recorders saved the day, successfully capturing every one of the readings.

The mediums weren't particularly surprised. Problems with recording equipment, they claim, are not uncommon when one "connects with the realm of the spirit world." In the absence of a plausible conventional explanation, we can't dismiss their hypothesis, especially since all four dysfunctional cameras worked fine when returned to their respective owners. Linda and I still scratch our heads over this one.

But I would be pleased when the video recording of later experiments worked without flaw, since the coincident failure of four separate cameras at Miraval left us open to charges of trying to hide our procedures.

## The Unknown Sitter: Silent Period

One of the Miraval sitters had a special connection to these experiments, and we had a particular reason for including her. The most telling session with this person was the reading with our well-known television medium, John Edward. (Parts of this reading will be familiar from the Preface.)

> *The first thing being shown to me is a male figure that I would say as being above, that would be to me some type of father image, I want to talk about the number seven, symbolic of the month July or the seventh of some type of month.*

Early in our experimental work, that type of statement made me uncomfortable. "July or the seventh of a month"—the either/or doubles the likelihood that the sitter will find something to resonate with.

But our scoring methods now took this into account. If July was right and the seventh wrong, the medium would be credited with one hit and one miss. So multiple guesses could just mean that much greater chance for a low score.

*I also want to talk about another father figure. Two fathers, could be like father and father-in-law to be acknowledged. One of these people must have had problems in either the valve of the heart or something that would pump in and out, and there is some type of connection that is outside of family, where they either had liver or pancreatic cancer . . . filtered bad or not filtered properly. . . . Showing me the month of May.*

*And when they show me dates, it's to acknowledge a passing, a celebration, some type of event that come. . . . They're telling me to talk about the Big H—um, the H connection. To me this is an H with an N sound. So what they are talking about Henna, Henry, but there's an HN connection. Some kind of out-of-state connection but I feel like I'm all over the place.*

A quick list of specific facts here. On the other hand, two different months were mentioned. Again, this sounded as if it could be just guessing.

But seven indeed figured into this family's life. The oldest daughter was born in July, the seventh month; the sitter's home condominium number was 708; her husband's office suite number was 7; and so on. In fact, the family in times past had spoken of seven as the "family number."

The "Big H" was Henry, who had been known to his professional colleagues as the "gentle giant." He had died in the month of May, and his mother's name was Henrietta.

What about other items mentioned by John—father figure, outside the family, died of pancreatic cancer? According to the sitter, this could well be her husband's esteemed colleague and friend, who had died of pancreatic cancer about two years after Henry.

What about the possible celebration, and an out-of-state connection? Those were to be explained soon enough.

All things considered, John's accuracy was already well above 70 percent. He went on to speak about "... very strong symbolism of teaching and books" and "there may have been something published." A physician and well-known educator, Henry had published two hundred papers and edited seven books—more clear hits.

Moving into the yes/no part of the session, John continued bringing in other family members.

> *Again, there is a father figure. Is there a biological father who has passed?*

> Yes.

> *Is there also a father-in-law who has crossed over?*

> Yes.

This would later be corrected. Not only do experienced mediums make mistakes, sitters make mistakes, too. It turns out that this particular sitter made a number of important errors that confused John.

> *And they're telling me to talk about the diabetes—but this is female. And there's an L connection around it—it's either Elizabeth, Ellen, Eileen—very L ... Do you understand?*

> No.

> *It's on your mom's side or connected with the mother figure or the mother-in-law—it's the same side with the other with the B name, either Betty, Beth, or Bobby.*

A few days after the reading, the sitter remembered that one of her relatives on her mother's side was diabetic and had an L name. The B name could have been the sitter's Uncle Benny, her mother's brother.

Or was I stretching to make the statement fit remote facts?

John then spoke of an out-of-state tie and "Gemini or the sign of the twins; they want me to talk about actual twins." The sitter's daughter, who was living in Boston ("out of state"), fit the rest of the description in two ways: she was born under the sign of Gemini, and she has twin children.

The reading ended here, having produced many hits of the kind we were now accustomed to. But the most interesting information came *after* the readings officially ended. The sitter, still unseen by the medium, was now allowed to ask the medium about specific topics, and John responded with something that seemed out of the blue.

> *. . . three properties, three real estate issues where two are like close and one's in a different place; two similar, one different.*

The real estate item made absolutely no sense to the sitter at the time. Later, watching the videotape of the session, she remembered that she and her husband had once owned two houses on Staten Island: one their residence, the other used as his office for thirty years. These two, which John had described as "close," were less than a mile apart. Years afterward, the couple had moved to a new residence in Boca Raton, Florida.

> If you could talk about the husband's image?

> *There're telling me to bring the Big S. Also that comes up around Henry or the H. There's a big S*

*that comes up—they're making me feel that it's important that I acknowledge this.*

The sitter's daughter and mother of the twins is the S: Shelley.

*They show me lab-related stuff, so whether there's someone who works in the health care field or they're in some kind of lab-related function but they're coming from a lab background.*

Shelley does indeed do lab-related work in the health care field. Holding a doctorate in molecular biology and psychopharmacology, she runs a medical school laboratory at Boston University.

Now, content came very fast.

*. . . a father dying in someone else's family, on the East Coast . . . someone who has his ties and done something funny with it, like frame it—but I feel I need to joke about this tie thing.*

This information initially made no sense to the sitter, but it turned out to be very meaningful upon reflection.

John then moved into the remarkable story detailed in the Preface about "something funny happening at the beach" involving her mother, which turned out to be a family story about the beautiful mother's reluctance to allow her legs to be seen at the beach, thinking they were not attractive enough, when in fact they were perfectly normal.

After that, John spoke about her holding something connected to her husband. She denied it, and John replied, "I'm just telling you what he's telling me." In fact, it was a matter of interpretation: she was *wearing* a ring of her husband's, but had her other hand wrapped around the ring, so in a sense she was indeed holding it.

John's contradicting of the sitter was consistent with his hypothesis that he communicates with living spirits who will correct not only him but the sitter, as well.

And suddenly, out of nowhere, John brought up the subject of tea that appears earlier but I think is worth repeating:

> *"And enjoy the tea." . . . I have no idea what that means, "enjoy the tea"—like I feel like I'm having tea but enjoy it. Like "drink" . . . I have no idea what this is, but I feel it's kind of inside humor: "Enjoy the tea."*

If John was not really communicating with her deceased husband, how would he have known that she had never liked tea when he was alive but had since developed a taste for it?

Moreover, the comments suggested that the husband was continuing to observe what was going on in her life.

What happened next suggested a limitation on what a medium can do. Or maybe it's just a limitation on what they are able to achieve with our present state of knowledge.

Earlier the sitter had twice asked about a description of her husband, and John had not responded. Again she asked for specific information, and John sidestepped. The exchange went like this:

> He doesn't have any messages for me as his wife, does he?

> *Before I will let anybody come through with any type of messages, my whole focus in the work that I do is to try to bring validation and facts through to show you that there is a survival of their energy and they're a part of your life. To me, that is the ultimate big-message bit.*

> *As far as giving you the flowery loving messages and whatnot, that's not gonna come through me. So I kind of provide the information and the acknowledgments of "here they are."*
>
> *Their biggest message is coming from a point of love and to let you know there is a reunion of souls here but also there. That's my big message.*

John's total accuracy for this reading appeared to be at least 70 to 80 percent. The amount of information was less during the silent period, but even there, it was clearly above 70 percent. Some of the information obtained during the yes/no period was both specific and meaningful. And it did not appear to be shot-in-the-dark guesses: less than 20 percent of what John received would have been correct for me, had I been the sitter.

## THE SITTER UNMASKED

A skeptic might contend that there was a serious complication with this session. The sitter not only was known to the experimenter but was family.

The sitter was Linda's mother.

We were deliberately interested in seeing whether the relationship between the sitter and experimenter mattered. This is an important scientific question, and it deserves a scientific answer.

If the experimenter and the sitter are unrelated, then two possible families of deceased people, or information about deceased people, are potentially in the same room—the sitter's and the experimenter's. Do the mediums sometimes get confused? Yes. But our findings to date suggest that the majority of information received does not depend on whether the sitter knows the experimenter.

For the record, none of the mediums knew we were including Linda's mother, Elayne, as one of the ten sitters in the experiment. And John had never met Linda's mother before she served as a sitter.

One final point about this unique reading: John had also spoken of a "G," whom he described as "from another family . . . whose father died on the East Coast" and "someone who has his ties and done something funny with it."

That person was not hard to identify. He is also a Gemini, his last name is also a "Big S," and he also works in the health field, in a laboratory. He even feels inspired to wear Henry's ties on special occasions, such as when he was filmed for the HBO documentary and for the Arts and Entertainment documentary special *Beyond Death*.

The "G" is me: Gary Schwartz.

The reading with Linda's mother was particularly special to us because it spoke to the reason why Linda and I began this research in the first place. It addressed Linda's desire, as well as her mother's and family's, to discover scientifically whether Henry is still here.

However, from a scientific point of view, the second sitter's readings were more interesting and important, as you shall see. The sitter was the author of *Infinite Grace*, Diane Goldner. She was also staying at Canyon Ranch, where the mediums stayed, and she encountered them the day before the experiment at a panel on mediumship we held that drew an audience of about a hundred people. The mediums, though, did not know that Diane would be a sitter.

Just before Diane's reading, John had a mental image and wrote down information about a man who had died in a fire, though he had no idea what it was connected with.

His session with Diane was curious: John was able to report absolutely nothing. He went completely blank. We might have expected that meeting Diane before the reading would have helped, but it didn't work like that. On a scale of 0 to 100, John got a great big zero.

If he were cheating, you might expect him either to have a great reading, or to deliberately make it look average. But why would he make it a complete failure? Was this the ploy of a great actor, or was John distracted . . . perhaps by an unknown man who had been killed in a fire?

## A Pair in Contrast

Two of the other sitters that day provided a contrast in extremes. One of them, an undergraduate at the University of Arizona, was deeply spiritual; the other, a physician, was notable most of all for his irreverent sense of humor.

Like many others, the story of Heather Rist, the undergraduate, reflects the heart-warming desire to connect with loved ones who have died, reminding us that conducting research in this area is not only science but also touches the core values we place on human relationships.

Heather told me that the night before the experiment she prayed that her loved ones would be contacted. She recalled that as she walked to her first reading she asked for a sign: "At that moment a bird jumped onto a railing, looked at me curiously, hopped a couple of steps closer, and looked at me curiously again, cocking its head to the side." She was well aware this was most likely just a bird doing its normal bird-thing but yet she couldn't help hoping it might be something more—the sign she had asked for.

The last medium Heather met with was John Edward, and she viewed this reading as her last chance to connect with her brother Travis, since none of the other mediums had conclusively identified him.

Like the other mediums that day, John mentioned Heather's great-grandmother and correctly cited her cause of death as breast cancer. He also reported the date of July 24 as being connected to a person with a C or K name, which at the time seemed like a complete miss. It wasn't until later, when Heather was talking to her boyfriend, that she realized the date was his birthday and that his last name began with a C.

However, her primary hope of hearing about her brother still hadn't been fulfilled. But it wasn't long before John provided these suggestive statements.

"I'm getting a young male energy coming through," she remembers John saying. "He says that he is the reason that you're here. He says he was just being polite in letting the others come through first, but he's the real reason you're here."

Heather fought back the tears as she continued with the reading, trying to remain a good research sitter and not reveal too much to the medium. Then John mentioned a yellow bird, and at that moment a bird again popped into view, outside a window visible to both John and Heather.

"Do you see this bird? Does it mean anything to you? He says he is doing this."

For Heather, this validated her experience with the bird before the experiment started.

After the session was over, John asked how her brother had died. Heather said he had died in his sleep during a fire.

"He just about fell out of his chair and said, 'Holy shit,' " she recalls.

John then reached for the pad of paper on which he had scribbled out the words "man in fire," which the previous sitter had said held no meaning for her. The videotape documents John's great surprise. For Heather, that was a dazzling moment.

According to Heather, the other mediums accurately reported the names and descriptions of several relatives. Many of the statements about her great-grandmother—for instance, that she had an injured leg—Heather later verified with her grandmother.

During one of the readings, Suzane Northrop reported that this grandmother was floating between the spirit and physical realms, preparing to cross over to the "other side." This same statement was also reported by Laurie Campbell.

In a later reading, Laurie reported a remark from Heather's dead brother that dying in his sleep had been peaceful and that he wished everyone could go that way. Heather not long afterward had the chance to share the remark with her grandmother and "had a weird, indescribable feeling." Telling me of the incident, she explained, "My grandmother died a week after that visit, in her sleep."

Does Heather's story just exemplify the human desire to hold on to the memory of our loved ones?

Did the mediums bring up Heather's great-grandmother because it was an easy guess? (Who doesn't have a great-grandmother in the hereafter?) Or was it Heather's "calling" to tell her grandmother that her mother and grandson were waiting for her?

As you can see, the silent paradigm turned out to be both baffling and quite stirring.

With the physician, almost at the very beginning of the silent-period reading, John said:

> *I'm . . . being shown the movie* Pretty in Pink. . . . *A pink connection. Pretty intense, this information. And dying the hair, dying the hair.*

A few minutes later, John came back to this idea.

> *I just want to stress very strongly the movie* Pretty in Pink. *It's a very predominant thing that's coming across to me. Do you have any ties to that movie?*

> No.

> *Very predominant connection to the movie* Pretty in Pink. *Huge. Not to be facetious, are you, like, wearing all pink?*

> Yes!

John broke out laughing at the ridiculousness of this. The sitter, despite his prominence in the medical world, had—as a joke, or perhaps as a test of the medium's abilities—come to the session dressed in pink trousers and a pink Hawaiian T-shirt.

The contrast between the student's sensitivity and tears and the doctor's irreverence served as a pointed reminder—if I needed one—that in this research I could always expect the unexpected.

# · 1 0 ·

# The Christopher Readings

Would it make any difference if the sitter was someone with a highly developed sense of spirituality? Christopher, a sometime staff member of ours, had been raised in a spiritual home and knew through firsthand experience both the gift and the curse of being brought up by an extraordinarily metaphysical mother. A devout Theosophist, she had lived her life as if life continued forever.

Christopher wanted to find out whether his mother was inspired or merely out of her mind—a question he had entertained about the mediums themselves.

Some moments from his readings that day remain with me still.

## WITH ANNE GEHMAN: "YOU SOMETIMES HAVE WRIST PAIN"

As required by the experimental design, Christopher sat quietly for the first ten minutes while Anne attempted to receive whatever information she could.

Her first impression was of a woman named Edith, whose face, Anne said, had become paralyzed shortly before her death.

She also reported sensing three Johns, one of whom was still alive.

Christopher didn't know who Edith was. John is such a common name that he knew several of them, living and deceased. What was unusual was the medium saying "three Johns, one of whom is still alive." Could Anne be referring to Christopher himself, then in the midst of a legal change from his given name, John, to his middle name?

Anne then said she felt the presence of a young man who had recently died an accidental death.

Could this be Joe, a friend who had died not long ago? "The accident may have involved drugs or alcohol," she added.

Christopher had not so far said a word to Anne, and yet she was suggesting a story quite consistent with Joe's personality and a lifestyle that had been free-spirited bordering on reckless.

"He wants you to know he's okay," she said. That kind of reassurance is what so many people turn to mediums for, every day.

Anne immediately changed the subject. Rubbing her left arm, she said that Christopher suffered from pain in his wrist and upper forearm.

Christopher was stunned. There seemed no way for Anne to have any clue who this sitter was, yet she had just described his pain perfectly.

Two years before, Christopher's soccer team had been ahead with less than five minutes to play when he was taken down by a defender's illegal tackle and had suffered a broken arm. He still had two pins in his arm and a pair of five-inch scars to show for it. No one, not even Linda and I, knew of this injury before the experiment.

"You need to let go of the pain and anger you have associated with this," Anne told him.

It was as if Michael Jordan had just made a three-pointer. According to Christopher, he had struggled ever since the incident to free himself of the anger and frustration he still felt toward the player who had caused his injury. And here was Anne—still during the silent period—laying it all before him as easily and smoothly as a walk in the park.

Hearing her words, Christopher found his feelings of anger, pain, and sadness unexpectedly rekindled. He had been prepared for the possibility of hearing from his deceased mother, his dead friend, and his late grandmother. But he wasn't emotionally prepared to have his history of pain and anger paraded before him.

Anne continued with more personal information. She spoke of Christopher's having had an out-of-body experience, and that he was interested in psychology, the higher mind, and extended consciousness. She said a person named Andrew would help him in doing some writing about healing and mental health. Save for the mention of Andrew, all the other statements were true.

Part way into the yes/no period, Anne suddenly broke off in midsentence.

"Two people are with me now," she said. "They're your grandparents. I'm getting the name Will . . . William."

"Yes."

"They died a short time apart," Anne said.

"Yes," Christopher confirmed. The previous year, his grandmother had died only three weeks after his grandfather.

Anne also reported the impression of Christopher's deceased mother and said that her name included the sound "Bet." Anne said she felt the presence of a "Ma."

His mother's name was Betty. And "Ma" is indeed what his mother's family affectionately called his grandmother.

Anne again focused on Christopher's personal life. Moving into an area that the mediums in our experiments have rarely gone to, she said that a suggested trip to Mexico was a good idea and urged him not to hesitate. She also said that it would provide useful information, and she predicted a return trip to Mexico with a group of people a year after the first visit.

Another three-pointer. Christopher's wife had for several months been pushing him to take her to Mexico.

At the end of the reading, Anne spoke of Christopher's grandparents on his father's side. "They want you to know they're here and that they love you," she said. "They've asked me to give you a hug."

Anne then got up out of her chair and turned around, seeing Christopher for the first time. They hugged, and then Anne placed her hand on Christopher's injured arm.

"You must let go to help this completely heal."

Christopher's emotions were now raw. And this was just the beginning.

## With John Edward: "Have You Ever Considered Raising Cows?"

During the silent period with Christopher, John provided some information with little emotion. Then the mood changed. "I feel a tightness in my lungs. It's really strong." He described the feeling as consistent with the difficulty of breathing before death.

And then he added an innocuous remark that was nonetheless stunning to Christopher. "She wants me to acknowledge your partner."

Christopher's mother had never met his wife.

Still during the ten-minute silent part of the experiment, John began offering names of family members. "Kathy, Karen . . . K, K names" matched the names of Christopher's sisters: Kathy, Karen, and Kandee. He mentioned a Jim or James, the name of Christopher's brother-in-law.

He said that Christopher's mother was worried about his sister, who was a great distance away. The youngest sister, Kandee, had recently moved to Seattle from Tucson, but Christopher had not heard of any problems. Not until Christopher was with the next medium, Suzane Northrop, would he get a possible answer.

John Edward continued, suddenly blurting out, "Your mom died in February. She says, 'I'm back, I'm radiant, glowing, and surrounded by pink roses.'"

John also reported an older man as a relative of Christopher's father, and the presence of a man who had died instantly in a possible "high to low accident." Could this be Christopher's beloved grandfather and his departed close friend, Joe?

Turning to people around Christopher's mother, John sensed a woman with an R name who liked to crochet—a description that fit his grandmother Ruth, who had crocheted his first baby blanket.

"Have you ever considered raising cows or cattle?"

Stunned, Christopher did a quick mental inventory and recalled a conversation he had had with his wife while driving through rural Colorado. He had announced, only partly in jest, that he might quit his job to become a cowboy.

He acknowledged to John that he had indeed considered raising cattle, and asked, "Did my mother hear our conversation?"

John replied "Well, your mom's teasing you about that."

Christopher was dumbfounded. He was experiencing as a sitter what I had experienced as an experimenter—bewilderment. There was no way John could have hired a secret detective to get *that* information. And no cold reader worth his salt is going to inquire out of the blue something as outlandish and unlikely as "Have you considered raising cows or cattle?"

Then John dropped a bomb of a question on Christopher. It was even more out of left field, and more shocking than asking about cows.

"Are you in a same-sex or transvestite relationship?"

"No." Christopher flatly responded.

"Are you sure? This is coming in really strong," he insisted. "Your mom says she knows about this."

At first, Christopher was completely baffled. John had really missed on this one—and what an incredibly invasive, offensive question to ask any stranger.

Two days after the reading, a possible explanation popped into Christopher's mind. About a week before the experiment, his wife had jokingly asked whether Christopher would remain married to her if she had a sex change operation. Christopher said no—that he wanted to be with a woman, not a man—and they had both laughed about it.

He was left to wonder, was his mother sometimes present during his conversations with his wife? What other explanation could there be?

John said that Christopher's mother wanted to assure him that she is with him all the time. This was a woman who throughout her life had been a big believer in the afterlife. If John was correct, she was living out her belief with a passion.

"She's telling me that I need to give you a hug, so I'm turning around now," John said.

When Christopher recounted this to me, I was astonished. Two readings, one after the next, and two spontaneous hugs from the mediums? Anne maybe, but not John—he does not regularly hug his sitters.

After they embraced, John told Christopher he was moved by his mother's powerful personality.

He added, "I don't give hugs." And, with a shake of his head, "Whew, your mom was a strong woman, wasn't she?"

## With Suzane Northrop: "I'm Seeing Goats in the Mountains"

Now with his third medium and more familiar with what to expect, Christopher was less surprised but even more impressed with Suzane's immediate detection of his mother and her family.

"I'm getting the name Rose or someone's fondness of roses," she said, quickly lighting on his mother's favorite flower. Suzane also confirmed that his mother had been in a coma before she died and that she had suffered from heavy swelling of the legs. Christopher hadn't said a word yet, and Suzane was getting precise and accurate details.

As Christopher quietly sat behind Suzane, she raised her hands in a tense, disfigured gesture. What was she doing?

"Your mom's hands were crippled. She had a hard time using them," she said. "They're okay now."

A long three-pointer.

Suzane spoke, often nonstop and at high speed, providing a barrage of information, as is her way. She reported the presence of a man that she initially believed to be a brother but soon corrected that to "like a brother and who had died quickly." Again this sounded like his friend Joe but the statement was too general to mean much.

She moved on quickly, jumping around abruptly from one deceased person to the next, to talk about a man on his father's side who had left behind a car he was very fond of. To Christopher, this could only be his grandfather, who had given him his special car two months before his death. In one breath, Suzane had gone from the general to the very, very specific.

Continuing to jump around as if she were on a spiritual basketball court, Suzane then came back to Christopher's mother, saying that she was concerned about the well-being of a sister who lived far away. This was the second time a medium had seemingly referred to his sister in Seattle.

"[Your mom] says there was a lot of upset surrounding her death and that she wants everyone to let it go. She knows there are things you would have liked to have said to her."

And then she added, as if talking about someone she had just met at a cocktail party, "Your mom's a pistol, isn't she?"

I was discovering that Suzane liked to use this word when describing a powerful woman. Yet I would in time recognize that in the three experiments when she used this word, each was very apt. Christopher's mother was powerful indeed, a veritable "pistol"—first in physical life, and now, seemingly, in the afterlife.

After reporting the presence of Christopher's grandparents, Suzane referred to a man whose name began with an "H" and said, "I'm seeing goats in the mountain. Does that mean anything to you?"

Christopher's maternal grandfather, Hugh, had been a sheepherder in mile-high surroundings.

And then—"Your mother wants to give you a rose." Her favorite flower. Even a skeptic might have quietly wiped away a tear.

Unexpectedly she then said, in her sometimes flip New York style, "Zip, that's it, they're gone."

And just like that, the reading was over.

Three readings, three sets of tears. Sorry/grateful, regretful/happy, he was unprepared for how moved he had been by the experiences. And he still had one more medium to go.

## With Laurie Campbell: "You'll Always Be My Little Boy"

Christopher was especially interested in what would happen with Laurie because she was the only medium he had met previously, though of course she was not told he would be a sitter. As in the case of the earlier John Edward reading with Diane Goldner, we were particularly interested in knowing whether their having met would make any noticeable difference.

The result was very much the same as with John and Diane. Laurie was unable to pick up information during the silent period—something that had almost never happened for her.

She began by "reading" Christopher as a professor or faculty member and had a hard time accepting that he was not. "I just keep seeing the university and a study. You're not a student?"

However, she was close: he wasn't then in school but had only recently graduated.

Laurie reported that Christopher and his wife had a dog that they sometimes "treat like a child." She described where they were living—the house with its wood floors, the yard with its odd shape, the area where the dog liked to play. All her statements were specific and accurate.

For me, the bit with the dog and the house was one of the subtle shots that true Michael Jordans make, which seem so easy when you watch them but you realize are very difficult when you think about them.

According to Christopher, Laurie was able to determine in many ways that she felt a distance between him and his father, and sensed he was closer to his grandfather than to his father, "almost a skip in generations." She confirmed that his grandfather had been healthy and that his death had taken the family by surprise.

"I see your grandpa at your graduation."

Again Christopher was fighting back the tears.

After the reading, Laurie told Christopher that she had pictured the graduation scene with his grandfather attending in the physical. Christopher explained that his grandfather had always stressed the importance of education—had even helped pay for Christopher's college—and Christopher had been very much looking forward to standing up at graduation with the beloved old man watching proudly from the audience. It was not to be; his grandfather died about a month before.

But the highlight of the reading, Christopher told me later, had come in a single statement of just a few words. According to Laurie, his grandfather had told her to say, "You'll always be my little boy."

These words, according to Christopher, "pierced my heart because it was an expression of love that my grandfather was not able to verbally communicate to me when he was alive."

If Laurie and the other mediums are correct, maybe Christopher's mother, friend, and grandfather are still with him in ways that they can see and we can only imagine.

## CHRISTOPHER'S EXPERIENCE

When Christopher finished the four readings, he said, "I felt like I'd just run a marathon. I was perspiring, I had muscle aches, my head hurt, and I was slightly weak in the knees."

Why did his experience produce so many physical and emotional responses? He said it wasn't the mediums' ability to give an accurate death tally that was most memorable. It was "the feeling in the room"—a feeling he called "indescribable except that it felt at times like we were not alone" and "like the feeling you get when you feel you're being watched, only to look up and find out it's true, that someone is looking your way."

He understood that it could have been just the experience of reliving the past: "an emotional response from deep within my consciousness, a place that wanted this to be true." And although a believer in the survival of consciousness as a strong possibility, he was stunned by the level of success. "The number of hits the mediums made was a shocking and surreal experience. There I was, sitting in a hotel room behind complete strangers who, while facing away from me, were able to give detailed descriptions of my life and family."

He saw the day as a story that unfolded reading by reading. Anne had provided the introduction, John and Suzane built with an update of loved ones' lives, and Laurie ended the day with a touching private time with his grandfather, when words previously unspoken were shared.

And how did Anne know about his wrist pain, John about the cows, Suzane about the goats on the mountain? How had Laurie described his house so perfectly?

But, again, the most unexplainable and breathtaking part of the readings came with statements about things unknown to the sitter until later. Three of the mediums had spoken of his mother's expressing concern for one of his sisters. When he later spoke to the sister, the message alarmed her. "Am I going to die?" she asked.

After some coaxing, she admitted there was reason for concern. The move to Seattle had been very difficult for her. Issues concerning their mother's death had resurfaced, and she found herself reliving old feelings of guilt and anger. She was also debating some important decisions in her life and wishing she could talk to her mother about them.

Christopher had been on a spiritual and emotional roller-coaster ride he would never forget.

# · 11 ·

# The Revealing Pat Price Readings

It was already late in the day when the time came for John Edward's reading with Pat Price. Everyone, I think, was beginning to feel drained from the pace of session after session. I was beginning to wonder whether we had scheduled too much, whether the remaining encounters could produce anything of value.

Two things would happen in this reading to make it memorable. We would get the answer to the question of whether the death of Pat's husband Mike would be sensed by any of the mediums.

And John's reading would contain a single, powerful phrase that would continue to resonate with me long afterward.

### WITH JOHN EDWARD

*I want to talk . . . through the husband's family. Okay? It's somebody connected through the husband. Also is there a Michael or a Mike. 'Cause it's like you need to acknowledge the Mike or the Michael.*

A bit later, John reported that other family members were also present.

> *Okay. I've got both of your parents here. They're making . . . this is what I referred to like when my mother died, it's a cameo appearance, she's like, "Well, let 'em know that they're here." Now, they're also making me feel like I've got this younger female that I want to talk about and they're also talking about teasing you about—do you ride a motorcycle?*

> Yes.

> *Okay. Your parents are teasing you about they didn't raise you like that—putting you on the back of a motorcycle. But it's like a wink, wink, wink, wink— kind of, kind of a connection. They're making me feel like they are here and they've got their younger male who is with them. So this is like their son, their grandson, but there's a younger male who's there.*

After a few more minutes came that memorable phrase, to me one of the most important statements of this or any other reading we've done so far.

> *They're trying to tell me that for me, doing this for you today is a validation of either your own experience or maybe I'm now validating what somebody else just did for you.*
> *But I'm validating a validation, is what they're trying to tell me.*

"Validating a validation." Powerful to me both for the meaning and for the ring of the language.

And then Pat's recently dead husband visited.

*Okay. They're making me feel it's very important—okay, you're gonna think I'm all right. I'm gonna tell you exactly. They're telling me to tell you your husband is here. Now I was going to tell you that your husband was like around me outside and to go get him, because this son figure, the son figure is telling me to tell you that he's here. This is what's coming through. And he's making me feel like, he's making me feel like he—wait a second. Your son has passed before his father?*

Yes.

*He's telling me he greeted his dad. This is what he's showing me, and he's making me feel like boom, [snapping fingers] one, two, three, somebody passes quickly. This is what's being acknowledged.*

Yes.

We had our answer. Mike had died so very recently, yet John had no difficulty being aware of his presence.

*And I also feel like this is something that was warned. You were warned about this. This was not something that . . .*

Yes.

*. . . And I feel like soon, very recent, soon. Very recent, like somebody just crosses and I bet this happened in the last three to six, three to six, three to six.*

Yes.

Recent, yes; but even more recent than he sensed. In a way, Pat's response was misleading.

> *And I feel like this is something that could not have been stopped . . . Your death views or your view on death and your experience with death and dying . . . helps him make a transition, and he's thanking you for doing that.*
>
> *And he's making me feel like they arranged for you to be here. This is what they're showing me. And that this is very, very important. That they arranged for this. And that nothing happens by accident. This is what they want me—want me to kind of come across with.*

"They arranged for you to be here"—it was only because of Mike's death that Pat had been invited to be a sitter.

> *Now they tell me you talked about "Michael times two." Now, is Michael your son?*

Yes.

> *Is there another Michael besides him?*

Yes.

> *Okay. 'Cause they say Michael times two. And they tell me to talk about—they tell me, your husband was afraid of this, but he believed in it, but he was a little put off by it at the same time, correct?*

Through most of his life Mike had, indeed, been a little put off by talk of a hereafter, and he had teased his wife about her belief in it for thirty years.

## WITH SUZANE NORTHROP

During Pat's readings with Suzane, the intense atmosphere was lightened briefly by a humorous moment when Suzane mentioned seeing a little dog. I assumed that she was seeing PeeWee, a replication from the HBO experiment. But when she went on to describe the dog as looking like a beagle, I changed my mind: wrong breed.

Relaxing after the readings, I asked Pat about the dog. She smiled and pulled out her wallet. PeeWee's mother had been . . . yes, a beagle, and Pat proudly showed us her picture. Once again, what seemed to be a mistake had a plausible explanation, after all.

Suzane also received some remarkable information about the passing of Michael, Sr. For example, she reported receiving communication with Pat's son, who had this message for his mother:

> *"I'm with daddy, and daddy just came over. But daddy was sick. Daddy knew he was gonna pass, and he didn't want you to have to take care of him."*
>
> *Proud man. Do you understand? Also successful, he tells me. He's not modest. Do you understand?*

Yes.

That must have brought a lump to Pat's throat because of conversations she and her husband had had in the months before his death—conversations I would not learn of until later.

Pat's readings with both Suzane and John had been wrenchingly emotional. But in the process, information was replicated from the HBO experiment and extended by the appearance of Michael Sr.

The skeptic will be quick to point to the obvious limitations in these two readings, and we would be the first to agree. But to dismiss the readings as due to fraud, cold reading, lucky guesses, or even memory from the previous HBO readings would be to ignore the remarkably high percentage of +3 hits obtained during the silent periods (the scoring would reveal them to be 77 percent accurate) and would also ignore the precise nature of the information received during the yes/no periods.

Your conclusions may be different from ours, but if nothing else, we see these readings as paying homage to the loving biker who came to believe in the possibility of survival of consciousness.

First, he witnessed research in our laboratory as the husband of the primary sitter in the HBO experiment. Then, he shared his new vision about the possibility of survival with his family and friends. Finally, he "participated" from the beyond in the Miraval Experiment, bringing new hope and vision to his wife and to the world.

Was Michael, in his own way, "validating a validation"? The story continues.

## RESULTS OF THE DETAILED SCORING

When the transcripts were ready and time had come for the scoring, we discovered a problem. The sitters, who had traveled from as far away as the East Coast and Hawaii, had willingly made their journeys for the experiment, but returning to Tucson to do the scoring turned out to be a different story. In the end, only Patricia Price performed the scoring.

She arranged to show up at our laboratory in September 1999, a few months after the readings had taken place. To ensure that skeptics and believers alike could verify our procedures, the entire scoring session was videotaped. Following the same procedure as before, Pat used the numbers from –3 to +3 to individually rate the more than two hundred items received by Suzane and John (Chart 11-1).

For the total readings, the two mediums achieved levels of accuracy similar to those in the HBO experiment. The control subjects' accuracy ratings from the HBO experiment are included in the center for comparison.

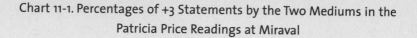

Chart 11-1. Percentages of +3 Statements by the Two Mediums in the
Patricia Price Readings at Miraval

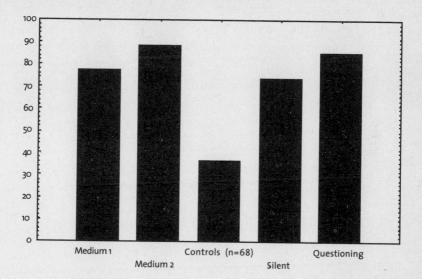

The chart also depicts the accuracy levels for the silent period, 77 percent, and the yes/no questioning period, 85 percent. Though the number of items was less for the silent period (64) than the yes/no period (157), the +3 accuracy level for the silent items was truly remarkable. (For the record, most of the silent items came from Suzane.)

Did John or Suzane figure out in the yes/no period that the person sitting behind them was Pat, one of the women they had read in the HBO experiment? As John put it, he does hundreds of readings a month and could hardly be expected to remember a particular individual months later.

At the end of each of the readings, I carefully pushed John and Suzane to guess who was sitting behind them. More accurately, I grilled them. Neither could identify the sitter, but when each turned around and saw who it was, they of course recognized her from the HBO experiment, when they had met not only Pat but her husband, Mike, as well. Each immediately realized that Mike was the dead husband they had just been talking about, and their pain was palpable.

We counted the experiment as highly successful, providing compelling further evidence. But would it be enough to convince a skeptic? I was sure not. What further controls could we put in place?

The question would haunt me for weeks.

## • 12 •

# Is There Such a Thing as Precognition?

I'm no longer sure who suggested something might have been said during Pat's readings in the HBO experiment that we should go back and take a look at. But we pulled the transcripts out to review them and found ourselves in a further quandary.

See for yourself.

### PAT PRICE WITH JOHN EDWARD, HBO EXPERIMENT

*Okay, the first thing that's coming through is they're telling me to talk about a male figure to your side. A male figure to your side would be a husband or a brother who has crossed over. Do you understand that?*

*They're showing me . . . one seems to be like a husband figure to you. Do you understand that?*

Yes.

Pat answered in the affirmative, though her husband was very much alive at the time; Mike's death was still months in the future.

Moments later, John referred to their son (the one who committed suicide).

> *There's a younger male figure, also connected to your husband who's crossed over, which either means it's his brother or there's a son who's crossed. But there's a younger male figure. Do you understand that?*

After John reported that the son had gone out "with a boom," he continued with the father/son connection.

> *Okay. They're coming through with your husband and they're showing me the month of May, actually what they're showing me is a five. A five to me represents the 5th month, May, or the 5th of a month has some type of meaning. Do you understand that?*

> Yes.

And Pat went on to make a connection with Mother's Day, the last time she received a gift from her son.

> *Okay. Did your husband have a dog [that] passed?*

Another PeeWee reference. In his next few remarks, John described some of the dog's personality, referring to a "he" who was telling him the information.

Much of the dialogue was with the son; yet, John at times appeared to be confused about whether it was coming from the father or the son.

Pat tried to intervene, asking whether she was allowed to say something, possibly wanting to correct the mistake. Thinking it would interrupt the flow and possibly break John's concentration, I asked Pat not to speak just then. John continued to talk about her husband as if he were dead.

*Now, was it your husband that was in the coma?*

Yes.

I did not understand this at the time of reading it, but would soon enough.

> *'Cause he's making me feel like his physical body was still running while he was kind of leaving the body. And that he was not of clear mind when he passes. But he's telling me to let you know that his passing was quick and peaceful. He shows me a peaceful passing. Okay?*

John was being very specific about Mike's passing, though Mike was still very much alive.

> *I see your son standing in front. . . . I see it's almost like your son greets the father figure. Whether it's his father or stepfather, the father figure is greeted by the younger male, is what's being shown. That's how it's coming through to me.*
> *And my feeling is to say that they're together, and that it's okay. And you need to have peace of mind with this. That's what I'm being shown. You need to have peace of mind, and that's what they're expressing to you.*

At the end of the reading Pat was allowed to ask questions. She wanted more information about her husband.

*What I was seeing is your husband was making a reference. Prior to leaving the body he shows me a male figure who is not of clear mind, the physical body is basically still running, but the soul is not in it. So I see this being like if the soul is the driver of a car, the car would be the body, the car was running, but the driver was not in it.*

The analogy to a car and driver would take on a haunting meaning.

Only at this point did Pat reveal to John that her husband was still alive. Despite this new information, John maintained the validity of his first impressions.

*Okay. Well, I'm getting this as being a male figure to your side. That to me would be like a husband figure.*

Why had Pat, on so many occasions, followed John's lead about her husband's being dead? I thought that perhaps, overcome with the emotions of the day, she had mistakenly given John the wrong information, and John went along with it.

The skeptic could argue that this was a classic case of intentional deception on the part of the medium. If John had been really communicating with the dead, he should have known that her husband was still physically alive—right?

One other possibility can be entertained here—something mediums claim happens from time to time. Could this be an instance of psychic precognition—of John's seeing the future and not knowing it?

He kept saying, "This is what I'm seeing" not "This is what I'm hearing." He also said, many times, "They're showing me this . . ." referring to other supposed spirits who were allowing him to view this image. So was John seeing the future through his "guides"?

John claims that he was a psychic before he was a medium. It was while he was doing so-called psychic readings that he began to notice "hearing voices in his head." He came to accept these voices as spirits connected to his clients after he realized he was able to provide the clients accurate details about their deceased relatives.

But what about Pat? Why had she gone along with it? This is exactly what I asked her when we went back to review the HBO transcripts and rediscovered her surprising lack of forthrightness. My question to her didn't bring the response I expected. Far from it.

Pat explained that while she was reluctant at first to accept the statements, she was forced to believe they might have confirmed a gloomy dream she had had about her husband a month before the HBO experiment. In a nightmare, she had seen Mike die in a car accident.

So she had understood when John said those things? She had known at the time of the HBO readings what he was talking about?

"Yes," she acknowledged. She hadn't spoken up because the truth seemed so somber and so personal.

Pat then told us the full story, which would haunt us long after.

## TWO CASES OF PRECOGNITION?

Years earlier, Pat told us, Mike had been mugged and almost killed. Since then he had suffered from chronic head and neck pain, and more recently the long-term effects of the incident had started to catch up with him. Severe headaches and blackouts, and occasional paralysis in the back of his neck, became more frequent. He was also losing coordination and sleeping a lot.

They had both considered the possibility that he might die, but they had never shared this possibility with the mediums, Linda, or me.

One day, Pat said, he had asked her directly, "You feel it, don't you?"

"It wasn't what I felt; it was what I didn't feel," Pat told us. "And that was light coming from him."

Three weeks before his death, Mike's usual habit of working from dusk until dawn changed. He started coming home early and began eating very little. When Pat tried to bring up making plans for their anniversary, Mike just shrugged them off. "You go ahead and make the plans, and I'll try to be there," she remembers him saying.

She remembered thinking, "What do you mean, 'You'll try'?"

One day he told her, "Baby, I'm not going to make our anniversary." He hugged her tightly, and walked away with tears in his eyes. A few days later, she heard him tell a friend the same thing. The chilling moment brought back recollections of the nightmare when she envisioned a white vehicle crashing into a tree.

The next Friday, Mike called several times to let her know his schedule, saying that if he stayed out late to tie up some loose ends, they could have the weekend free. She called him several times, pleading for him to come home. "Every time I said, 'Come home,' the phone would cut out. I'd call back and it would happen again. He just kept saying, 'I'm almost there, baby, just a few more stops.' "

But she hadn't heard by midnight and could barely keep her panic in check. When she looked at the clock at 12:29, a feeling of death overpowered her. She said out loud to the elderly aunt who was sitting with her, "Mike just died." She knew, because she had just heard him say, "Baby, I will always love you."

Pat awoke at 3:55 to hear Mike's voice saying, "Baby, the police are coming to tell you I died." She got up and woke the aunt to warn her, and the two sat together in the living room. Soon, car headlights came down the street and turned into the driveway. She opened the door to find two policemen. They confirmed what she already knew: "My husband of twenty-nine years died on June 5th at 12:29 A.M. the day before our 30th wedding anniversary."

The police said he had veered off the road and smacked head

on into a tree. He was dead by the time the emergency squad arrived.

## More on Precognition?

Here's where the story becomes haunting.

During the HBO readings, John Edward had reported impressions of death "around the man with the beard," before he knew Mike and Pat were husband and wife. After the end of the readings that day, Mike Price and John Edward met and got into a discussion about auras, during which John mentioned that he sometimes sees a dim aura instead of a normal one around a person whose death is not far away.

In response to the request I had made of Mike that day at the HBO session to write down his impressions and send them to me, he wrote a letter just a few weeks before his fatal accident. In one part, he wrote:

"John said something about people having an ora [aura] around them and the closer the event to the death was, the less the ora around them. There was a few times when he would look at me but I felt like he was looking past me. He looked a little uncomfortable whenever he looked my way. I had the feeling that he wasn't seeing the ora around me. I really don't know why I thought that, I just did."

Mike was obsessed with this conversation up until his death, Pat said.

In the letter, Mike also wrote:

"John looked at me and said, 'Your son really needs to talk to you. I am willing to sit with you if you are.' I told John, 'No, thank you. I knew what Mike [his son] wanted to say, and I didn't want to hear it.' "

What did he mean? Did he sense that what his dead son wanted to say was something like "We're going to be together soon"?

A portion of Pat's reading with George Anderson contained what could be further support:

*He speaks about his dad; does that make sense?*

Yes.

*I don't know why yet. I don't know if he's trying to tell me his dad is there or if he's calling to his dad. So don't say anything, I want them to say it.*

*It . . . there's talk of the son that passed on. That is correct?*

Yes.

*Okay, he's claiming to be the first male who came in the room. That would make sense? 'Cause he's . . . that's why I was hearing him talk about Dad. Now that's why I didn't want you to explain. Let him explain where his father is.*

*His father is on the earth. "Please tell Dad you've heard from me, whether he believes in this or not." Who cares? It's the message that's important, not the belief system. And as your son says, besides, "He'll find that I'm right as usual, someday, anyway."*

One February day, Mike Price awoke holding the same belief he had held for more than forty years—that when somebody dies, that's it. They're done. But by the end of the day, he had been witness to something so unbelievable yet so convincing that his entire worldview had been turned upside down. Not only had he experienced strong evidence of an afterlife, but some of his own son's communications had suggested that he might be waiting for Mike to join him . . . very soon.

If that weren't enough, his head injury from a mugging more than a decade earlier was beginning to catch up with him, with painful migraines all the time, and a pinching pain in his neck that was slowly paralyzing him. And now, because of his wife's day with a group of self-proclaimed mediums, he was truly scared.

I could well understand how that single day was enough to change Mike's perceptions and turn him into a believer.

And me—was I ready to believe? I had seen a great deal of convincing evidence. But I was still a scientist above all else.

# PART IV

# The Canyon Ranch Totally Silent Sitter Experiment

# · 1 3 ·

# The Canyon Ranch Experiment: What if the Sitters *Never* Speak?

## A Magician as a Scientific Consultant

The history of research in this subject is filled with examples of careful investigators who later turned out to have been duped as a result of their own blindness, or by their inability to recognize the ways they were being fooled, or by using investigative techniques that were less precise and demanding than had appeared.

All things considered, Linda and I had a problem we couldn't ignore: our results to date were too good.

The +3 accuracy percentages were so high for both the HBO and Miraval experiments, and the quality of the material often so penetratingly accurate, that we were suspicious. And then there were the truly strange, apparently precognitive incidents that seemed to require extraordinary paranormal explanations.

Were our results so good because we were being fooled? We had to find ways of determining whether we were the unwitting victims of error, intentional or inadvertent. We had to rule out any possibility of deception, cues from the sitters, errors in the scoring technique, or some other hazard we couldn't even imagine.

How to proceed when the researcher doesn't know where the source of errors, if any, might lie?

We decided it was time to seek the advice of a skilled psychic magician, a "cold reader" who doesn't profess to be in contact with the spirit world but blatantly uses trickery. Our first efforts turned up a local source: Tucson magician Ross Horowitz, who among other things teaches a course on psychic cold reading at a local community college. An academic magician? I was intrigued.

I was able to attend one evening of his two-evening course. There I learned many of the subtle tools and tricks a magician uses to lure clients into revealing more information than they realize, and was fascinated by how easy it can be "to fool some of the people all of the time."

Besides the materials Ross provided for his students, he also procured for me a more extensive set of manuscripts and books that teach the techniques of being a fake medium.

Needless to say, I studied this material carefully. Yet, the more I investigated the secret tactics of psychic trickery, the more I became convinced that the mediums I had been observing in our laboratory could not, and were not, using these age-old tricks.

Later, Ross agreed to examine the video footage collected to date and help us design procedures aimed at eliminating the possibility of deliberate deception by mediums or sitters, as well as any other possible trickery he could envision.

But when this master of illusion visited the laboratory, the tables were turned. I wasted no time in asking him to see whether he could extract some of my personal history, with the requirement that he couldn't ask me any questions for the first ten minutes.

He quickly explained that his techniques were useless unless he had the opportunity of obtaining secret information beforehand, or of holding a dialogue with the sitter, or preferably both. I pushed him to try, and he reluctantly agreed. Giving it his best shot, his +3 accuracy was well under 20 percent.

When Linda and I told him that the mediums we had tested produced specific and accurate information during a silent period, when the medium did not even know who the sitter was, we had his full attention. He wanted to see the videotapes, to witness this for himself and to see whether the tapes would allow him to figure out what trickery was being used.

The first tape I played was Suzane's HBO reading of Patricia Price, the one in which she asked only five questions yet generated over 120 pieces of specific information, of which more than 80 percent were accurate.

The look on Ross's face as he watched this videotape was actually funny to see. After only a few minutes, he told me he could not find any indications that Suzane was using psychic cold-reading tactics. The only explanation he could provide for her accuracy was that she might have obtained information about the sitter before the experiment.

He told us that none of the tricks or tools he knew would allow him—or any psychic magicians he knew of—to score as high as Suzane did. However, he did suggest that we consider one possible way the mediums, en masse, might have been cheating. He asked if it was possible that they could have had access to the sitters' personal information before they arrived at the experiment.

I did not believe that this was plausible. I told him that in the HBO experiment, even the laboratory staff did not know who HBO had selected as the sitter until shortly before the experiment. Moreover, we had deliberately made sure that HBO did not know the identify of the sitter from Tucson we had selected, whose identity had been kept secret from the production staff until the day before the experiment.

And in the Miraval studies, even if information had secretly been obtained about some of the possible sitters, during the silent periods the mediums had no idea which person was sitting behind them on a given reading. How could they have made use of any information gained ahead of time?

He asked simply, "Do you know for sure that your personal phones, the laboratory's phones, and HBO's phones, weren't tapped?"

No, I couldn't be sure.

On the other hand, I pointed out that the five mediums would have had to agree to a conspiracy. They would have had to hire a private agency to tap our phones and HBO's, monitor the phones over an extended period to secretly learn the identifies of the sitters, then assign researchers or private detectives to obtain information about each of the sitters, and finally pass this information to each of the mediums so that they could each fake the process of retrieving information from the deceased. And they would have had to have several people watching which sitter entered which room, and somehow secretly pass this information as well to each of the mediums on the spot at the beginning of each reading.

He agreed that those hurdles presented some very considerable challenges. Yet he admitted that he himself uses some of these very techniques. Ross told us how he prepares for his psychic magic shows as a performer for large private functions. He doesn't use private investigators, but only because he plays private detective on his own.

Before a show, he gets a list of the names of as many of the people who are planning to attend as possible. Then through various methods, including innocent-seeming conversations with relatives, he unearths specific details about the individuals, which he uses to put the audience members in awe during the show.

With the help of Ross's critique as well as our own observations from the previous experiments, we set out to construct a new research design—one that would erect much more certain barriers against fraud and deception.

## DESIGNING THE NEW EXPERIMENT

We decided to make more certain there could be no possible way for the mediums to find out the identity of the sitter during a session. Though the mediums never turned around to see the sitters in our second experiment until the end of a reading, we had to rule out the possibility that secreted mirrors or other sneaky techniques (for example, a reflection off a window) might have enabled them to somehow "sneak a peek." Even though the experimenters had observed no evidence that this occurred, we wanted to completely eliminate the possibility.

To achieve this assurance, two sets of doubled white sheets would be attached wall to wall and floor to ceiling in each of the rooms where the sittings were to take place. The medium would be stationed on one side of the screen, back to the screen and facing the video camera, and the experimenter would escort the sitter through a door on the other side of the screen, making it impossible for the medium to have any visual contact.

Once the sitter was in place, we would again use the Russek silent paradigm from Miraval: the first ten minutes of the reading would be conducted with the sitter never speaking. And for the yes/no period of the experiment, we would add a new restriction: the medium would never hear the sitter's voice. This way, the medium would have no clues about the sitter's age, sex, or emotional state at any time during the session.

We considered many ideas for doing this, from ringing bells or blowing whistles to computerized voices or flashing lights. The challenge lay in finding some method that wouldn't become a distraction to the medium's concentration. We ultimately went with the least distracting and most straightforward method: the experimenter would simply watch for the sitter's silent nod or shake of the head, and call out a yes or no as appropriate to the medium on the other side of the screen.

So that the voice heard by a particular medium would be as constant as possible, each medium would have the same experimenter throughout. We trusted we would be better able to control the tone of our voices than the individual sitters, since we were emotionally detached from the information being received.

Again there would be five research sitters; they would write down in advance the details of the lives and their relationships with the deceased people they hoped might take part. These records would be sealed, unseen by any of the experimenters until the scoring session, much later.

One room would be set aside as a "sitters' sequestering room," where the sitters would wait between readings, thoroughly protected from being heard or observed by the mediums.

## A New Type of Sitter

Another lesson from the Miraval experiment was that sitters from remote parts of the country brought complications when it came time to score the data. Also—though we had no reason to doubt that their scoring had been sincere and reliable—even so, most of the previous sitters had no professional experience evaluating data.

This time we would use research-oriented, scoring-minded sitters. What's more, we would expand the scoring procedure in a novel and important way.

We invited five people to become our first dedicated team of research sitters—a group varying in age from twenty-two to fifty-five, all of whom lived in the greater Tucson area. Not only were they open to the possibility of contact with the other side, but they really wanted to know whether or not the phenomenon was real. This time, though, they wouldn't have the protection of remaining anonymous: all had to agree that they would, if asked, confirm the experiment by taking part in interviews with skeptics and the media.

The youngest was Juliet Speisman, an undergraduate student who had taken my course on the psychology of religion and spirituality. From the moment the topic of mediumship was mentioned in the lecture, she expressed a deep enthusiasm to participate in our future research. She had a previous connection to John Edward, who had conducted a reading with a family friend after a traumatic death; after that, she had tried for more than two years to get an appointment with John. Her deep desire to participate in the experiment ultimately secured her a research sitter position.

Sabrina Geoffrion was a member of the research and administrative team of our laboratory. I knew her commitment to research and knowledge and knew I could trust her; trust was key.

Sabrina's ties to the University of Arizona run deep. Her

mother is a professor and former chairperson of the art department, and her father was associate dean of the College of Science and had served as a university associate vice president and as the university integrity officer. Given her family background and her extensive training in experimental science, she seemed a strong choice.

The number one component in selection was integrity. That's why it was easy to select Janna Excel, who works as a grief counselor at a local cemetery and leads a large monthly near-death experience group at a local church.

I had met Janna two years earlier when she had been a guest speaker for Professor Robert Wrenn's popular course on the psychology of death and loss. She related some personal experiences involving a particular form of mediumship, which she was interested in investigating scientifically. Her knowledge of death, both personal and professional, made her an excellent research candidate. She also had an interest in experiencing mediumship firsthand, since it is often discussed as a possible therapy to aid in the grieving process. Janna wanted to know whether mediumship was something she could or should recommend to clients. What better way to make the decision than to experience mediumship as a research sitter, and experimentally test the phenomenon firsthand?

The fourth person we selected was an old friend of Linda's, Terri Raymond. A very spiritual person with a background in clinical hypnosis, Terri was fascinated by our research and asked to witness it herself.

The final sitter was a professional colleague, Lynn Ferro, a research coordinator in Dr. Andrew Weil's program in integrative medicine at the medical school. She is a well-trained clinical researcher, who has worked for several years at the Arizona Cancer Center. Given her background in both conventional and alternative medicine, we invited Lynn to participate as a sitter and to serve as chair of the research sitter team.

One issue we hadn't previously addressed had to do with unintentional bias in the scoring: the possibility that sitters might believe so deeply in the experience they had undergone that they would rate as correct statements that were in fact not correct. (There's a card trick in which the magician has an audience member pick a card, and later, on purpose, shows the wrong one; when the person says, "No, that wasn't my card," the magician flips it over and, presto, it has changed into the one selected. But the trick sometimes backfires: occasionally the person thinks the magician has made a mistake and, hoping to save him embarrassment, accepts the wrong card as correct.) In the same way, consciously or unconsciously, our sitters might have been scoring bad information as good, a process we termed rater bias.

Because we were deeply concerned about the possibility of rater bias, we decided to require that each reading would be scored not just by the sitter of that reading, but by the other four sitters as well. We knew it would be a burden on the sitters, who would have to score their own three readings plus every item from the twelve readings of the other sitters as well—a total of fifteen readings to be scored by each person. We made this clear in advance to each person we were considering; all five said they were willing.

However, none of the sitters reflected the extent of loss experienced by the sitters of the HBO session. Hence, we anticipated that the mediums' +3 accuracy might be reduced. We hypothesized that the "pull" for the deceased to speak might be less for these sitters. Yet if positive results could be obtained under these conditions, this would provide the foundation for establishing a standardized paradigm that we believed could be applied to a wide range of sitters and mediums, including magicians. We hoped, too, that it might prove effective enough to be replicated independently in other experimental centers around the country.

Large expectations. A lot to hope for from a one-day experiment.

## THE ROAD TO CANYON RANCH

Canyon Ranch spa once again generously came through with an arrangement that provided funding and accommodations for the experiment. They turned over for our exclusive use their Dream Street House, a large, rambling ranch house standing by itself among the trees.

Some of our faithful mediums were available for the selected dates, but not all. George Anderson would be in Europe on his book tour for *Lessons from Heaven,* and Anne Gehman had a conflicting commitment. But Laurie Campbell, Suzane Northrop, and John Edward would be joining us.

We gathered at the Canyon Ranch house on a Saturday morning in December 1999, with the millennium celebrations not far away. The plan called for the mediums to give five readings in a row, though John insisted that he would tire and that his later readings would not be as good as the first.

Because of an on-again/off-again discussion about whether we should hold one group reading with all three sitters at the end of the day, John was also convinced that his accuracy would not be as high as for the HBO and Miraval experiments because he was now stressed.

While the day produced its share of disappointments, two readings in particular proved memorable—both of them, coincidentally, by John Edward, the medium who had raised the greatest concern over the chances for success.

I offer the first of these two readings with great reverence and affection because of the people involved: the sensitive young Sabrina Geoffrion, and her beloved departed grandmother.

## SABRINA WITH JOHN EDWARD

I brought Sabrina into the room, and she sat down quietly. Once the videotape and audiotape recorders were turned on, John gave his standard brief introduction and launched into the silent-period reading.

> *Okay. The first one I want to acknowledge is that there's an older female that's coming through*

*to me, I would say either being an older sister or a*
*mother figure, there's an older female above you*
*that's coming through. They're telling me to ac-*
*knowledge somebody having the same name or ini-*
*tials being passed down in the family.*

Coupled with other verification remarks John provided later in the reading, where he makes reference to "the middle name," the sitter connected this to her son's middle name, which is taken from her grandmother's maiden name.

Still in the silent period, John made another reference that the sitter believed was connected to her grandmother.

*They are acknowledging that there are two dogs,*
*not one, two dogs who have passed, but there's a*
*two-dog connection that's coming through.*

In the yes/no period, even though John heard only my voice and never the sitter's, the information became more specific, just as we had expected. John was able to extend his first impressions by providing extremely detailed information about the departed grandmother, including more information about the dogs. For example, John got that one of them was a "large white poodle" who was "bad" and would eat everything from "shoes to wood chips." He also identified this grandmother as playing a strong motherly role in the sitter's life.

*Oh my god, talk about a love bond. This is like,*
*"The princess has arrived." I mean, there's a feeling*
*of this girl must have been like the apple of this*
*woman's eye, or something.*
*I also want to acknowledge that there's a wed-*
*ding, 'cause they're showing me there's a wedding.*
*So I don't know if this person is now married or*

> *they're getting married, but Grandma wants to know—wants me to acknowledge the wedding.*

In fact, since her grandmother's death, the sitter had gotten married.

> *So it means she was at the wedding after, you know, after she passed, but there's a, a connection to the wedding. And she's talking about . . . some type of flowers connection. And what's weird is she's showing me flowers that I wouldn't think about being at a wedding, and these are daisies. Um, they're showing me daisies . . .*
> *So I don't know what the reference is to daisies, but they're showing me daisies.*

It turned out that when the sitter's mother got married, her mother, the sitter's grandmother, sewed a ring of daisies into her daughter's hair. When people think of weddings, daisies are not the flowers that usually come to mind. The reference to daises at a wedding is a highly improbable one. In the formal scoring session later on, the sitter determined that nearly 90 percent of the information John provided about her grandmother was +3 correct.

However, at this point in our research, I had experienced striking and accurate information about so many departed loved ones as to make this particular reading seem almost routine. Deceased family members, especially grandmothers, often appear in this kind of work, and when a deceased loved one is described by a medium with such specific details, it's not an occasion for calling a press conference.

We've discovered that sometimes, quite unexpectedly, there are "anomalies within the anomalies" as the data unfold. When you conduct research in such a way that you are open to uncovering the strange within the strange, you sometimes come upon an extraordinary class of data—information that does not easily fit the conventional "anomalous" explanations such as reading the mind of the sitter. While these kinds of data are the most difficult to detect, produce on demand, and evaluate, they are the most exciting and sometimes the most definitive.

That notion came even more to mind with John's next reading.

## SITTER NO. 4 WITH JOHN EDWARD—AN ANOMALY WITHIN THE ANOMALIES

At the end of the session, I took the sitter back to the waiting room to relax before her next session. It appeared she would have about half an hour to wind down until her next reading.

I then escorted John's next sitter into the room, and we began the same procedure. But after his usual introduction, John sat silent for quite a while. Finally he said, "I'm carrying the . . . other woman's grandmother with me."

The next moments were quite baffling. John asked me verify that the person now behind the curtain was a different sitter, and a person not related to the previous sitter. He wanted to be assured I wasn't playing a trick on him.

He also wanted me to note the time so we could check later to see whether the previous sitter had gone to her next reading at the time of this incident. "Write down exactly what time it is right now, 'cause that woman's grandma, that person's grandmother, is still here," John said.

He reported some further information about the *previous* sitter: that she was connected to an S-A name, and that "The only thing I play in my head right now is 'On the Good Ship Lollipop,' " a tune best remembered in connection with the 1930s child star Shirley Temple.

About the only other information he received during the silent phase was *Sabrina, the Teenage Witch,* the title of a contemporary television show.

We then moved into a brief yes/no period, and John quickly

determined that neither of the two titles meant anything to either the sitter or me. He suggested it might be a message from the previous sitter's grandma, though he couldn't suggest any meaning.

> *I don't even know what that is, like I don't know if that's a movie, I don't know what that's from. I mean I thought that was Shirley Temple, so I don't know if that means we're supposed to talk about a cute little kid with ringlets or if I'm supposed to be talking about someone with the name Shirley, um, which is not how I normally would get that, so I want to go on record saying that.*

John apologized for not being able to receive any information for the current sitter. He added that the previous sitter's grandmother had told him he was not the right medium for the current sitter, whom he correctly identified as a woman. He also claimed that the previous sitter's grandmother had taken a liking to him.

> *I just, I just have a very protective feeling of this woman, as if she's, ironically, protecting me.*

While John accounted himself completely bewildered by the information he was getting and frustrated by his inability to get anything else, I began to have an inkling of what might be going on, though I concealed my thoughts from John.

By the end of the reading, John had received virtually zero information for the sitter. This was a complete failure in terms of the experimental design. His zero percent accuracy for the session would obviously pull down the averages overall.

Still, maybe the overall averages wouldn't be so bad in the end. The previous sitter, after all, was Sabrina Geoffrion, so *Sabrina, the Teenage Witch* looked like an incredibly good hit. But what about "On the Good Ship Lollipop"? I could hardly have anticipated what I was about to discover.

When I went back to the sitter holding area, Sabrina was still there, waiting to go to her next session. So it was at least logically consistent that John might have continued a communication with her grandmother even after her session had ended.

## Searching for an Answer

I sat down beside Sabrina and asked if "On the Good Ship Lollipop" meant anything to her.

She broke out in tears.

Gaining control, she explained that as a child, her hair had been in short, curly locks. When she sang and danced, her grandmother would tell her that she looked like Shirley Temple. She had actually sung Shirley Temple songs for her grandmother.

*Sabrina, the Teenage Witch* didn't seem much of a mystery, but I asked anyway. There turned out to be more of a connection than just the name Sabrina. I explained to her how John had received the show title, believing it was just a way that had been used to convey her name to him. In fact, he says he's often shown movie titles to convey a message—something he attributes to having worked in a video store at one time. But it turns out that the movie had a more direct significance.

As I watched more tears stream down her face, Sabrina explained that some of her teenage peers had teased her by calling her *Sabrina, the Teenage Witch.* And then she would run to her grandmother for comfort and understanding.

When I returned to John, I could not help but tell him that some of his misinformation with the fourth sitter had been a dazzle shot for the previous one. Showing no surprise, he took the information in stride, claiming that Sabrina's grandmother was still in the room as we were speaking.

To take John's statements at face value, I realized that the grandmother might hang around, disrupting his readings, until Sabrina began her next session with another medium. It turned out she was then on her way to her next reading. Indeed, the grandmother did appear to be gone; John was able to regain his concentration and to accurately receive information for his next sitter.

I was deeply touched by this unexpected experience. Although I had just witnessed John Edward ruin our research data with one sitter, I had seen him present fascinating information that is surprisingly consistent with the hypothesis of a universe populated with the living souls of our loved ones.

And there was more to come. In the last reading of the day, John was to receive information that came home to me personally.

# More Canyon Ranch: An Unexpected Visitor

Most mediums inform their clients—maybe "warn" would be a more appropriate term—that they have no control over who might choose to come through in a given reading. They simply open up and tune in, much like an antenna, receptive to whoever and whatever may come through.

We've learned how important it is to be prepared for surprises in this kind of work. This predictable unpredictability sometimes complicates the process of reporting the data when unanticipated information arrives.

As we saw with Sabrina, one source of unpredictability is that the loved one of a sitter might not be ready to leave when the sitter does. Another is the chance that the deceased loved ones of someone else in the near vicinity might appear and interfere with the medium's attempt to reach the loved ones of the sitter. This is what seems to have occurred in John's last reading of the Canyon Ranch experiment.

## AN UNINVITED GUEST

As we reached the fifth and final reading of the day, John and I were both tired and looking forward to wrapping up. Nonetheless,

John went ahead with the reading, picking up images and names of people that the sitter recognized.

But it wasn't long before he acknowledged a difference in what he was experiencing.

> *This is not flowing like in my normal conversational style, it's being given to me in, like, big blurbs, kind of like what I wrote down on the paper before everybody came in.*
>
> *They're telling me that the female S-sounding name is here, acknowledging her boys. One must be in the medical field, 'cause he's a doctor. That she has her husband there. She talks about the sign of Gemini, which either means somebody's a Gemini or is a twin. But that's not for the sitter. Gary, it might be for you.*

I was both stunned and secretly pleased. My mother, whose name starts with S, did have two sons, one of them a doctor—me (though not a physician but a Ph.D.). And I am a Gemini. But was the information really for me?

John continued with more from the same person.

> *And somebody wants to be called "the milkman." And that's weird because he's not trying to show me that he delivered milk. He's the milkman . . . I have two moms here. They're not related at all. Gary, for you . . .*

Startled and intrigued, I encouraged John to continue with what he was receiving, regardless of whether it was for the sitter or me.

More of this occurred during the yes/no period, and since John identified this as being for me, the answers I spoke were my own, not the sitters.

*. . .was your gallbladder removed?*

Not it specifically.

*I'm sorry? Was there stomach surgery like gall-bladder, appendix removed?*

Yes.

*And your mom has passed?*

Yes.

*Is she the "S"?*

Yes.

*Do you have a brother?*

Uh huh [yes].

*I am not sitting with your brother; correct?*

Excuse me?

*This is not your brother?*

No.

*Okay. This is for you. The milkman is for you.*

Hmm.

*Your dad also passed*

Yes.

*Is there a Morris in that family?*

Yes.

*What I see is it being like an uncle or a grandfather.*

Uh huh [yes].

After this dialogue, John requested permission to ask my mother to be quiet so he could receive information for the sitter. But he continued to have trouble. And then he identified the source of the problem: as he had suggested earlier in passing, *two* mothers were present.

*One for the person, one for you. Your mother is louder, Gary.*

His interpretation was consistent with my mother's personality. She had often been the dominant person in a conversation.

John was then able to focus on the actual sitter of the session and receive significant and accurate information for her, but he continued to report information that was accurate for me, as well. He confirmed that the milkman he had mentioned earlier was for me, and he said my Uncle Morris was known by two other versions of his name; which sounded like Maurice or Merle.

After the experiment I called my brother, who in turn called our cousin, Uncle Morris's son. The cousin confirmed a version of what John had said: his father was sometimes called Moshia or Moe. Not the same names that John had given—and perhaps it's debatable whether his versions were close or not—but about the man's being called by two names other than his own, John was right on target.

If I applied our standard scoring procedures to the information John said specifically came from my family for me, the rating would be at least 80 percent +3 accurate. The combination of information—mother "S" name, one son in medical field, a Gemini, appendix out, a brother, deceased father, Uncle Morris, two or more names—also had no connection to any of the sitters or the other two experimenters. The combination applied only to me. The conditional probability is way less than one in a million.

Did John fake receiving this information from my deceased mother—information that he had located on the internet or in some other way?

Knowing how open I am in the search for meaningful facts, did he secretly place this fraudulent information in the readings at the last moment so that a gullible scientist would report it as an experimental finding?

If you are a skeptic, you might say, "I told you so—it has to be fraudulent."

If you are a believer, you might say, "John's accuracy for the sitters he did not know was equally high."

If you are an agnostic—a scientist like me—you would place all the hypotheses on the table, and say, "I don't know. Let's do more research."

But there's another chapter to this story.

## THE MILKMAN, MY MOTHER, AND THE MYSTERIOUS SIXTH SITTER

Most of the information about my family was interesting and even accurate, but what about the reference to "the milkman"?

When we checked with all the sitters and experimenters to see whether any of them had a relationship or connection to a milkman, none did.

But I hadn't expected any of them to report a connection; I was pretty sure from the first that the information was for me. Indeed, it brought back a fond childhood memory, something I had not thought about in years.

As a youngster, I had developed great enthusiasm for collecting glass milk bottles, which I used for storing the kinds of things little boys tend to collect—favorite plastic cowboys and Indians, old pennies, assorted deceased Japanese beetles and lightning bugs.

I had a large collection of those bottles, which must have put me on a special blacklist with the milkman, who was constantly asking for them back. The day the glass milk bottles were replaced by plasticized cartons was a jolting time for this young child and for his sympathetic mother.

Was John's mention of a milkman a specific reference to a childhood memory of mine? Obviously, we can't know the answer. But I was inclined to think the answer might be yes . . . in part because of a secret procedure we had planned for this experiment, even though in the end it never took place.

The mediums had originally been told there would be six sitters. At the beginning of each session, the experimenters would enter the room of the medium they were working with, escorting the next sitter. The plan was that at some point during the day, the experimenter would actually come in alone; because of the screening, and because during the yes/no period the procedure called for the experimenter, not the sitter, to speak the answers, the medium would not know that the sitter for this session was in fact the experimenter. So the information reported by the medium would potentially relate to the deceased family members and friends of the experimenter. I would finally have a chance to ride the rollercoaster.

After the morning's stress on the mediums about dropping the intended group readings, we decided that pulling this surprise might be both unwelcome and unfair. Hoping for an opportunity to try this in a later experiment, we never told the mediums of the plan.

Nonetheless, John received information about my deceased loved ones without knowing we had hoped that this might be part of the original experiment.

Is it possible that the change of plans might have upset my

mother, who had been looking forward to talking to me? Even more remote, is it possible that the milkman of my childhood—who did indeed have reason to remember me above the other children on his route, for the troubles I caused him—might have accompanied her? While I, as the experimenter, had decided that I could put off being a sitter until another day, maybe my mother was looking forward to having the opportunity to speak through a medium and showed up anyway. I remembered how, in one of our first formal experiments with Laurie, when she was attempting to communicate with my father, my mother came in unannounced and more or less dominated the conversation, precisely as she had done in life.

My response to my mother's barging in on John's reading could have been one of disapproval, since her interruption contaminated the experiment and decreased the accuracy-score ratings for that sitting. But instead my response was a smile, accompanied by the hope that my dear mother was well and that John would be pleased, not annoyed, by my mother showing up so unexpectedly.

One other item that was to remain with me as among the most memorable incidents of the day occurred with Suzane and the sitter Janna Excel. At the beginning of the silent period, Suzane reported the presence of a man with a mustache and piercing blue eyes who was showing her a police uniform.

On the other side of the double-sheeted screen, Janna was at that moment holding two items in her lap: a photo set of a man with a distinct mustache and striking blue eyes, and the man's leather police jacket.

Yes, I know a skeptic would shrug off the incident. Yet to be present and witness a moment like this is a chilling experience, never to be forgotten.

## RATING THE DATA

Written transcripts of the videotapes provided 317 pages of material from the fifteen readings, each medium having met with the five sitters individually. For the silent periods alone, this gave us over five hundred pieces of specific information. Using computer spreadsheets, our staff prepared an item-by-item listing of each piece of information the mediums provided, grouping items by medium and sequentially as they were reported. Chart 14-1 shows a selection of items from one reading

We again used the same categories and scoring system, each statement of a medium being classified as Initial, Name, Historical fact, Personal description, Temperament, or Opinion, and each then being rated from –3 for a complete miss to +3 for a correct hit. Once again the sitters were directed to leave an item unscored if they did not know, and to lean toward assigning a negative score when uncertain.

Clearly our focus was on the results of the silent periods, to see whether the mediums had achieved a significant accuracy rate when they did not know who the sitter was, and were speaking without receiving any feedback. If the mediums during the HBO readings had been obtaining clues from the sitter's voice, response, and perceived emotional state, they had none of that to rely on during the silent periods at Canyon Ranch.

The five sitters and three experimenters spent an entire grueling weekend doing the ratings for the silent period alone. Each sitter and experimenter individually rated all fifteen readings, giving us more than 4,000 rated items.

We calculated the percent number of certain hits (+3) and certain misses (–3) in two ways. As usual, the sitters rated their own readings. In addition, each sitter rated the readings of every other sitter. And all three experimenters rated every one of the readings, as well.

Would the results be significantly different? Would there be a greater percentage of hits for their own readings versus the control

## Chart 14-1. Sample Spreadsheet for Scoring Data from the Canyon Ranch Experiment

| Item No. | Medium's Statement | Category | Rating |
|---|---|---|---|
| 20 | sitter is a female | historical fact | |
| 21 | sitter's grandmother is in spirit | historical fact | |
| 22 | incredible bond, love between sitter and grandmother | historical fact | |
| 23 | pain in sitter's heart from her passing | historical fact | |
| 44 | sitter has pain from her relationships with men | historical fact | |
| 45 | sitter needs to be more self-sufficient, not look to others | opinion | |
| 46 | sitter needs to find self, become stronger person | opinion | |
| 47 | see men walking all over sitter | historical fact | |
| 48 | sitter must take center stage, move into the light | opinion | |
| 54 | see mountains .. | description | |
| 55 | and a person walking in white tennis shoes | description | |
| 56 | and there is sun on her face | description | |
| 57 | sitter's father is tall man, with dark hair | description | |
| 58 | see father in a suit | description | |
| 59 | sitter wanted more bonding, love from father | historical fact | |
| 60 | feels like restraint, or separation of father | historical fact | |
| 61 | can't tell if it's physical or emotional distance | historical fact | |
| 62 | sitter's mother is very demanding | historical fact | |
| 63 | she kind of runs everything | historical fact | |
| 64 | I get a very strong woman | description | |
| 65 | she was in control, took care of everything, he was quiet | historical fact | |
| 66 | I see her as the doer and him more quiet | temperament | |
| 67 | is his mother also passed over? | historical fact | |
| 68 | I keep seeing an older woman on father's side | historical fact | |
| 69 | she's very strong, and opinionated ... | temperament | |
| 70 | but loving in her own way | temperament | |
| 71 | woman give sense of invincible, iron strong | temperament | |
| 72 | she feels like a smaller woman | description | |
| 73 | her husband is also passed | historical fact | |
| 74 | they are together and are very happy | opinion | |
| 75 | both are smaller people in appearance | description | |
| 76 | sitter called this couple by a different name | historical fact | |
| 77 | everybody is concerned about sitter's emotional state | historical fact | |
| 78 | all these people knew this dog | historical fact | |
| 79 | dog a type of terrier | historical fact | |

| Item No. | Medium's Statement | Category | Rating |
|----------|--------------------|----------|--------|
| 80 | dog a mutt... | historical fact | |
| 81 | with short legs and a pointy nose | description | |
| 82 | but it was spunky, outgoing, and loving | temperament | |
| 83 | special ball game dog liked; bounce ball off floor, it catches | description | |
| 84 | and see the dog in the house | description | |
| 85 | if sitting on the couch, there is a chair to the left | description | |
| 86 | feel someone would sit there when playing with dog | historical fact | |
| 93 | hear David | name | |
| 94 | David has dark hair | description | |
| 95 | David like a soul mate | historical fact | |
| 96 | that was close | historical fact | |
| 97 | sitter's broken heart related to him | historical fact | |
| 98 | but sitter's heart is broken, needs healing | historical fact | |
| 99 | connection with David and a car | historical fact | |
| 100 | he came to medium before experiment | opinion | |
| 101 | this is who sitter came to talk to today | historical fact | |
| 102 | David die in a car | historical fact | |
| 103 | sitter has painful experience connected to a car | historical fact | |
| 104 | medium feels pain around David | historical fact | |

readings of others? If so, it would tell us whether the information that the mediums were getting for Sabrina, say, was specific to Sabrina or whether the information could apply just as well or even better to someone else.

Medium 1 generated substantially more items (approximately 60 items per reading on the average), compared with Mediums 2 and 3, who averaged about 25 and 20 items each session, respectively. The total number of items generated during the silent periods for the three mediums over the fifteen readings was 528.

In terms of items per reading, the average number of +3 hits was 12 for the actual readings versus 6 for controls. The three mediums individually ranged from a low of 25 percent to a high of 54 percent of +3 hits, with an overall average of 40 percent.

When the sitters rated one another's readings as a control group, they detected an average of half as many +3 hits per reading (6 for the control group versus 12 for the mediums). In other words, as expected, the mediums' actual readings rated significantly higher than the control readings, suggesting that the mediums' results were not achieved by guesswork.

This was the first time we had conducted an experiment where simultaneous readings occurred in a relatively confined area. The findings suggested the hypothesis that "cross-talk" could be slipping in—a question that deserves to be systematically investigated in future research.

My mother's unexpected appearance turned out not to be the only example of what might be called "cross-visits" during the day. On several occasions, the medium was able to identify that the information was not for the sitter in the room but for someone else in the house. For scoring purposes, though—even when the information turned out to be virtually 100 percent accurate for the absent sitter—such statements were rated as misses. In future research, we will specify what kinds of misses can be scored as hits; for example, if the medium specifically states that the information applies to someone other than the sitter.

Even so, to put these findings in context, it's worth remembering that Michael Jordan averaged 45 percent hits and 55 percent misses—and this was when he could see the basket. Our mediums could neither see nor hear the sitters at any time. Yet their hits averaged 40 percent.

We can also ask the question, did these results replicate for each of the five sitters?

The answer is, yes. Each of the five sitters scored his or her own readings as having higher numbers of hits compared with the control readings, and each sitter scored his or her own readings as having fewer numbers of misses compared with the control readings.

And yet, for all that, the results were significantly worse than in the HBO or Miraval Experiments—in fact, only about half the percentage of +3 results: about 40 percent compared with about 80 percent. If the mediums are really doing what they claim, is it reasonable that the silent-period results should be so much worse? Or are there other factors that might have influenced this result?

Although it was not something we had frequently experienced before, it happened in these readings that the mediums sometimes got nothing—zero—for a given sitter. The question arises, if these are the Michael Jordans of mediumship, why do they sometimes miss every possible basket with a given sitter? How are we to explain these dreadful performances?

In a traditional scientific publication, we would simply report the lowered averages, period. We would not be allowed to offer background descriptions of what actually happened in the sessions when the mediums missed everything. Yet sometimes key evidence is revealed in the errors. Sabrina's grandmother and my mother illustrate these mistakes—anomalies in the anomalies. Sometimes the truth is revealed in the mistakes. We just have to be willing to listen to what the data are telling us.

But despite the disappointment with the overall averages of the silent-period data, the Canyon Ranch experiment represented a major step in the development of our experimental techniques. And the silent-period results, after all, had been well above anything that could be explained by chance or guessing. In that sense, the experiment had been a rousing success and had given us every reason for being eager to figure out what would come next.

# PART V

# Discovering the Larger Reality

*Death is only a horizon*
CARLY SIMON

*Look up from your life.*
JAMES TAYLOR

*Give us more to see.*
FROM *SUNDAY IN THE PARK WITH GEORGE* BY STEPHEN SONDHEIM

# · 15 ·

# What's Fraud Got to Do with It?

John Edward once told me in an e-mail that he was tired of being perceived as a freak. I replied with a question: "What would you rather be called? A freak? Or a fraud?"

If science could establish that fraud is not involved in what our group of mediums is doing, and they are able to do something so special and unusual that it is almost freakish, this would actually be a significant advance.

It's our fervent hope that future research will enable us to establish definitively that some of the people who call themselves mediums are neither frauds nor freaks but may actually be among humankind's greatest friends by providing confirmed evidence of the existence of a larger spiritual family.

Clearly, science must explicitly address the fraud hypothesis and examine it through controlled, replicated laboratory experiments if the work of mediums is ever to be accepted. We expect that everyone interested in this question—especially people knowledgeable about the subject and about past research efforts—will carefully examine our data, help us discover flaws in our experimental methods, and support us in developing better experiments.

Or, at the very least, find out what we're doing before launching virulent attacks.

Probably our greatest surprise and deepest disappointment was the unexpected discovery that some of the people who are most convinced that this entire subject is based on fraud were willing to criticize our work without ever looking at our data.

## THE LESSON OF MR. WIZARD

When I was eighteen and a freshman electrical engineering student at Cornell University, a close friend made the claim that she knew a "Mr. Wizard" who, in a phone call, could tell me my birthday without my ever speaking a word to him.

Curious, I accepted the challenge. My friend asked me for my birth date, I told her, and she placed the call. After a short wait, she said, "Hello, can I please speak with Mr. Wizard?"

Then she was silent again for several moments, and I was willing to wait until the mysterious Mr. Wizard was available to take the call. Meanwhile, ever suspicious, I carefully watched her lips, throat, and fingers, and listened carefully to make sure she wasn't making any little noises or sending any subtle taps. She wasn't.

After a bit, she said into the phone, "Is this Mr. Wizard?" Another pause. I wondered whether she had called a pay phone in a dorm hallway, and someone had grabbed the wrong "Mr. Wizard." Or maybe she was just confirming that this was, indeed, the real Mr. Wizard.

Then she spoke once again: "Thank you, Mr. Wizard. Now I'll give the phone to my friend."

When I put the phone to my ear and gingerly said, "Hello," the voice on the other end simply replied, "This is Mr. Wizard. Your birthday is June 14th," and hung up.

Which was correct.

I couldn't believe it. How was it possible? She had only referred to me as "my friend" and hadn't even asked him to give my birth date.

Totally dumbfounded, I thought I might have witnessed some form of psychic communication. Or maybe super-electromagnetic communication (after all, I was an electrical engineering student). Could Mr. Wizard be for real?

I pleaded with her to tell me the truth. Finally, after some amount of teasing, she gave away the trick.

It turned out there had been nothing psychic or scientific about it. I had just been fooled by a familiar ruse known to every magician.

When she asked to speak with "Mr. Wizard," the person on the other end never left the line. Instead, he knew he was to assume the "wizard" role and began slowly naming the months of year: January, February, March. . . .

When he said "June," she simply interrupted with the next question: "Is this Mr. Wizard?" Her accomplice then knew the month, and began slowly counting days: "1, 2, 3 . . ." At 14, she again interrupted.

Then all she had to do was hand me the phone and prepare to have a big laugh at my expense.

In the end I managed to laugh, too, but I had learned a life-altering lesson that stays with me to this day. The seemingly innocent experience opened my eyes to the larger world of deceit, even among "friends," and it frankly left a bad taste in my mouth.

## EXAMINING DECEIT

Whenever I think about the Mr. Wizard incident, it reminds me of what attracted me to science in the first place. Science is a systematic approach to obtaining knowledge. It was developed to be the ultimate proving ground for discerning the true and real from the false and illusory.

All things being equal, I prefer to trust people, both scientists and nonscientists alike. When I meet new people, I want to be able trust them. Whenever possible, I attempt to give them the benefit of the doubt.

Still, I know perfectly well that not everyone acts on trust. History documents that the world has always had an ample supply of deceivers and cheaters. We need to ask, "Is fraud involved in the mediumship experiments we've been running?" As is clear by now, that's a question we've asked constantly.

The question applies not just to the mediums but to the scientists, as well: "Are the scientists being fooled by the deceivers (the mediums), or, even worse, are the scientists deceiving themselves?"

The realm of deception doesn't necessarily stop at the doors of academia. It sometimes makes its way into the halls and laboratories of science. This is the university environment that modern society has created. We've seen enough examples of scientific deceit to know it does happen.

All things considered, we must regularly ask the question, both in science and in daily life: Are we being deceived?

In the case of science, especially in controversial areas, research must be designed with the possibility of deception and fraud in mind. The possibility of deception by mediums, sitters, and even the experimenters themselves has always been in the foreground of our awareness. With each succeeding experiment, the possibility of deception operating at any level was increasingly and stringently addressed.

All this, and more, went through my mind as I witnessed the research unfold.

When I watched the five mediums in the HBO experiment provide astounding results, as the first scientist ever to conduct such an experiment under a controlled setting, my thoughts immediately brought me back to Mr. Wizard.

I wondered, was I being fooled again? This time, if I was being made the butt of a joke, it wasn't just for laughs—my scientific career as well as the credibility of everyone in our laboratory was on the line.

There was only one group that I was 100 percent sure of: we, the researchers, were not engaged in deliberate deception. We consciously live the motto "Let the data speak, whatever the data say."

It's an accepted matter of faith in a free society that reporters and the media have the same dedication to truth that scientists do.

Unfortunately, that faith is not always justified, as we were to find out to our regret.

## AIR TIME

In October, HBO invited us to attend an advance screening of the documentary, just before the air date, and we flew to New York for the occasion.

We felt like celebrities, as if we were attending the Academy Awards and had been nominated for an Oscar. We all took our seats, the lights in the theater went down, and for a while we were captivated. HBO had made a beautiful, inspiring show.

But the science was sandwiched in the middle and lost nearly all its impact. We had expected that the show would leave the audience feeling "Science can be brought to bear on these issues" and "Wow, those mediums were tested by science and actually were found to be doing what they claimed."

Instead, the show was good entertainment but little more. We had thought HBO really cared about the science, but discovered what the producers most wanted was to see how many people were crying when the lights went up. After all, HBO didn't really care about making a scientific statement.

When the screening was over, the audience wanted to talk about the science. The discussion was cut off so everyone could go to the cocktail party.

## DOUBLE DECEPTION

Meanwhile, a producer for a television show on the Fox network hosted by the well-known professional skeptic Michael Shermer called and said he was interested in addressing the possible truth of mediumship, and wanted to do a segment focused on Suzane Northrop. Maybe the outcome would be better this time; we could always hope. The approach, the producer said, would be to compare her techniques with those of a skilled psychic magician who claimed that he had no contact with the spirit world, yet could retrieve the same kinds of information as Suzane.

On the face of it, this sounded like an excellent idea. Fox had a professional magician, skilled in the secret tricks of psychic cold readings, who might be able to help us determine whether Suzane was as deceptive as that "Mr. Wizard" of my college days, or the real thing. This was someone possibly even more skilled and knowledgeable than the Tuscon cold reader we had earlier consulted.

Since magicians are ordinarily unwilling to share the tricks of their trade with non-magicians, we saw this as an opportunity that could perhaps lead to a collaboration with a professional trickster, who might provide useful insights about what we were observing in our laboratory.

We agreed, and the Fox unit sent a film team to Tucson. On one long, tiring day, the team filmed me in the laboratory, interviewing me on camera for five hours.

When they heard about the HBO experiment, they asked if they could use scenes from it. We gave them access to a copy of the complete, unedited footage so they could make their own selections.

What we later saw on the air knocked us off our feet.

The producer let us know in advance that he had screened the entire HBO footage. He had seen Suzane speaking virtually non-stop for over ten minutes, asking only five questions, yet producing more than 120 specific pieces of factual information with over 80 percent accuracy.

But instead of using any of that footage showing Suzane under laboratory conditions during a scientific experiment, Fox made arrangements on the side to film her at another time as she offered readings to callers over the phone. In between short clips of Suzane's statements, the program cut to the psychic magician, who claimed that her statements were typical generalizations that could be used to fit most people. He claimed she was saying things like "I'm getting an M name" for someone "who may be living or dead."

Our HBO footage made it clear that she was doing nothing of the kind—so the program never used that footage. Apparently Michael Shermer and the producers thought it made better television to use a pick-up magician who knew nothing but the deceptive tricks of fake mediumship as a tool for debunking Suzane, rather than to use the authentic footage that revealed her remarkable successes.

At one point in the show, the same magician was seen in a busy mall, posing as a medium and giving "psychic readings" to passersby. The edited portion of his readings showed him asking many people whether they know a "Charlie, living or deceased." At the end of each reading, the magician admitted he had no psychic powers, and that he always used the name Charlie because almost everyone knows a Charlie.

Yes, those people had been fooled by the magician, just as "Mr. Wizard" had fooled me many years ago.

But the producers knew that Suzane was not using trickery, as the psychic magician claimed. They also knew the results of the Miraval studies, in which no questions were asked of the sitter for the first ten minutes. Nonetheless, they allowed the impression to be created that Suzane was doing precisely what the psychic magician was doing: using trickery, deceiving the clients.

And all, presumably, because trashing Suzane seemed like better "entertainment."

## A CONTROL STUDY IN THE CLASSROOM

To explore one aspect of what that misleading, harmful television show claimed our mediums couldn't do, I decided to conduct some research with a group of approximately seventy students in one of my classes, using an incident from the Miraval experiment. In John Edward's reading with Patricia, he reported that her mother was showing him a box of Parliament cigarettes with something "hidden inside the carton." This was clearly an unusual statement, but Patricia immediately understood it and knew what the hidden item was.

Could the students duplicate anything of the kind?

I told the class that they were each to pretend they were a medium and should write down on a piece of paper what kind of cigarettes they thought Patricia's mother smoked.

How many do you think guessed Parliaments? 50 percent? 10 percent? The data from our sample yielded *zero* percent. People picked Winstons, Marlboros, Camels, and even Newports, but no one out of the group of seventy students guessed Parliaments.

I then asked them to write down what was unusual about the cigarettes. None guessed that something was hidden inside the carton. The answers the students gave were almost as varied as the number of people in the room, but not one guessed right.

For the record, John never said what the hidden item was, but Patricia told us later. Her son—the one who shortly after committed suicide—had spiked his grandmother's Parliament cigarettes with marijuana to help ease the pain and nausea of the lung cancer she was dying of. (Virtually no one in the family knew that the grandson had done this; it was illegal, and was kept secret even from most family members.)

But was this the kind of information that viewers of the Fox program heard? Does Suzane tell all her clients that her deceased grandmother is pulling out her false teeth? Does John tell all his clients that something is hidden inside a box of Parliaments? How can these stunning examples in any way be compared with the psychic magician's asking all his clients if they know somebody, living or dead, named Charlie?

It's infuriating. But I was discovering that this kind of accusation comes with the territory when you attempt to do research in one of the "forbidden" subjects.

## AFTERMATH

The epilogue of this story was unexpected. In spite of what we saw as the deceit of the Fox show, we were nonetheless impressed by the psychic magician's command of the tricks of his trade.

What we had anticipated in advance was now confirmed. We were more certain than ever that someone with his abilities could be enormously helpful in our studies. Watching our raw videotapes, he could advise us whether the mediums were using any trickery he could identify. And we hoped he might be willing to serve as a medium under our controlled conditions, to see whether he could do as well as the research mediums we had been working with.

So we asked the network to put us in touch with the psychic magician who had appeared on the show. And then we asked again. We asked repeatedly, and were stonewalled. Perhaps the network realized the show segment had been irresponsible, perhaps the magician thought we were angry and were trying to trap him somehow, perhaps he knew from the footage that Suzane was really doing things he could not and was simply embarrassed for accusing her of using the same kind of tricks he was using. Whatever the reason, the network would not put us in touch with the magician, and we finally gave up trying.

Double deception—first from the host and producer of the show, and then from the psychic magician. This creates a powerful deceptive combination that misleads viewers.

We had requested from the producer of the Fox show the same things we had requested from the HBO producers—that we be provided a copy of the entire raw footage shot in our laboratory, and that we be allowed to view and comment on a rough cut before the show was aired. The HBO team was glad to have our input, so they could be sure the program presented our work in a scientifically accurate fashion. The script and footage was actually revised three times in response to our inputs. We had not expected such integrity from HBO. But perhaps there was a downside: it left us not wary enough.

At this point, you won't be surprised to learn that the Fox producers did not provide us a copy of their footage. Instead, they let us have just the few brief moments from the segment in our lab, taken out of context. What they did not provide us with was the majority of the segment that revealed the false impressions they had created by their too-clever editing.

# • INTERLUDE •

## "Re-Contact"

Earlier I offered thoughts about a scene in the movie *Contact* that showed how difficult it can be to justify scientifically the subjectivity of our first-person consciousness, such as how you would prove that you love your spouse.

There was in this film another scene that also affected me deeply. Both were scenes that expressed the wonder of the visible and invisible universe, and both expressed the coming together of love and integrity.

The second of these scenes comes near the end of the movie. The scientist Dr. Ellie Arroway has risked her life to make contact with the intelligent beings who provided her with the plans for constructing the massive machine that would take her to them.

But when she returns from her remarkable journey, she learns to her dismay that her scientist colleagues insist there is no proof she has gone anywhere. She has experienced a journey to distant stars; yet to the observers on earth, her spacecraft appears to have simply dropped into the sea.

Has she imagined the eighteen hours of her journey, the life-changing epiphany? Has she hallucinated the whole thing? Almost no one believes that her experiences were real. And her scientist colleagues only require from her the very same kinds of proof she has always required from others.

Of course she understands their concerns; she is, after all, a scientist. As a scientist myself, I appreciate their concerns, as well.

But Dr. Arroway also understands that she has undergone a profound set of personal experiences. She cannot, with integrity, simply discount them. She knows that her experiences in the space capsule, and beyond, were as real and strong as the love she experienced for her father.

Another aspect of this fictional episode also affected me strongly. The story portrays how a few select politicians and senior scientists, some her so-called friends, actually see hard data from a video recorder indicating that eighteen hours have, indeed, inexplicably elapsed. Though the camera recorded nothing more than noise, that eighteen hours of noise supports the time frame of her experience. Yet this vital information is deliberately withheld, not only from the public but from Dr. Arroway herself.

Carl Sagan seemed to be writing from his own experience about the deceptive duplicity and the hypocrisy of people in power, including unscrupulous skeptics.

The research we are conducting on the possibility of survival after physical death is not much different from Dr. Arroway's research in *Contact*. We, too, are looking for conscious intelligence beyond our limited physical existence and awareness.

But unlike Dr. Arroway's situation, our research journey is documented by many hours of available videotapes that reveal things unexplainable by any currently accepted knowledge—videotapes available for anyone interested in seeing them. These tapes show things that scientists and nonscientists alike have never seen before. We have made the actual raw footage available to the public so that you may see and judge for yourself.

# ·16·

# Answering the Skeptics

## Diagnosing and Treating "Skeptimania"

It's one thing to be skeptical—open to alternative hypotheses. It's another to be *devoutly* skeptical—always "knowing" that cheating, lying, fraud, and deception are the explanations for any not-yet-explainable phenomenon.

What does it mean when a person concludes that an event "must be due to fraud" no matter how strong the data are? At what point does the instinct to dismiss data reflect a bias so strong that it begins to border on the pathological?

Simply put, when does skepticism become what I would call skeptimania? When does skeptimania become so strong that a person will engage in double deception rather than report the facts as they actually occurred?

These are important questions, and they affect us all. Science will die if it does not follow the data with integrity.

If it ultimately turns out that survival of consciousness is true, the potential for duplicity will no longer be possible. We will enter a new era where love and integrity become an integral part of our lives, where science and spirituality will become two sides of a universal coin, and where the abundance of eternal possibility and opportunity will become increasingly evident.

## AN EARLY CHALLENGE

As a young faculty member at Harvard I was once asked by some senior people in a transcendental meditation school to conduct research on the physical and mental health benefits of TM. I was to learn their specific brand of meditation and was told that I would receive prized professional secret information when I joined their group. There was a caveat: I would have to maintain complete confidentiality of all information.

I explained that I could not accept their secrets and become one of them. Part of the reason was for credibility—who would trust a scientist doing research on his own particular school or sect? It would be like having the police studying the police. Even though the law enforcement officers of course know the truth about what's going on in their own department better than anyone else, how can we expect them to oversee themselves with integrity? Outsiders are needed to maintain balance.

But there was also a second reason I couldn't accept. Consider the importance of openness—what Marcel Proust called "seeing with new eyes." Sometimes children ask great questions precisely because they have a "beginner's mind." Moreover, they're not afraid to ask "stupid" questions. I remembered the story I heard as a youngster about the child who was willing to say that the emperor was wearing no clothes. It's difficult for people to mature and grow wiser yet still retain an innocence of observation.

I explained my thoughts to the leaders of the meditation center, using a metaphor of a blind man trying to assist a study on color vision. The sightless person has to listen very closely to what is being said by others, and then often asks seemingly innocent questions—questions that only a blind person would ask. The very fact that a person can see results in much being taken for granted.

People can be blinded by their own sight; I had committed to seeing more in life by staying "blind."

Our Friendly Devil's Advocates committee raised the usual questions that have been asked for at least a century of scientific research in this fragile area of research: about fraud, and self-deceit, and whether there might be errors of some other kinds that we weren't even able to conceive.

But now and again, just as we'd hoped, a member of our Devil's Advocates committee has asked a really penetrating question that advances work as only the blind or innocent can. Here are a few of their powerful questions, our responses, and how our research addresses these issues.

## Question 1

**Can mediums read skeptics? If mediums can read only believers, this raises serious questions about the claims.**

One way of responding to this valid challenge is to turn to psychological studies on what's called "the perception of weak stimuli," which deals with how people respond to very faint inputs.

Experimental psychologists have conducted research with very soft sounds—so low that it takes careful attention to detect them. If a loud sound is played just before the soft sound, the listener will miss the following gentle sound. The previous loud sound serves as a distracting stimulus.

Distraction operates for strong stimuli as well. Basketball players tell us that it's harder to make foul shots when opposing fans are screaming for them to miss.

In the same way, mediums tell us that in order to receive information, which is typically soft and subtle, they must get their own thoughts and emotions out of the way. Their own feelings deafen them, so to speak, to the subtle information they're trying to receive.

Our dream team of mediums tells us that when they face hostile clients or a hostile audience, they get anxious. They have negative thoughts and feelings that distract them from getting the subtle information they're trying to receive. Some say they're reminded of being teased when they were children; they worry about missing the shot and then being laughed at, or worse. And they know the skeptics will claim "See, you can't do it—it must be fraud."

Of course, if the mediums were engaged in fraud, it shouldn't matter whether they were reading believers or skeptics. If they had detectives secretly getting information ahead of time, for example, the facts obtained in advance would be there for the mediums to use no matter how skeptical the sitter.

On the face of it, at least, the mediums' explanation of why they don't like to read for skeptics appears reasonable. Maybe it really is more difficult—for well-established cognitive information-processing reasons. But this will be a valuable question to be addressed in future research.

## Question 2

**If mediums can really hear dead people, why don't they ever hear and speak in foreign languages or make medical diagnoses from a dead physician? If mediums can hear only what they know, maybe they're just replaying their own memories and fantasies.**

Mediums claim that the stimuli are there for all to perceive, but they're low-level and subtle, and most of us are too distracted by the outside world as well as our own thoughts and feelings to sense them.

Much of what we hear is incomplete, but we're usually able to fill in the gaps. For example, if you're watching a romantic movie on television in a noisy room and you pick up an incomplete group of sounds—"I ov er"—you would very likely be able to fill in what's missing and, without even realizing you didn't get all the sounds, understand that what the character really said was "I love her." This kind of "fill-in" phenomenon has been substantially investigated in contemporary cognitive psychology.

Now, instead, imagine that the character in the film has said a group of sounds which, over the noise in the room, reached you as "J a or." You wonder, "What did he say? I missed it." But if you knew French, your mind might have been able to fill in the gaps to complete the sentence—"Je l'adore"—which means the same thing as before: "I love her." (Well, okay, it could also mean "I love him" or "I love it." Leave it to the French to be nonspecific, even about love.)

Experimental psychology tells us that we often unconsciously fill in subtle or incomplete information with the information we know—the information from our own memories. That is, at least, a reasonable-sounding explanation of why mediums shouldn't be expected to relay messages in languages they don't understand, or highly technical jargon or medical terminology unfamiliar to them. Again, a subject for future experimentation.

In this regard, our team of mediums tell us that symbols from their own personal lives often come to them, and they learn how to interpret these symbols. I've found John Edward especially surprising and often amusing in this regard. As we've seen, his video-store job as a youngster sometimes leads him to get the names or images from movies that have a connection with something a deceased is trying to communicate—which is what happened with the *Pretty in Pink* incident (and it is, in fact, one of my personal favorite anecdotes of the mediums at work, perhaps because it's not just poignant but funny, as well).

## Question 3

**Why do dead people always give such boring information like messages of love and the like? Why don't they give us information about new science or technology? It sounds as though the mediums are just giving the clients what they want to hear.**

I can remember exactly when one of our senior Friendly Devil's Advocate committee members, a person who typically asks searching questions, threw this at us in a seminar, challenging our research to date.

This is a troubling question. Perhaps the answer might lie along the following line of reasoning: Imagine a deceased person, a father who has been waiting for months or even years to communicate with his daughter. His time with the high-priced medium is maybe five minutes or, if he's lucky, perhaps as much as fifteen. There are other deceased people who want to communicate, too.

What will he want to tell his daughter? The latest scientific discoveries? The great books he's been reading in the afterlife? That's not what his daughter came to hear. And she probably wouldn't believe any of it even if true.

He and his daughter are with the medium for one reason—to give and receive expressions of love. He is there first and foremost to somehow prove to his daughter, in a way she can understand, that he still exists. Not only that, but he wants to prove to her that he still cares—that he is still her father, and that if he has anything to say about it, he will be her father forever.

So he attempts to show the medium who he is, identifying himself by relating information the daughter would know. He then shows his daughter that he's still around by acknowledging present things in her life that she can verify to be true. And he tells her, in his personal way, that he loves her. This is what he wants to do during the little time he has with the medium.

If I were that parent, this is what I would want to do. This is consistent with what Linda's father did for Linda, what Susy's mother did for Susy, what Christopher's grandfather did for Christopher, and what my mother did for me. It's what loving parents do.

However, my colleague's question is a thoughtful, provocative one. What would happen if we took the suggestion seriously? What would happen if we took a group of great mediums and invited them to communicate with departed great scientists like Sir James Clerk Maxwell and Professor William James? What would happen if we honored the possibility of the living soul hypothesis and asked them for their help?

Is it possible that we will one day be able to get information in this way, to help sick people whom modern science has no answers for, to solve perplexing problems in the sciences and technology, perhaps to offer suggestions toward furthering world peace? True visionaries are people who conceive of things that most people consider impossible.

We are already planning experiments to pursue these possibilities. It seems too much to hope for, and yet . . .

## Question 4

**Even if there appear to be a few "white crow" mediums, so what? Since we know that really good conjurers can fool other conjurers, who's to say that your lily-white mediums are really not just "whitewashing" your experiments?**

I vividly remember the day in January 1997 when Professor Daryl Bem of Cornell University gave a colloquium at the University of Arizona on his analysis of telepathy studies conducted by established researchers. Bem is an exceptionally sophisticated social psychologist who also happens to be an accomplished psychic magician. In his presentation, he performed some remarkable feats of mentalist magic to show his audience—faculty and students— that smart minds can easily be deceived by well-trained conjurers.

He also showed, equally convincingly, that the combined results of exceptionally well controlled studies on telepathy were extraordinarily significant. The statistics produced values in the billions. By comparison, values required for publication of mainstream findings are in the hundreds.

After the talk, I asked a senior member of our Friendly Devils' Advocates committee what he thought of Bem's views. His comment was priceless. He said, "We must remember, just because the probability values are less than one in a billion, they still could have occurred by chance."

In our latest mediumship experiments, we performed statistical analyses indicating that the results could have occurred by chance fewer than one in a 100 trillion times. And I say to myself,

"But they still could have occurred by chance." These words haunt me.

Carl Sagan's phrase (apparently picked up from Marcello Truizzi, a distinguished skeptic) that "extraordinary claims require extraordinary evidence" raises the question, How extra-ordinary must the evidence be in order to quality as extraordinary? When is enough enough?

A young research medium, Allison Klupar, when asked this question, replied, "It's *never* enough."

## UNDERSTANDING SKEPTICISM

When mediums themselves have trouble believing that what they're doing could be real and come to the conclusion that "It's never enough," how can we expect well-conditioned agnostics and professional skeptics ever to conclude, "I've seen enough to change my mind?"

It's understandable why professional skeptics like James Randi and Michael Shermer, who make money and build reputations by trumpeting that all paranormal claims are due to conjuring, will push the "deception hypothesis" as far as it can go. In *Skeptic* magazine, for example, Randi wrote of John Edward "pretending" to talk to dead people.

To justify his claim that John Edward was pretending, Randi had to ignore the research conducted in our laboratory—which is precisely what he did.

Yet research suggests there are deep psychological reasons why many of us, not just professional skeptics, have a hard time believing.

Recall the familiar experiments a hundred years ago by Russian physiologist Ivan Pavlov, who conditioned dogs to salivate whenever they heard a bell. I've come to realize that many people in contemporary society, including myself, suffer from an insidious form of conditioned neurosis. We've been conditioned since childhood to pair words like *soul, spirit,* and *survival of consciousness* with negative terms like *stupid, impossible, fake, crazy, shameful, sinful, superstitious, mistaken,* and even *"too good to be true."* Our beliefs are so thoroughly conditioned that even in the face of controlled laboratory experiments, strong negative emotions are triggered by the findings. We think "impossible" or "fraud" or "it's too good to be true" automatically and uncontrollably.

When someone experiences repeated emotional trauma, this can lead to PTSD: post-traumatic stress disorder. What happens when a whole culture experiences repeated conditioned emotional conditioning to certain ideas? Do we develop a PESD: post-*educational* stress disorder?

Thoughtful skeptics who are serious scientists are beginning to ask the same question. Professor Ray Hyman, one of the most distinguished academic skeptics, has told me, "I do not have control over my beliefs." He had learned from childhood that paranormal events are impossible. Today he finds himself amazed that even in the face of compelling theory and convincing scientific data, his beliefs have not changed. His repeated disappointments with past genuine frauds prevent him from accepting genuine science today.

Perhaps professional skeptics share a hazard with professional civil engineers: if a civil engineer designs a single bridge that falls down, he almost certainly loses his reputation and his livelihood. If science reveals that one of a skeptic's biggest conceptual bridges has fallen down—for example, the conviction that all mediums are "pretending"—the skeptic could lose his reputation and his livelihood. And once that bridge has fallen, who knows what else may fall?

Professional scientists, on the other hand, don't face such consequences. Theories come and go. The earth was flat; then it was round. The sun revolved around the earth; then the earth revolved around the sun. Material objects were solid (classical physics); then material objects were mostly empty space (quantum physics). If one conceptual bridge falls down, scientists just find another.

In fairness to professional skeptics like James Randi and Michael Shermer, they claim that they will give in to compelling data. They have certainly played a valuable role by revealing tricksters and deceivers. However, if John Edward, for example, turns out to be the real deal (and all of our experiments suggest he is as real as steel), we hope the Amazing Randi won't turn out to be the "Amazing Deceiver."

The purpose of science is not to confirm our conditioned beliefs but to reveal truths, whatever they are. Fortunately, times are changing, and children today are living with technology like radio telescopes, theories like quantum physics, movies like *The Sixth Sense,* and television shows like *Crossing Over.*

Thanks to Linda and her dream to know scientifically, one way or another, whether her beloved physician father is still here, years of surprising research have emerged from the laboratory. In the process, she has helped me discover the deep conditioned emotional scars that lead many to dismiss data, and their implications, as "insane." The fact is, if anything is insane, it is our collective inability to repair the damage and heal the wounds caused by mistaken conditioning. If humans have a fundamental spiritual nature, our future as a species will depend on whether we can "look up from our lives" (to paraphrase James Taylor), or "rise above it" (as Linda's father put it), and celebrate our potential to learn and evolve.

We're still at the infancy of this science, and haven't yet found out whether we can, by pursuing it, develop the techniques for obtaining information of value to us as individuals and to us as a society. But we're making progress.

# The Campbell White Crow Readings

When a scientific experiment is being considered, the researchers and the scientists involved in the project make decisions about what's required, which procedures will be most appropriate, and how to go about accomplishing what's needed.

That's the usual way. Our next experiment wouldn't include much that was "usual" about it.

Laurie Campbell mentioned while visiting us one day in December 2000 that she had been using a novel procedure at home in her telephone readings with clients. She had begun to notice that she was receiving information even before a reading got under way—specific information such as names, relationships, causes of death, personal descriptions. A lightbulb went on; she had started doing a "pre-reading" in which she would meditate for fifteen minutes or half an hour before beginning a reading, and write down whatever information came to her during that period.

When the call came in from the sitter, Laurie would explain how she conducts a reading and then would go over what she had received in the meditation period. Only after that would she begin the usual reading.

At the time we learned this, Laurie had already collected data on more than a hundred sitters, and said that her accuracy rates on the pre-reading data were ranging between 50 percent and 95 percent.

I came to term this design the Campbell Procedure to acknowledge that Laurie had come up with the idea herself. It seemed to be an extension of the Russek Procedure, where the first ten minutes of the readings are conducted in complete silence.

Needless to say, Linda and I were eager to test Laurie's idea in the laboratory, and we conceived a controlled, blinded experiment to investigate her claims. The idea was to combine the Russek Procedure and the Campbell Procedure in the same experiment.

The data gathering took place soon after, in Tucson, on Sunday, December 20. Three sitters were used, from various locations, and they each agreed to remain at home, ready to participate. Extreme care was taken from the first to insure that no one but the experimenters knew the sitters' identity. Laurie stayed at our house, where we were able to observe her, and she had no cell phone or other communication device we could detect.

The plan was fairly straightforward. Half an hour before a scheduled reading, Laurie would meditate, in seclusion and in silence, and would then write down the impressions she received during this meditation period. With the sitters each at some distant location, all possible cues—visible, auditory, even olfactory—were eliminated. That appeared to totally rule out any accusations of cold reading, subtle cueing, or medium fraud as possible explanations of the findings.

After about a half hour of pre-reading, we established telephone contact with the scheduled sitter. A Sony digital videotape recorder was used to record the initial reception of the sitter and the conduct of the Russek Procedure.

The sitter was reminded that the phone would momentarily be placed on mute (so that the sitter would not be able to hear Laurie speaking), and that for the duration of the ten-minute silent-sitter period the person was to hold the phone to his or her ear. Each time before passing the muted phone to Laurie, we checked to make sure that the mute button was working to cut off the sound, and that neither Laurie nor the sitter could hear any voices.

With mute activated, the handset was passed to Laurie, who chose to hold the phone turned away from her ear to minimize any noises or static on the phone line.

The Sony video camera recorded the ten-minute Russek Procedure while Laurie described out loud the impressions she was receiving. At no time did the experimenters refer to the sitter by name, and of course Laurie had not yet heard the sitter's voice.

On completion of the sitter-silent period, the phone was taken off mute, and Laurie then introduced herself and explained how she conducted a normal medium/sitter dialogue reading. She then read, item by item, the notes she had made from the pre-reading contemplation, and asked the sitter to confirm, question, or contradict the information.

What we most wanted to know was whether Laurie would be able to generate discrete and specific accurate information during the pre-reading period.

## The George Dalzell Reading

Of the three readings, the most striking was the one in which we had arranged for the sitter to be another medium, George Dalzell. He was a uniquely appropriate choice for several reasons. A professionally trained and licensed clinical social worker, he comes from a highly educated academic family. He himself was educated at Northwestern University in Chicago, and his father, grandfather, and great-grandfather were educated at Yale University. And he has been active as a medium for the past few years—but in secret, for fear of endangering his professional standing in the social work community.

At the time of testing, Laurie and George had never met face to face, nor had they communicated by phone, fax, mail, or e-mail. Laurie was aware of George and knew that he worked as a medium, but she was not informed that he would be one of the sitters selected to participate in this experiment.

George had "invited" four deceased people to participate. A plethora of documented information would be available to us; we could easily verify the data that Laurie might receive.

The session with George took over an hour. After Laurie's meditation period, she wrote down that the sitter (who had yet to be telephoned) was concerned with "truth that is held within the soul's journey—journey of the soul's path—truth from someone with an M name" and that the sitter was preparing to "stand up and be counted." She also wrote the names George, Michael, Alice, Bob, and Jerry, and mentions of "a small dog" and "candles burning."

We would soon learn that *every one* of the names of the deceased people invited by George was absolutely correct. In particular, she had received George's own name and the name of his best friend, Michael, who had recently passed. George had lit a candle just before the beginning of the experiment—something that, he said, he very rarely does. About the "stand up and be counted," though this might be a stretch, there is a sense in which we knew he was at the time preparing to do this: he had written a book, *Messages*, about his experiences as a medium and was looking forward to having it published.

During the Russek Procedure silent period—with Laurie holding the phone but still not having heard the voice of the person on the other end—she produced a large amount of data.

By now we had experienced over and over mediums producing a large amount of correct information—nothing new about that. The crucial distinction here lay in the sitter's not being in the same room—the sitter and medium in fact being in two different parts of the country with no contact at all or, at most, connected only over a muted telephone. This would seem to answer the doubts of even the most suspicious skeptic.

The amount of totally correct information Laurie reported was mind-boggling. All these statements were correct: That the reading was for a person named George and that the primary deceased person was Michael. That there was an East Coast and a California connection (George comes from the East Coast, and he currently lives in California). That his father is deceased. That both he and his father have had connections with science and with books.

And more: That Alice was the name of an aunt. That there was a dog, and it had an "S" name. And that there was someone with a strange name that sounded like "Talya," "Tiya," or "Tilya."

Still, as usual, the reading was by no means perfect. Some of the statements were general and could apply to many people—for example, that the sitter was loving and caring. And she made outright mistakes, such as that George's mother was deceased, when in fact she was living and in good health.

When the reading proper began—both people on the phone and able to speak to each other—Laurie first reviewed the pre-reading information she had received, and then started the reading by mentioning that someone named Jerry had passed recently, and that Michael was a "partner" to George, and George's "muse." She described Michael's personality accurately—not only as loving and caring, but obsessively neat and "pristine"—all correct, and George particularly agreed that "pristine" was an accurate description. She saw him in a white kitchen that was cozy and done with stone, also correct.

Laurie then moved to Jerry. She saw him from the Brooklyn area. Once again, here was a fact that the sitter, George, did not know about his friend but was able to confirm after the reading. Laurie saw him as sitting on bar stools, drinking and smoking, and often intoxicated, but that he had stopped drinking before he died. Every one of these statements was right on the money.

Even more remarkable, I thought, were statements by Laurie that Michael showed her where he had lived somewhere in Europe; he showed her a big city and then was traveling through the countryside to his home. Along the road to his house Laurie was shown a river, an old stone monastery on the edge of the river, and "centuries-old stonework." She reported his parents as having a heavy accent.

George had visited Michael at his parents' home in Germany,

and knew Michael's parents did indeed speak English with a heavy accent. He could also confirm the parts about the big city, the countryside, the road to his home alongside a river, and their living in a village. However, he did not recall anything about an old stone monastery along the river.

Laurie then described the older Aunt A, her great sense of humor (true) but related that A was experiencing "compassion and sorrow" for her granddaughter (true). Laurie correctly gave the exact name of the granddaughter, who she said was having difficulty, was "uncontrolled," and was currently receiving "healing."

George was unaware of any such situation.

Moving back to George himself, Laurie said she was being shown by Michael that George's life was about to become "noisy" and be "turned upside down." Indeed, with the publication of George's book, his secret life as a medium would become a matter of public record, and he might have to face professional complications in his role as a psychiatric social worker in good standing with the Los Angeles County Department of Mental Health, or with his other job as psychiatric admissions coordinator at a hospital in Glendale, California.

Laurie reported Michael showing her George and "white-coat" clinicians in a hospital. It turned out that George had performed psychological evaluations in the emergency room of a Los Angeles hospital just before the reading.

She described a small dog—description of personality and colors reported by George to be accurate—and saw the dog being near a favorite tree and water. George later informed us that he and his dog had spent many hours at a special tree near the water, where his former dog was buried.

There have been times in this work when it has been difficult to retain a scientific detachment. This was certainly one of them. The precision of the details, and their accuracy, was simply awesome.

But there was more. After the reading, George placed three phone calls to seek out information about statements Laurie had made that he was unable to confirm or refute.

One of these was to the mother of the young woman who was supposedly having difficulties. The mother confirmed that the young woman was indeed having serious problems and had sought psychological counseling in the week before the experiment because she was in crisis.

He also asked about the granddaughter's name. While Laurie had given the name correctly, it is one that has two common spellings, and George believed that Laurie had given the incorrect spelling. Wrong—George was mistaken about the spelling of his own relative's name. Laurie had spelled it correctly.

The second call was to Michael's parents in Germany, who confirmed that there is, indeed, a monastery-like old church built of stone along the river's edge on the way to their house; George had simply never noticed it as he sped past on the autobahn en route to visit them. They also mentioned that they had held a service for Michael in this building a few weeks before the experiment.

The third call, to a friend of Jerry's, confirmed that Jerry had indeed lived in Brooklyn.

Laurie Campbell, the housewife who had at first been worried about trying to do readings in the company of esteemed mediums with national reputations, had accomplished a feat of mediumship that may well be remembered in the history of the field.

## SCORING THE READINGS

The formal scoring of these readings showed that two of the three were in every way up to the standards of what we had come to expect.

The third, with George Dalzell, not only met that standard but went far beyond it. Laurie had provided over a hundred specific details, with an accuracy that ranged between 90 percent and 100 percent per deceased person.

As an example, Chart 17-1 shows every name given by Laurie in all three parts of her reading with George.

## Chart 17-1

| Name | Relationship | Living/Deceased | Rating |
|------|-------------|-----------------|--------|
| Pre-reading | | | |
| George | Self | Living | +3 |
| Jerry | Friend | Deceased | +3 |
| John | Great-grandfather | Deceased | +2 |
| B name (Becky, Barbara, Betty) | Friend | Living | +1 |
| Maureen | Friend | Living | +1 |
| Robert/Bob | Father | Deceased | +3 |
| Talya/Tily/Tilya | Friend | Living | +3 |
| S (Suzane) | Dog | Deceased | +2+ |
| S name (Sherm?) (Laurie spelled) | Known | Living | +1 |
| | | | |
| Sitter-silent | | | |
| Michael | Friend | Deceased | +3 |
| Jerry | Friend | Deceased | +3 |
| Joyce | — | — | 0 |
| Fred | Friend | Living | +2 |
| Francis | Friend | Living | +3 |
| Albert or Alfred | Friend of friend | Deceased | +3 |
| Elaine | — | — | 0 |
| | | | |
| Actual reading | | | |
| Michael | Friend | Deceased | +3 |
| Marcus | Friend | Living | +3 |
| Jerry | Friend | Deceased | +3 |
| Albert | Joel's friend | Deceased | +3 |
| Alice | Aunt | Deceased | +3 |
| George | Self | Living | +3 |
| An "A" name (Arthur) | Friend of friend | Deceased | +2+ |
| (name suppressed for privacy) | Granddaughter | Living | 3 |
| Joe/Joseph | — | — | 0 |

Of the thirty-one names or variations Laurie reported, only three had no connection at all with George, while thirteen were absolutely accurate. The names of the four people specifically invited by George—Michael, Alice, Bob, and Jerry—were received by Laurie during the most challenging of the three phases: the Campbell Procedure pre-reading and the Russek Procedure silent reading. In addition, it turned out to be factually correct that George had a friend with an unusual name that sounded like "Talya," although Laurie muffed the spelling; also that George had a dog with an "S" name (Laurie's guess about the actual name was similar in sound but not precisely correct).

As in the previous studies, and not unexpectedly, the most extensive and detailed information was provided during the traditional reading, with both Laurie and George on the phone and able to hear each other. During this period, Laurie provided four examples of information not previously known to George but later verified as correct.

One curiosity is noted for the sake of completeness and integrity. In the actual reading phase, Laurie brought up the names of three deceased well-known scientists. George later advised us that he had also invited "spirit scientists" to help facilitate the experiment, without specifying any particular people. She gave the names of Albert Einstein, Carl Jung, and David Bohm (an internationally renowned physicist who had once taught at Princeton, but a name Laurie could hardly have been expected to know).

Any skeptic watching the videotape of this experiment would have great difficulty explaining how Laurie came to mention the presence of three scientists—something she had never done in the context of any previous research reading since we had begun our work with her three years earlier.

## SUMMING UP

The new method we had termed the Campbell Procedure blocks any possibility of input from the sitter of the kind relied on by cold readers—anything that might suggest whether a particular statement is close to the truth or out in left field. Not even an inadvertent noise like a shuffling of body position or an unconscious sucking in of breath would become a clue.

Also, the procedures used in this experiment completely answered the issues that psychic magician Ross Horowitz had raised. Even if the medium or an investigator working for her had found out in advance who the sitters would be, Laurie could not know which person we had dialed.

George later wrote: "If you score the reading overall on the basis of naming the intended spirit collaborators, Laurie scored with 100 percent accuracy. . . . It was one of the great thrills of my life to have a medium bring through my Aunt Alice, who was the dearest love in my life, like a second mother to me—and with such strength and accuracy in the reading."

Linda and I were elated. In our most persuasive experiment to date, in terms of safeguards against deceit or trickery, this procedure seemed to answer almost every challenge a skeptic could throw at us.

## THE ULTIMATE DESIGN

In medicine, what's called a double-blind procedure is considered the "gold standard" research design. Not only do none of the patients know whether they are being given the drug under test or a placebo, but the experimenter, as well, does not know which patients are taking the drug and which the placebo. This is termed evidence-based medicine.

The same kind of procedure can be created for mediumship science. We call this evidence-based mediumship.

The elegance of the Campbell Procedure is that it could be used in a double-blind manner. It thereby completely rules out any accusations of fraud. In fact, some months later, we devised and conducted a complex double-blind design with Laurie once again as the medium.

There were six sitters, one of whom was George. As in previous experiments, Laurie was not told who the sitters would be. She was "blind" to the sitters.

However, this time not only did Laurie never hear the sitters' voices, but the sitters never heard Laurie's voice. As a further safeguard, Linda and I were blind to the order in which the six subjects were to be run. The phone calls, muting, and taping were conducted by staff in the Human Energy Systems Laboratory.

Once the tapes of Laurie's statements had been transcribed, each sitter was mailed two transcripts—one of his or her own reading, and one "placebo" transcript, which belonged to one of the other sitters. The papers were intentionally not marked to show which transcript belonged to which sitter, so the sitters did not know which reading was their own. They were told to score both transcripts, blindly. The question was, even under blind conditions, could the sitters determine which of the readings was theirs?

The findings were breathtaking. Once again it was George Dalzell's reading stood out.

During the pre-reading period—with medium and sitter not in contact in any way, and Laurie having no idea who the sitter was—the information she obtained was 60 percent accurate; the accuracy increased to 65 percent during the sitter-silent period. George's double-blind ratings of Laurie's misses during his reading were only 13 percent for the pre-reading and 17 percent for the sitter-silent period.

When George scored the control reading—that is, Laurie's reading of one of the other sitters—he rated Laurie getting zero hits in the pre-reading period and the same—zero—in the silent-sitter period. In other words, only one of the readings strongly matched George's history, and that was his own personal reading.

Again, George did not hear his reading at the time it occurred. As a result, he did not know which of the transcripts was from his reading and which was from another sitter.

This provided incontrovertible evidence in response to the skeptics' highly implausible argument against the single-blind study that the sitter would be biased in his or her ratings (for example, misrating his deceased loved ones' names and relationships) because he knew that this information was from his own reading.

The skeptics' complaint becomes a completely and convincingly impossible argument in the case of the double-blind study.

It appeared to be the ultimate "white crow" design.

# · 18 ·

# How Our Lives
# Might Change

There is an off-beat assignment I like to present my classes, for the challenge it gives them and for my own pleasure in seeing whether any students will come up with refreshingly original ideas. And sometimes, to relax, my colleagues and I also enjoy this mental game.

The challenge is to imagine life without any boundaries between this world and the next.

Try it. Imagine that one day in the not too distant future, you pick up your local newspaper and your eye is drawn to a banner headline something like this:

## SCIENCE PROVES HUMAN SOUL LIVES FOREVER
### Conclusive Lab Experiments Show Consciousness
### Survives After Death

The lead paragraph of the article reports that over the past few months a collaborative team of scientists has been conducting a series of highly controlled, replicated experiments in multiple laboratories across the United States and abroad. Just as starlight from distant stars continues forever, the scientists have noted, so does human consciousness. The final results of the experiments are reported to be clear-cut and positive.

According to the report, the multi-centered, double-blind mediumship experiment rules out any possibility of fraud, deception, subtle cueing, or statistical coincidence. The experimental design of the research has been vouched for by a team of Nobel laureate scientists.

Related stories fill the front page and most of the first section of the paper. You realize that similar articles are also being run simultaneously in distinguished newspapers like the *New York Times,* the *Washington Post,* and the *Times* of London. Hundreds of millions of people around the world are reading this news.

Imagine that after all the inevitable challenges, it turns out that it's not dust to dust, but energy to energy—as predicted in my first book with Linda, *The Living Energy Universe.*

How would this discovery change your life if you knew, once and for all, that consciousness stayed with us forever?

You would realize and believe that life in your physical body, relatively speaking, reflects just a brief moment in time. That your time here on the earth is for the purpose of learning advanced lessons of love and compassion, and for you to honor the many gifts you have received by learning how to give to your family, friends, community, and the world as a whole. And that as the caterpillar eventually becomes a butterfly, you too, will in time be able to take flight in ways we cannot yet fathom.

The questions go beyond how you yourself would change. Consider: If all this and more were true, how would these facts change education, science, medicine, the legal system, religion, and the rest of human institutions?

As Linda and I have pondered this question and posed it to our colleagues, students, and friends, we've come to realize that if the living soul hypothesis turns out to be true, virtually everything we know and live by will change.

Albert Einstein used to propose "thought experiments" to explore hard-to-imagine subjects. So from time to time we conduct our own thought experiments on how our results might affect individuals and the world as a whole.

Many of the answers to the questions we pose are not self-evident, and will necessarily remain unanswered for the immediate future. I personally believe that if and when the living soul hypothesis turns out to be completely beyond doubt, it will take the collaborative and integrative effort of our greatest scientific, educational, business, political, and spiritual leaders—both present and past—to evolve the practical philosophies and ethics needed to guide us toward peace, wisdom, and health.

But here are some of our own conjectures.

## How Would This Knowledge Change Our Daily Lives?

Knowing that life continues after death (the phrase is contradictory, of course, but by now you understand what I mean) would give us permission to slow down. We would now know that life on earth isn't a race, and we would no longer feel an intense pressure to achieve as much as possible in the shortest amount of time.

When I was a professor at Yale and my schedule became increasingly overcommitted, I realized one day that it was impossible for me to fulfill my parents' dreams. I had been brought up to believe that the number one goal in life was to reach one's personal potential. It occurred to me that my busy schedule didn't allow me the time to conduct all the scientific research I had the potential to do, not to mention all the other personal goals I had set for myself.

I came to appreciate an intriguing irony. The more potential a person has, the more impossible it is for that individual to reach this potential in a single given lifetime. I realized it's ill advised to attempt living one's life only to fulfill one's potential—each human has too great a potential; yet there is too little time on earth to manifest it all.

At that moment of realization, I gave up trying to "reach my potential." I decided that it was more reasonable to make choices in life and to focus on the interests that are most precious and prized.

During the time I was at Yale, if I had had a vote in the universe, I would have voted that something like reincarnation be possible, because then I wouldn't have had to worry about reaching my potential in this lifetime. I could wait, knowing that I wouldn't be wasting the talents and abilities I had been blessed with. And neither would anyone else have to worry about wasting his or her talents.

If the living soul hypothesis could be proven true, it would logically follow that people no longer need to worry about cramming every bit of experience into their current physical life.

If you are, or ever were in your life, in conflict about spending more time with your children, for example, versus getting a bigger house, and you take a view that transcends physical death, it becomes easy to determine which is more important. If we knew for a fact that survival of consciousness is real, this would enable us to stop looking to outside societal pressures as our life's primary guides. Instead, we could turn our attention to finding meaning and purpose in our own lives, realizing that we have the potential to be compassionate human beings with a supreme capacity to love.

The process of slowing down, if appreciated globally, would benefit everyone as well as the earth as a whole. My friend Christopher likes to say that many of us spend hours a day commuting to and from jobs we hope will earn us more money so that we can buy a bigger house farther from the city, demanding even more time commuting.

Yes, we often try to accomplish all this and more in the name of love. But one can rightfully ask, is this truly loving? If we could fully accept that the goal of obtaining material goods is less important than the quality of time we spend with the ones we love, we would be happier and healthier. As we've seen from the follow-up to the Harvard Stress Study, having loving relationships appears to bring the added blessing of better health.

If we could spend less time "racing to the grave" as we exploit the earth's resources with abandon, we would then slow down, take it easier, and give the earth a Sabbath, too.

The global economy has put an extra strain on the earth, and our planet never gets its essential rest. On any given day, around the clock, automobile and truck traffic, airline traffic, commercial shipping and even use of the internet contribute twenty-four hours a day to polluting our air and using the earth's valuable resources to power the global connections we've come to depend on and expect to be accessible forever.

It's clear that the living soul hypothesis and its many implications could potentially benefit our personal lives, the lives of our loved ones, and our entire planet. It gives us new reasons to act in ways guaranteed to make us feel better in our hearts.

As for the way we value human relationships, it will no longer be justifiable to view acquaintances in our lives, especially in business, as competitive obstacles between us and what we want out of life.

The living soul hypothesis encourages people to re-evaluate how kind and compassionate we are. It becomes more possible that these values will take priority in our evolving relationships. For example, if you had been cruel to a given person, who then died, how would you feel if you knew scientifically and without doubt that he or she would still be around?

Would you feel comfortable about having this person looking over your shoulder—not merely metaphorically but literally?

Would you want to face him or her when it was your time to "cross over"?

## DO EMOTIONAL CONSEQUENCES CONTINUE
## AFTER DEATH?

If the pain we caused in others still lives within them after death in their info-energy systems, we may continue to resonate energetically with their suffering. Since relationships can continue between physical systems (us) and info-energy systems (the deceased), this possibility leads us to reconsider how we treat others in the physical world.

The resulting emphasis on kindness and compassion also includes new consequences related to deceit and lying, with far-reaching implications for all human interactions.

Theoretically, if the living soul hypothesis becomes accepted truth, it will be more difficult for us to justify behaving in deceitful ways, since we will have strong reason to expect that those whom we deceive today will catch up with us in the future. Moreover, it's possible that we won't have to wait until we die to face the consequences of our deceptions, since our departed loved ones, as well as the departed loved ones of those we are deceiving, will be witnessing our lying "on line," in real time.

And is it also possible that mediums may serve as deceit detectors, giving us messages from beyond that confirm who is lying to us?

As people everywhere become skilled at receiving information from the departed, help from the other side could in principle give each of us, directly or indirectly, the ability to discern who is being fair and honest with us, and who is being unjust and deceptive.

If the living soul hypothesis is true, and we develop our abilities to "hear" what the dead have to say to us, perhaps human deceit might come to an end. It's possible that we could enter a new era of human caring that Linda and I call integrity love. We would be strongly encouraged, to put it mildly, to take responsibility for our actions, transforming the way we live our daily lives. And as more of us openly look to the deceased for everyday guidance, this potential could make life easier, safer, and more rewarding.

Receiving communication from the other side could help our everyday decision making in both our personal and our professional lives. And knowing that our loved ones were always close and available to listen to us would allow us to feel less alone. The ache of being lonesome for our loved ones would be diminished.

The intuition of all people would be fed and nourished into full bloom.

Of course, we would then have to seriously reconsider and accept where some of "our" thoughts come from. Perhaps it's time for us all to humble ourselves and consider the possibility that to various degrees we may already be receiving communication from those who have walked this earth before us.

If the living soul hypothesis is proven accurate, we'll need to awaken to the realization that the distinction between "our" minds and "their" minds may be far less clear cut than previously imagined. Is it possible that contemporary scientists, artists, physicians, and educators are receiving information from departed individuals skilled in these areas and devoted to our evolutionary potential? Logic requires that we entertain the idea that those of us who are open to the possibility may unknowingly be receiving ideas from great minds of earlier generations.

Some of what follows may sound laughable and unworthy. We know from our initial experiences with Susy and Laurie how hard it is to suppress a negative judgmental response when confronted with mediumship experience. Few things are more serious than death, few more awesome than the thought of talking to the dead. But if a given suggestion seems ludicrous to you, please remember that all of them are offered with a clear purpose. Though the question of the living soul opens a veritable Pandora's box, it is a box that, for better or worse, must ultimately be opened if it truly exists.

## The Spiritual Legal System

Historically, courts have selected juries without ever asking questions about the beliefs of the candidates' *deceased* relatives concerning prejudice, the death penalty, and other opinions related to a given case. But an interesting question arises: If the deceased can hear the trial, is it okay for the jurors to be open to receiving opinions from their deceased loved ones during the jury deliberations?

And might those contributions help jurors more consistently find the path to the truth of guilt or innocence?

In addition to instructing jurors not to discuss the trial with friends or relatives, will judges advise juries not to confer with deceased friends and relatives about the case? Or might they, on the contrary, *insist* that jurors attempt to communicate and seek advice from the departed?

Deceased people will have been witness to crimes, especially if they are the victims in cases of murder. If scientifically documented and licensed mediums become accepted in the future, then theoretically a medium's account of the deceased's testimony regarding the crime could be considered by the court. This sounds like science fiction; in fact, some imaginative sci-fi writer has probably used just this premise.

A victim's afterlife testimony could be a critical factor in determining the conviction or acquittal of the defendant, especially if the testimony could be obtained scientifically and validated independently by multiple certified mediums.

The living soul hypothesis has implications for sentencing, as well. If life after life exists, we can no longer presume that the death penalty is society's worst punishment. And, just as there are victim's family rights, the courts would have to decide to what extent the deceased's rights should help determine an appropriate punishment. The victim might not be in a hurry to see his murderer in the afterlife. The ultimate punishment—the death penalty—might need to be reconsidered, not just in regard to its appropriateness for the defendant but from the viewpoint of the deceased victims.

Lawyers and business people will also need to reconsider what to do about intellectual property rights. Imagine that a scientist, engineer, inventor, or creative person dies and then, from the beyond, communicates a discovery that can be patented—a concept for a book or movie, an idea for a new form of art work, a plan for a new building, a plan for reducing crime or rehabilitating criminals. Who should receive credit? Will patents be owned jointly, between here and there? Will the Writers Guild arbitrate between living and departed contributors to a script? Will people win acclaim and promotions for ideas received from "over there"?

This issue extends as well to wills and estates. Though we acknowledge that you can't take the money with you, if the living soul hypothesis is true, maybe you should be able to have input regarding how what you leave behind is spent. After you die, should you be allowed to continue making decisions about how your company is run or how your estate is handled? Should deceased people be allowed to change their wills after they've died, adding codicils or amendments if they don't like the way the benefactors of their estates and foundations are spending their money? This, of course, would open up a whole new arena of law.

Will we begin to speak of "deceaseds' rights" and see future legislation emerge to protects these rights?

## New Marriage Vows

The most familiar marriage vow still contains the words "till death do us part."

But what if death doesn't part us? How far does the commitment to marriage extend?

We can envision a system that provides a new level of marriage vow, one that goes beyond "till death do us part." It would reflect a true spiritual contract that would join the loved ones eternally. Here the couple would be making a commitment to the continued evolution of their relationship with each other, regardless of their respective ups and downs, here or there.

If Sir Isaac Newton and the many other intellectual and spiritual giants before him are correct, astrophysics and metaphysics may reflect two sides of the same coin: the universal currency of love.

## Spiritual Education

In contemporary society, children are regularly exposed to violence and death, not just in films, television, comic books, video games, and the like but also in their real-life neighborhoods and even their schools. Yet if it turns out that there is no death of the personality, then the way the media portrays violence and death might change. The consequences of these changes would influence the minds and hearts of our children . . . possibly in negative ways as well as positive.

Children often report having imaginary friends as well as seeing ghosts and angels. Adults discredit these experiences and interpret them as "make-believe." But if the living soul hypothesis is true, it's reasonable to entertain the thesis that children may be more open to receiving this kind of information. Encourage the young to cultivate these experiences, and by the time they reach adulthood, these latent talents might be developed into meaningful skills that could substantially aid society.

How would the world change if increasing numbers of adults had a deep connection to these living info-energies? Educational scholars, such as Howard Gardner at Harvard's School of Education, have documented at least seven different kinds of intelligence, which directly influence how children acquire skills in everything they do, from reading, talking, and walking to their ability to function in a complex society. Educators may wish to consider adding an eighth category of intelligence to describe the realm of psychic and spiritual abilities that reflect inherent capacities of the living soul.

On the other side of the equation, what if a youngster is depressed, and knows that the living soul hypothesis is true—would he or she feel more comfortable about committing suicide?

According to recent figures, about thirty thousand people a year in the United States take their own lives. Is it possible that suicide will increase if the living soul hypothesis is discovered to be true? How can children be educated and encouraged to sustain a passion and reverence for physical life if what they experience in the world is increasing violence, apathy, and discouraging messages about the future of our planet?

There are no simple answers here. But if our personal lives continue beyond the physical, children can be taught to appreciate the many adventures and life gifts that can be experienced only in the physical.

In Suzane Northrop's book *The Séance: Healing Messages from Beyond,* she reports that in her work with clients, many of whom wish to contact a person who committed suicide, the deceased often regret leaving the physical realm so soon. According to Suzane, the reason the deceased give is not that where they are now is so bad. Rather, they realize that they cut short their natural life's path and failed to complete the journey they set for themselves, or that was set for them, before they were born.

The humanist in me cringes at the idea that proof of the living soul hypothesis might encourage some unstable people or zealots to decide to get to "the other side" early by taking their own lives, like the Heaven's Gate cultists. Still, this is a possibility, a dark side of the reality that we must recognize.

It should be possible to teach children at an early age what a truly profound gift our time on earth is. Because of their unique openness, children may be able to learn things faster than their parents. Just as the young frequently have an easier time learning new languages, so might they also find it easier to learn the language of the soul.

## Spiritual Biobehavioral Sciences

Children who report "seeing things" sometimes grow up to be adults who are labeled as psychotic and delusional by mental health professionals. When such experiences are dismissed and labeled as delusions and hallucinations, this rejection often increases dysfunctional behavior. The people having the experiences become fearful of their own consciousness, and they literally feel crazy.

The human mind is extremely inventive, and a subset of people who report seeing things may well be seeing the creations of their own imaginations. However, if the living soul hypothesis turns out to be true, the diagnoses of delusion and hallucination will have to be reconsidered. Not only will mental health professionals have to become more open-minded and scientific, but it may be necessary to have skilled mediums added to integrative mental health teams to help differentially diagnose and treat people in general, and also help those who are especially fearful of seeing aspects of spiritual reality.

Doctors in the future will need to seriously entertain the possibility that their patients do not show up for their sessions alone. What if a therapist's client is bringing along one or more deceased persons to his sessions?

Can psychotherapy be improved in the future if the deceased are more actively incorporated into the therapeutic process? And into psychological research, where both the investigators and the subjects may have deceased individuals witnessing the research? Is it possible that the living souls may complicate the findings, making them more difficult to replicate precisely because of the unique combination of people involved, not only here but there?

In the physical, chemical, and biological sciences, ambient electromagnetic energy levels created by nature and technology can cause "contamination" to experimental findings. It would be curious if a new form of experimental "contamination" turned out to be the living souls of earlier investigators.

## Spiritual Medicine

When someone dies in a hospital, the medical staff people say that the patient "expired." But this term describes only the physical process and would no longer tell the whole story. Would it be more appropriate to say that the person has "crossed over"?

If physicians didn't see death as the end but as a new beginning, the way they approached treatment for the seriously ill would dramatically change.

Would saving someone "at all costs" always be the best solution? If the living soul hypothesis is true, should spiritual practices be included in medical procedures at the time the living soul is separating from the physical body? The implications for hospice and the care of the dying are vast.

Another area in medicine that becomes significant is what is termed medical intuition. Sometimes physicians are capable of providing diagnoses well beyond the available scientific information. Are these merely informed lucky guesses, or is it possible that more is involved? Could the ability of physicians, nurses, psychologists, and even lay healers who make such diagnoses be consciously or unconsciously tuning in and receiving information from deceased health care providers?

I recall very clearly, as if it was yesterday, the realization that came to Linda and me about her father. Dr. Russek was known to be uncannily good at making decisions concerning the diagnosis and treatment of his cardiac patients. The complexity of the decisions he reached often went well beyond the available scientific data. The simple explanation Linda and her father entertained was that he had extraordinary intuition.

However, let's take into account three factors: Dr. Russek's devotion to nightly prayer (he always thanked the "Great Experimenter" for the blessings he received in his life), his fondness for philosophy (he regularly read Spinoza and Victor Frankl), and his secret curiosity about the plausibility of astrology (he used to enjoying reading horoscopes and keeping track of which predictions fit specific family members). In the light of these three additional facts, it's perhaps no surprise to know that he was a man who seriously entertained the possibility of the existence of spiritual reality. The fact that he was receptive to these kinds of phenomena could mean that he was open to unknown sources of information that he didn't realize he was receiving.

If the living soul hypothesis is proven true, it follows that what Linda and I affectionately call spirit-assisted medicine, or SAM, could also be true. As health care providers become better skilled at communication with the other side, medical practices could be enhanced through guidance and assistance from departed physicians and therapists.

We have initiated scientific research that attempts to establish whether collaborators such as Dr. Russek can be documented as being present in healing sessions, and whether measurable effects on clinical outcome can be attributed to their participation.

Though the research is in the exploratory stage, the data are interesting and consistent with the hypothesis.

The living soul hypothesis has implications for re-evaluating the "placebo" response, which along with cases of "spontaneous healing" are effects that are persistently observed in ancient as well as contemporary medicine. Attempts to explain placebo and spontaneous healing incidents in terms of known phenomena, including belief and expectancy of the patient, and social variables such as the warmth of the doctor, have been insufficient to account for all the findings.

Having formal training in psychophysiology, and having published over two hundred scientific papers that employ psychophysiological measures, I certainly appreciate the role such processes can play in healing. But the question remains: Do "mind-body" explanations provide the whole story, or do we need to expand our vision to include "mind-body-spirit"?

Once we open the door to the possibility of a living soul, many possibilities deserve our serious consideration. From energy medicine to parapsychology, the theories and findings should be, as Proust said, "seen with new eyes."

Is it possible that our health and illness are affected, at least in part, by our interaction with living info-energy systems or souls? Is it possible that unconscious attachments with "negative" souls can contribute to the presence of disease as well as behavioral health problems in certain individuals?

These are startling possibilities to entertain, and it's tempting to dismiss or ignore them by simply labeling them as weird or worthless.

### Spiritual Religion

If we do not primarily spend our time in the search for more money, a more beautiful partner, and a bigger house, or in a competition with people who get in our way, how will we spend our time? Is it possible that we'll spend more time revisiting questions that have troubled us since the beginning of humankind?

Where did we come from? When did consciousness begin? Why are we here? Where are we going? As science and spirituality come together, this will enable us to make a collective spiritual advancement that could be greater than at any other time in recorded history.

Most of us have been taught that the first person to be resurrected, who would continue to serve as a bridge between the physical earth and God, was the profoundly loving and caring Jesus. However, if the living soul hypothesis is true, it's possible that other spiritually enlightened persons, including Moses and the Buddha, may be included among the large community of deceased spiritual leaders who deeply care about the family of humankind and are ready to further assist us if we are prepared to receive their wisdom. Not only did this extensive community of spiritual leaders precede Jesus, they might have assisted him when he walked the earth.

As we entertain such ideas, we are led to posit that truly loving people from all religious faiths may be contributing to the evolution of human consciousness worldwide.

If the living soul hypothesis is true, we all will face the need to re-examine the history and evolution of religious institutions. No doubt it will be recognized that many religions may be more interconnected spiritually than even their leaders currently appreciate. In the same way that workers in the health care community are coming to appreciate, slowly but surely, that they must combine conventional, complementary, and alternative medicines in an "integrative medicine" framework, so spiritual care may one day combine conventional, complementary, and alternative religions in an "integrative spiritual" framework.

# · 19 ·

# Looking Forward
# and Outward

On January 1, 2000, Linda and I made an unusual New Year's resolution, or more precisely, a New Millennium resolution.

We decided we would try to live our lives as if the living soul hypothesis were true, so long as there was no convincing data to the
contrary. From that day forward, so long as the survival hypothesis
was plausible, we would attempt to make personal decisions with
the awareness that our lives might continue after we physically died.
We would live our personal lives as a great experiment.

If our decision is mistaken, and the truth is really ashes to
ashes, dust to dust, we will never know that the experiment failed.

However, if our assumption is correct and the living soul is a
doorway into the existence of a larger reality, a living spiritual/en-
ergy reality, then when we die, we will be aware that our consciousness continues. And we will be relieved to discover that the
choices we made were wise ones.

One of the members of our anonymous Friendly Devil's Advocates committee informed us that this same decision was arrived
at many years ago by the great seventeenth-century mathematician

Blaise Pascal. We reasoned that if the logic was good enough for Pascal, it should make sense for us, as well.

There's also another reason for conducting our lives as if the living soul hypothesis is true. This, too, comes from the canons of science in the form of a principle known as Occam's razor, after the thirteenth-century English philosopher who first enunciated the idea. One way of stating his principle is this: "All things being equal, the simpler hypothesis is usually the correct one."

Here's a favorite example of the wisdom of this simple statement. When stargazers of the Middle Ages went about gathering the evidence being revealed to them by the newly invented telescope, the earth-centered model of the universe became ever more complicated as the observers tried to account for the ever more contradictory data. One advantage of the new but highly controversial sun-centered model that landed Galileo in so much hot water was just that it was *simpler* in the sense that it could account for more of the data. One idea could account for so many observations—the idea, in a word, was elegant.

The same logic applies to the emerging data unfolding not only in our experiments, but in the history of mediumship research over the past hundred years. As described in Alan Gauld's book *Mediumship and Survival,* a definitive history of a century of investigations addressing the living soul hypothesis, the number of different explanations needed to account for all the data is itself extraordinary. The best experiments on this subject can be explained away only if one makes a whole series of assumptions:

- Some of the findings would require that mediums were secretly using detectives who were so good as to be themselves undetected by other detectives—"super cheating."
- Some of the findings would require that the sitters were falsely remembering specific facts of their personal histories, including relatives' names and causes of death—"super sitter bias."

- Some of the findings would require that the mediums were extraordinary guessers of information, even when the sitters were not saying a word and the mediums could not see them—"super guessing."
- Some of the findings would require that the mediums were interpreting subtle changes in the sitter's breathing so as to figure out, for example, that the sitter's grandmother had brought daisies to her mother's wedding—"super subtle cue reading."
- Some of the findings would require that the mediums were reading not only the unconscious mind of the sitters, but information that the sitters themselves could not remember or remembered wrong, only later to verify it through a conversation with another relative—"super telepathy."

However, if we were to apply Occam's razor to the total set of data collected over the past hundred years, including the information you have read about in this book, there is a straightforward hypothesis that is elegant in its simplicity. This is the simple hypothesis that consciousness continues after death. This hypothesis accounts for all the data.

If we are to take the process of science seriously, there comes a point when it makes sense to accept the principle of Occam's razor: sometimes the simpler hypothesis is the correct one.

And sometimes it is the tiniest piece of data that reminds us of this simple truth.

## REMEMBERING "POPSICLES" AND THE LIGHT FROM DISTANT STARS

If there is any one single piece of mediumship data that led me to accept the living soul hypothesis, it is a brief and seemingly silly incident that occurred in a John Edward reading on television.

He was speaking with a woman who appeared to be in her

early thirties and was receiving information about one of her older deceased relatives. He then said something like "She is showing me a little dog. Did your relative have a little dog?"

The woman looked confused. She did not know whether her relative had a little dog or not.

Then John said something that truly surprised me. He said, "She's telling me that the dog was named after a food. A food name."

A food name for a dog? What could it possibly be? Lettuce? Banana? Hamburger? Here, little Carrot. Roll over, Grits. Tortilla, play dead!

Not likely.

After the reading, the sitter was then shown calling her aunt to ask about the deceased relative's dog. The relative had, indeed, owned a little dog. When the sitter asked for its name, the relative replied, "Popsicles."

That sounded almost as weird as Grits or Tortilla. The sitter asked her aunt about the strange name, and she replied, "Because the dog loved popsicles."

Being the enthusiastic agnostic that I am, I ticked off the skeptical possibilities about detectives . . . or some deceit off camera to make it look as if John had done something remarkable when he was really cheating . . . or reading the mind of the audience member . . . or an amazing guess . . .

Or was this just another innocent and tiny little piece of data suggesting that John really does talk to dead people?

What do you think?

Here's what I think, as a scientist.

The probability that John is the real thing—and that Laurie, Suzane, Anne, George, and certain other mediums are engaged in something honest and truly spiritual—is as great as the probability that the light from distance stars continues in some form, forever.

And I remember what Professor William James wrote about Mrs. Piper, a medium he studied very carefully:

*I should be willing now to stake as much money on Mrs. Piper's honesty as on that of anyone I know, and I am quite satisfied to leave my reputation for wisdom or folly, so far as human nature is concerned, to stand or fall by this declaration.*

## Celebrating the Final Score

After three years of conducting the experiments laid out in these pages, Linda asked me one day how I could see all these data and still not believe.

Believe. The truth is, I couldn't believe. Couldn't, because I'm a scientist, and the data, though highly supportive, are not 100 percent certain.

She accused me of writing about Occam's razor but not actually putting the razor to use.

And she was right. I had so far avoided facing the data as a whole, which was enabling me to maintain my safe position of not committing to a belief one way or the other. Metaphorically, I was hiding behind my beard and wasn't about to conceptually shave with Occam's razor—or anyone else's.

The truth is that I was being scientifically hypocritical. I had failed to do the very thing I always try to encourage my students and colleagues to do.

Why did I resist summarizing the data as a whole? How could someone who had a reputation for being a big-picture person resist painting the big picture? I discovered that the reason was simple: I was experiencing a growing professional and personal fear.

No, I wasn't afraid that the skeptics were right. The data seemed clear enough on that point.

And, no, I wasn't afraid that the mediums and skeptics might be in a dead heat. That would actually be quite comforting. If that were the case, I could remain on the fence, and my most skeptical colleagues would be reassured.

My growing fear was that if I actually summarized and integrated the entire set of observations, I might be forced to conclude that—at least concerning the specific research mediums we worked with—the skeptics were completely wrong.

I was brought up from an early age to believe that scientists are not supposed to *believe* in things—in the sense of belief as opposed to accepting specific ideas and facts that current science has acknowledged as being scientifically verified.

Linda was asking me to face my fear about believing in mediumship. And if I were to believe, in what sense? To "believe" can range from simply holding views or opinions about something, to having confidence in the facts or ideas, to accepting on faith.

I realized that concerning belief in survival of consciousness, I was at the "opinions" level. Scientific theory strongly indicated the plausibility of the hypothesis, and the data were clear enough to enable me to hold the opinion that survival, in theory, was true. That was my reasoned opinion.

In terms of belief as having confidence—no, I did not have confidence in that reasoned opinion. The truth is, despite all the experiments and all our controls, for some reason I still doubted the mediums, the sitters, Linda's and my co-investigators, and even what I had witnessed with my own eyes. My degree of doubt in the presence of all the data was frankly irrational. I was experiencing skeptimania. I knew it, but I hadn't been able to do anything about it.

It was time to tally up the score and see what the data revealed—whether the claims and accusations of the skeptics now seemed valid, or whether we had already made such a strong case that I could change my own skepticism to some form of belief.

I went through all the experiments—each and every reading, both within and beyond the formal data collection periods—and examined it all on the basis of eleven key points that form the core.

I can no longer ignore the data and dismiss the words. They are as real as the sun, the trees, and our television sets, which seem to pull pictures out of the air.

So what do I recommend?

That we celebrate the Big H, memorable moments on the

beach, the "Good Ship Lollipop," the cow in the backyard, and daisies at the wedding.

That we celebrate the billions of trillions of stars and the physical miracle that their light shines forever.

That we celebrate the existence of the human mind, which not only raises scientific questions but also evolves the wisdom to know when it's time to stop obsessively questioning and accept the truth of the answers.

That we celebrate the existence of living souls in a living and evolving universe.

And that, with humility, we thank a Loving Essence that makes all of this possible.

## THE ELEVEN KEY SUMMARY POINTS

1. Fraud
2. Cueing
3. Selective memory
4. Vague information
5. Lucky guesses
6. Experimenter bias or mistakes
7. Motivation of the mediums
8. Motivation of the skeptics
9. Mind-reading by mediums
10. Memory in the universe
11. Talking to dead people

In the following analysis, it's important to understand that we are not analyzing the work of *all* mediums. Many mediums—perhaps even *most* mediums—are giving their clients what the clients want, very much in the same way people go to a magic show to have the magician dazzle and please them. The principal difference is that the paying customer at the magic show knows that trickery is being used, and the paying customer in the medium's living room wants to believe.

No, it's not the psychic medium using cold reading techniques we're evaluating here, but only the small, highly select group of top mediums who have been willing to risk exposure and humiliation by allowing scientific examination of their work under highly controlled circumstances.

So here's what the data show about the experiments involving this small group of mediums:

## Point 1: Fraud

### Skeptics Speculate

They somehow get information ahead of time, by detectives or other secret means.

### Mediums Say

We do not know who the sitters are, not only in the laboratory studies but also in our daily practices.

### What the Experiments Actually Reveal

In parts of the experiments, the mediums could indeed have cheated by having taps placed on the lab's phones and our home phones so they could obtain the names of all the sitters in advance, then scouting or hiring a detective to get useful information, and memorizing all the information.

But this would not have helped for the silent periods in the Miraval and Canyon Ranch experiments because the mediums could not see who was sitting behind them or on the other side of the screen. And they could not know the order in which the sitters would be brought to them (which was decided only at the last minute, on the day of the testing). Since the sitter did not speak during the silent period, the medium had no clues to age, sex, emotional state, or anything else that would have been revealed by seeing or hearing the sitter.

What's more, in the Campbell "white crow" experiment, the sitters were not even in the same location as the medium, and the most impressive data were provided even before any telephone contact was established.

## Point 2: Cueing

### Skeptics Speculate

The mediums get information by studying facial expressions and non-verbal cues, analyzing the verbal content, interpreting tone of voice, and using other tricks of cold reading.

### Mediums Say

We do not need to see the sitters, or even hear their voices, to get accurate information, and the experiments were successful even when we could not see the sitters and they did not speak.

### What the Experiments Actually Reveal

In the Miraval and Canyon Ranch experiments, the mediums were deaf and blind to the sitters. Yet, in the absence of any verbal or visual cues, they still provided a very large amount of data, of which 40 percent to 80 percent was scored as +3, absolutely accurate. In the HBO study, one medium in particular, Suzane Northrop, asked only five questions but reported more than 120 pieces of information that were rated over 80 percent accurate. Again, in the Campbell experiment, the barriers between medium and sitters were even more distinct, yet the medium's accuracy was astonishing.

## Point 3: Selective Memory

### Skeptics Speculate

The sitters primarily remember the hits and forget the misses because they're grieving and want to believe. This inflates their remembered accuracy, creating a self-fulfilling illusion that is completely false.

### Mediums Say

Except for information that seems sensitive and should be kept private, we convey everything we receive. Our clients mostly remember the hits because there are so many of them.

### What the Experiments Actually Reveal

The scoring techniques used in the laboratory in these experiments did not rely on the sitters' overall memories of the readings but were scored from the transcripts of what the mediums actually said. The sitters carefully scored every piece of data; when the medium said something like "the number six, which could mean the month of June or the sixth of a month," the sitter would score each of the statements, likely scoring one of the items as a hit and the other as a miss. Data evaluated this way, and showing high rates of accuracy, cannot be explained by selective remembering.

## Point 4: Vague Information

### Skeptics Speculate

The information mediums claim to receive is so vague and general that it can apply to a great many people.

### Mediums Say

Cold readers give vague and general information. We often get very specific pieces of information—initials, exact names, historical facts such as causes of death, personal descriptions such as size and appearance, personality characteristics such as shy or outgoing—that match the deceased loved ones of the sitters.

### What the Experiments Actually Reveal

When the sitters carefully score the data for initials, names, historical facts, personal descriptions, personality characteristics, and the like, the data turn out to be very specific for individual sitters. This became clear when readings were scored by control groups; the control group accuracy ratings were consistently much lower.

## Point 5: Lucky Guesses

### Skeptics Speculate

The high rates of accuracy, if they occur, must reflect lucky guesses. These must be accidents, the result of fishing. They are not replicable.

### Mediums Say

We are most definitely not guessing. We are getting specific sights, sounds, and feelings. Sometimes we interpret what we see, and sometimes the information is faint. But the process does not involve guessing.

### What the Experiments Actually Reveal

Our experiments provided replication by having sitters read by as many as five mediums. After precise scoring, the findings showed remarkable replication across mediums and sitters, and across experiments, as well. Probability values extend from the millions to the trillions. Guessing and chance cannot account for the accuracy of the information being provided.

## Point 6: Experimenter Biases or Mistakes

### Skeptics Speculate

Either the experimenters are engaged in fraud or they must be deceiving themselves. They are somehow unconsciously influencing the results, giving information to the mediums or encouraging the sitters to inflate their ratings.

### Mediums Say

The experimenters have all along been suspicious of us, never accepting on faith what we said but building ever-tighter controls to ensure the studies would be medium fraud-proof and sitter rater-proof. The scientists running the experiments are quite reluctant to believe, and they keep challenging our honesty and integrity.

### What the Experiments Actually Reveal

Despite ever tighter experimental controls, consistent efforts to have the raters give less favorable scores when in doubt, and, in the Canyon Ranch experiment, having the raters silently score their own transcripts as well as the other sitters' transcripts (thus eliminating any cues from the experimenters), the data still came out remarkably positive. Nonetheless, the experimenters are still uneasy about concluding that the data are genuine, reflecting their own cautious approach and their own fears.

## Point 7: Motivation of the Mediums

### Skeptics Say

Mediums are motivated to cheat the public; to take money from gullible, grieving people; and to be famous. They are participating in faulty lab experiments to feed their egos and raise their fees.

### Mediums Say

The description of taking money from gullible people may fit some, perhaps many, who call themselves mediums. Those of us who have been involved in the experiments do this work because we have discovered a gift for it and because it helps people realize that life is eternal.

### What the Experiments Actually Reveal

The mediums who participate in this research are putting their careers and reputations on the line. If we catch them cheating, we will expose them, in keeping with our lab motto of "If it is real, it will be revealed; if it is fake, we'll find the mistake." We have never found any evidence of fraud or cheating in our highly select group of research mediums. They know that if we ever do, they will be publicly embarrassed and their careers will suffer.

## Point 8: Motivation of the Skeptics

### Skeptics Say

Our motivation is to protect the public against fake mediums and voodoo science. Mediums are frauds, and scientists who study them are gullible or worse.

### Mediums Say

The skeptics have their minds made up and are not willing to examine the data from the experiments. They are unwilling to be open-minded in the presence of compelling data.

### What the Experiments Actually Reveal

Skeptics often ignore essential details of the scientific methods. They typically dismiss data that are positive, and they engage in irrational arguments to hold on to their personal beliefs. Extreme skeptics practice what could be termed voodoo skepticism, which lacks integrity and humility.

For example, the man who styles himself as the Amazing Randi, a "demystifier of paranormal and pseudoscientific claims," emphatically insists that all mediums "pretend" and engage in "deceptive art." He appears so committed to this view that even solid data will not change his mind. The professional skeptics have discovered that, as skeptics, they can make money selling books and magazines. Their careers are on the line.

## Point 9: Mind-Reading by Mediums

### Skeptics Speculate

If the mediums are doing anything paranormal, they must be reading the minds of the sitters. They can't be talking to dead people, because dead people are dead, period.

### Mediums Say

If we were reading the minds of the sitters, we would get only the information the sitters know about and were hoping to receive. Often we get people the sitter knows but was not expecting. Sometimes we get information that the sitter thinks is wrong or doesn't know about, which later turns out to be correct.

### What the Experiments Actually Reveal

Careful analysis of the experimental data shows many examples that mind-reading cannot explain—among them, who the sitters hope to hear from versus who they actually do hear from, information provided by the medium that is not anything the sitter had been thinking about, and information that the sitter did not know but was later able to confirm. Many such examples make it clear that telepathy can not explain all the data.

## Point 10: Memory in the Universe

### Skeptics Speculate

Physics remind us that light and energy extend into space, and photons as old as the birth of the universe have been recorded as "background" radiation. Maybe mediums, if they are doing something paranormal, are simply reading dead memory traces of information and energy in the universe

### Mediums Say

Maybe we are reading some information from memory banks in the universe. However, it often doesn't feel like that. The information seems too alive and playful. Not only that, would dead memories disagree with us when we mishear or misinterpret what is communicated, as often happens in our readings?

### What the Experiments Actually Reveal

The research to date does not eliminate a possible memory retrieval process from the "vacuum" of space. However, careful analysis of the language used by the mediums, plus examples like Sabrina's deceased grandmother seemingly continuing to communicate during the reading for the subsequent sitter, suggests that the "information" is not static or "dead" like information stored on a hard drive or CD.

## Point 11: Talking to Dead People

### Skeptics Speculate

Since we know that death is final, what the mediums report must be their imagination. Or worse, the mediums are making it up. If the mediums really believe in what they are doing, they must be deceiving themselves.

### Mediums Say

It truly feels as if we are talking to living souls. They seem as alive as the skeptics are, only usually more loving and accepting. Dead people often show us and tell us things that surprise us as well as the sitters. The deceased often correct us, contradicting the sitter.

### What the Experiments Actually Reveal

In the experiments, information was consistently retrieved that can best be explained as coming from living souls. In the Campbell procedure, information was obtained before the medium ever spoke with the sitters. Information sometimes comes that the sitter disagrees with but that turns out to be correct. Also, mediums are sometimes corrected by deceased people. The data appear to be as valid, convincing and living as the mediums, sitters, skeptics, and scientists themselves.

That's what the experimental data unmistakably show.

Again, this analysis applies only to the mediums who have agreed to be the subjects of our controlled laboratory experiments: five "white crow" mediums—Laurie Campbell, John Edward, Suzane Northrop, Anne Gehman, and George Anderson.

If there are five, there are probably many more.

## BRAIN FIRST OR MIND FIRST?

Probably the single most important implication of the living soul hypothesis has to do with the fundamental question of the origin of mind and its relationship to the brain.

The issue struck me as the result of a remark by Beth Costello, executive director of the Mind Science Foundation, in San Antonio, Texas. She asked me a question about the nature of consciousness that I immediately saw was as significant for me as Linda's question about the survival of consciousness.

The question was seemingly simple yet profoundly important: "Why should a foundation concerned with the study of consciousness consider funding research in the controversial area of mediumship?"

When people ask me, "Why study mediumship?" it is usually

in the context of the fear of death, the grieving process, the possibility of repairing relationships that were not healed on the earth, or to explore implications for how we might live our lives differently. But no one had ever asked me a question that turned on what mediumship research has to do with the essence of the mind itself.

The answer, I realized, had to do with the reason the foundation was dedicated to mind science instead of brain science. Raised as I was in the traditions of Western science, I had been taught that mind is a creation of neural structure and function, and of neurochemistry, that mind plays a small role in human behavior, and that when the brain dies, the mind disappears. Case closed.

This is the "brain first, mind second" hypothesis. It is the prevailing model in contemporary science. It is assumed to be true and, for all practical purposes, it is taken on faith by modern Western science. Until a few years ago, I took it on faith, too.

However, there is an alternative model, as current as today's visionary science yet as old as recorded history, looked on as truth by scholars like Plato and Pythagoras more than two thousand years ago. And it was held by scholars like Sir John Eccles, the Nobel prize–winning neurophysiologist, and Dr. Wilder Penfield, the distinguished neurosurgeon, in the last century. It was also held by Dr. William James; David Bohn, Ph.D., the distinguished quantum physicist student of Einstein's; and Tom Slick, who established the Mind Science Foundation.

This model says that mind is first. Consciousness exists independently of the brain. It does not depend upon the brain for its survival. Mind is first, the brain is second. The brain is not the creator of mind, it is a powerful tool of the mind. The brain is an antenna/receiver for the mind, like a sophisticated television or cell phone.

Scientifically, the key question is what kind of experiments enable us to decide which model is correct: brain first, or mind first?

History reminds us that sometimes a single experiment, appropriately replicated, can change our vision of the world. Columbus's voyage, sailing into the beyond, was just such an experiment.

What kind of experiment in consciousness research is like sailing into the beyond?

Mediumship experiments.

The experiments with mediums described in these pages strongly suggest that metaphorically, the earth is not flat, it is round. The brain is not primary, mind is. Mind extends like the light from distant stars. This single fact is more earth shattering than the discovery that the earth is round.

According to the data collected in our laboratory, Dr. William James has survived to tell the tale—consciousness continues after physical death. And now that Susy Smith has physically departed, new data collected in our laboratory indicates that she, too, has survived to tell the tale.

Flat, round; brain, mind—the parallels are worth pondering. If the mediumship studies continue to be positive, our vision of the universe and our privileged place within it will never be the same again.

## When Is It Time to Consider Changing Our Minds?

Is it wise to wait until definitive studies have been completed before we humans begin to work and play and love and parent as if the living soul hypothesis is already proven?

When people ask us "Are you advocating survival of consciousness" we say, "No—what we are advocating is survival of consciousness *research*."

It's true to say that the experiments at the University of Arizona have brought forth some remarkable events—so many, in fact, that to dismiss them is to commit the ultimate scientific sin. When a researcher is fortunate enough to repeatedly witness and collect extraordinary data in many experiments over many years, she or he has the responsibility to respect the reality of those facts.

That is exactly what we set out to do in these pages: we have recorded the facts.

All the experiments that have been described here may one day be looked on as representing a stage so primitive that it corresponds to the first lever ever used by a human being contrasted to the machines and computers of today.

What good does it do us to have confirmed that this spirit or that one knows about the dog that died or the son who committed suicide? Only in offering seemingly convincing evidence that the continuity of the consciousness may be true, that the survival of the soul may actually be real. The confirmation, if valid, would be earth-shaking—equal to proving the earth round rather than flat. It would be one of the most profound revelations of science in human history.

But the information about the dog and the suicide is inconsequential in itself. What we really want is to obtain knowledge from the other side about things we don't already know. To know those things will be to understand immortality.

To prove these things will be to gain knowledge of our own immortality.

Will this one day be mankind's gift?

The quest continues. . . .

# Integrating Science and Spirituality

*The following is derived in part from published scientific articles developed with Linda Russek.*

The origin of the word *science* comes from the Latin *scire*, which simply means "to know."

Science is first and foremost concerned with discovering truth. The process of science involves searching for information and then repeating the search—i.e., "re-searching"—in order to replicate the observations. The purpose of science is not to validate the way we *wish* nature to be—it is to discover *the way nature really is.*

This is the reason for choosing as the motto of the Human Energy Systems Laboratory *veritas,* the pursuit of truth—borrowed from Harvard's motto—and why we choose to be guided by the principle "Let the data speak."

The history of science reminds us that sometimes research leads to discoveries that challenge the way we think about virtually everything. When this happens, it is often tempting to put our heads in the sand. We prefer to make believe that nature is the way we want it to be (which is typically the way we were raised as children to believe it is) rather than the way nature really is. It has been said that ignorance is bliss. The truth is, it is often easier to hold on to the past than to face the discoveries revealed through science.

Science as a process, and survival as a hypothesis, have a unique relationship. The living soul hypothesis has profound implications for how science is conducted; in turn, science has profound implications for our understanding of the continuation of consciousness. The research that we've described in this book can be thought of as the tip of a gigantic prism, creating a rainbow-colored spectacular possibility that transcends virtually anything we have imagined. It is more than just poetry that we scientifically pursue *Lux et Veritas*—Light and Truth, Yale's motto—because the key may literally be light.

The key to predicting survival of consciousness happens when we understand the concept of a system.

## SYSTEMS THEORY: UNDERSTANDING THE MAGIC AND MIRACLE OF "WATERNESS"

How is it possible for two or more things to come together and create something—a whole—that is truly different from the individual components that constitute them?

The concept of a system is used to explain the exchange of information and energy, which, in the process, creates ever more complex wholes.

In the process of sharing information and energy, the components become a couple, or a unit. As they develop a relationship—a teamwork of mutual sharing of information and energy—novel dynamic possibilities emerge that are different from, and go beyond, any of the components by themselves. The phrase "the whole is greater than the sum of its parts" is one way to express these "emergent properties" of systems.

Our earlier book, *The Living Energy Universe*, explains how at every level in nature—from the micro levels of atoms and molecules to the macro levels of solar systems and galaxies—and everything in between, including people, when things come together and connect, they can develop long-standing bonds that "bring out the best in each other." Through this systemic, emergent property process, we witness novel and unpredictable phenomena that emerge only when the components develop a stable relation and become whole.

My favorite illustration of systemic emergent properties is "waterness."

At room temperature, hydrogen and oxygen, the two gases that create water, are undetectable with our human senses. We can't see, taste, or smell them. But when they join forces and become the "simple" molecule called $H_2O$, what emerges at room temperature is a novel liquid that represents 70 percent to 80 percent of our bodies and is required for all physical life as we know it.

Water is a special molecular system, expressing a unique pattern of properties unlike any other. At room temperature, it's a liquid, but when it freezes, it creates complex crystals of ice that float when placed in the liquid—unlike most other solids, which sink in their respective liquid forms.

Water also has the capacity to create exquisitely beautiful and complex crystals: snowflakes. Each flake is unique and reflects a pattern of structures that dazzle the eye. I have a book that contains photographs of thousands of individual snowflakes, and no two are identical.

Where does this breathtaking capacity for organization, structure, and the other unique properties of waterness come from?

Can we predict them by examining hydrogen and oxygen by themselves? No. It is only when these two gases are brought together and allowed to circulate their energy and information as $H_2O$ that the novel patterns of waterness emerge.

But what does waterness have to do with the living soul and the survival of consciousness after death? As you are about to see, the answer is "everything."

## Feedback Loops: Understanding the "Magic" and "Miracle" of Living Memory

When we combine the idea of eternal energy (see chapter 1) with the idea of a system, we discover the novel, emergent idea of "dynamical energy systems theory." Isn't it curious that the very idea of systems theory itself predicts that when it is combined with quantum physics, novel systemic properties will be revealed, and the whole will be greater than the sum of its parts?

Quantum physics tell us that everything vibrates and is never completely at rest. Even at the temperature of absolute zero, atomic systems vibrate. Subatomic systems such as photons and electrons act more like disturbed waves or fuzzy clouds than discrete objects or particles. Depending on how they are measured, they can resemble waves, distributed in space, or particles, localized in space. Photons and electrons seem to dance around in space, so to speak, waiting to be "materialized" into matter.

When we look closely at how information and energy circulate within a system, we discover something remarkable. Photons and electrons can circulate within a system by "feedback loops." One explanation for how neurons in the brain learn is that they are arranged like complex networks of components interconnected by recurrent feedback loops. So long as the feedback loops are connected, the information and energy will circulate, and memories will accumulate. What systems science tells us is that the reason neurons learn is precisely because they are arranged as systems containing feedback looks. When information and energy are continually circulated within a system—neural or otherwise—this constantly transforming information and energy will be stored in the system, and it will evolve over time. In other words, a history or "memory" of the interaction of the components in the network will be retained in the system and revised over time.

All systems, from the simplest atoms to the most complex organisms and beyond, contain feedback. Since feedback loops create memory, all systems should contain dynamic memory to various degrees.

The simplest way to describe this process is by using a two-component system, with components A and B.

The theory allows for A and B to be literally anything: two atoms, such as the relationship between hydrogen and water; or two cells, such as between two neurons in the brain; or between two cardiac cells in the heart. They could also be two organs, such as between the brain and the heart; or two people, such as between Linda and her father; or even two huge masses, such as the earth and the sun, or one galaxy and another.

The scale doesn't matter. Size isn't important. What matters is that one of them is A and the other is B, and they have the possibility to relate, to interact through feedback.

The key to remember is that to create and maintain a system, component A must be able to send information and energy to component B, and B must be able to send it back to A, over and over, time after time.

Note that the process of sending information and energy from A to B and back again takes time. Even when the process occurs as quickly as the speed of light (or even faster, as some physics now speculates), it still takes time. Once A's information reaches B, B will interpret it and send it back to A in revised form. Save for special-purpose digital circuits in artificial devices, the information returned to A will have been somewhat revised by B.

Let's say that A represents Albert (after Einstein) and B represents Betty (after Susy Smith's mother). Imagine that they are speaking to each other. They are becoming a two-person system.

Let's take the simplest case: After Albert says something to Betty, Betty responds by repeating what Albert just said.

What will Albert hear?

Albert won't hear exactly what he said because Betty's voice and intonation will reflect her interpretation of what she heard Albert say to her from their immediate past. Even if Betty simply repeated, word for word, whatever Albert said, the energy of her response would be somewhat different from Albert's. In this sense, during each cycle of their "conversation," the energy from the past will be revised and incorporated with the present. Sometimes this energy can be additive.

For example, a familiar example of energy memory with feedback is what happens when an amplified speaker (A) is connected to a microphone (B), and the microphone is then pointed toward the speaker.

What will you hear emerging from the speaker?

The rapidly emerging "wow" sound is a simple expression of the accumulation of information and energy as the sound travels between the speaker A and microphone B, over and over, amplified and revised rapidly with time.

The logic of systemic memory can also be expressed with two tuning forks of the same pitch.

If tuning fork A is struck in the presence of tuning fork B, the vibrations from A will travel to B, making B begin to resonate a sound. However, now that B is vibrating, its waves will journey back to A, carrying the history of A's initial vibration plus B's new vibration, creating an "AB" history.

Once this new vibration history returns and interacts with A, it will revise A's initial history and start back to B.

To summarize, what returns to A is the history of A as interpreted by B and returned to A in revised form.

This represents what has been termed a dynamic recurrent feedback interaction.

Here is an unexpected and novel observation. Quantum physics tells us that the tuning forks, once they have begun to vibrate, never will be completely at rest. They will continue to vibrate.

Each tuning fork represents a complex material system containing billions of atoms arranged as a network of vibrating feedback loops. When quantum physics is then combined with our analysis of feedback in systems, it logically follows that a history or vibratory "memory" of their interaction will remain in each of the tuning forks to various degrees.

This logical construction—that emergent properties in systems represent the dynamic accumulation of circulating relationship interactions as systemic memory—is consistent with current chaos and complexity theory, which evolved from general (feedback) systems theory. The challenge is to explain how these dynamic memories can be retrieved, be they from "neural" networks as structured in the brain, or any other "systemic" network containing recurrent feedback loops existing in natural or artificial systems.

Since all feedback networks theoretically store information and energy to various degrees, any system containing feedback will generate memories and will evolve.

But how common are feedback network structures in nature?

The universal living memory theory suggests that feedback network systems are the rule, not the exception, at every level in nature. Simply put, this means that all systems will store memories and evolve. In this sense, all systems can be seen as "alive."

Think about it. When we combine quantum physics with systems theory, we realize that what we experience with the naked eye to be "inanimate" things may actually be "invisibly animate."

Let's repeat this; it is key. What we see with our limited naked eyes as "inanimate" may actually be "invisibly animate."

Hence the vision of a living energy universe.

Of course, it follows that the complexity of the structure will dictate the complexity of its "memory" storage, and hence its "aliveness." A chair will not store as complex information as a plant, a plant not as complex as a dog, and a dog not as complex as a human. Increased complexity leads to increased complexity of memory and increased "aliveness."

But what exactly is being stored? What is being "re-membered?"

We use the terms *information* and *energy* to describe what is traveling between A and B.

What is information? It is "in-form," a pattern with a recognizable structure.

And what is energy? Energy is power, the capacity to do work and overcome resistance.

Both information and energy are "invisible" until they manifest their organization in physical systems. Information and energy are most effective as a team. Information without energy is "powerless," and energy without information is "purposeless."

Even though we can't see most information and energy per se, we know they exist through their effects on physical systems that we can see. Once information and energy, in the form of photons, are released into "space," they will hold the same properties as starlight, which we see with the naked eye, or star radio waves, for example, which we cannot see with the naked eye but can measure with radio telescopes.

Science tells us that humans, just like the stars, generate radio waves that can also be measured precisely with radio telescopes.

Photons are photons; waves are waves—whether they come from huge stars such as our sun or tiny stars such as ourselves. However, the brightness of a huge star may block our perception of the dim stars all around us.

In the morning, when our sun appears to rise in the east, the night sky appears to become blue and the starlight seems to disappear from our consciousness. At the end of the day, when our sun appears to set in the west, we discover that the starlight has "reappeared" as if by magic. In the same way, the patterns of information and energy are always there, though we are sometimes blinded by figurative bright lights that keep us from experiencing the deeper truth.

Where does all this take us? Well, let's consider a controversial topic: the purported existence of "ghosts." When are such entities purportedly seen?

History tells us that they typically appear in dreams, during meditation, or in the darkness when the light is dim. These are precisely the stimulus conditions, predicted by contemporary physics, that would allow us to potentially detect the subtle but nonetheless persistent info-energy patterns of the history of the universe that literally surrounds each and every one of us.

The hypothesis of ghosts in energy systems terms is ultimately no different than the idea of distant stars in astrophysical terms. Even though we may see ghosts or stars only under very special conditions, theory dictates that their info-energy patterns are still there, whether we are aware of them or not.

The pioneering work of Dr. Raymond Moody involves putting people into a dimly lit room with black velvet curtains and a mirror above their heads and inviting them to look, so to speak, into the infinity of space. Dr. Moody claims that when people who have lost loved ones sit quietly in this comfortable blackness, with just the slightest amount of light to allow for minimal perception, between 60 percent and 80 percent (depending on the experimental set-up) report seeing and hearing things that seem to be ghostly experiences of departed loved ones— experiences normally missed under normal white-walled, well-lit conditions.

Do these perceptions merely reflect the amplification of a person's own memories or fantasies? Or are people actually seeing the existence of the living souls (information) and spirits (energies) that constitute the continued evolution of the living energy systems of their beloved?

## THE SCIENCE OF "SOUL" AND "SPIRIT" IN THE VACUUM OF SPACE

This work clearly suggests that the "soul" and "spirit" of a living person will continue after bodily death as a "living info-energy system" in the vacuum of space.

Let's briefly return to our consideration of A and B so that you can make the jump from the visible to the invisible.

By definition, when A and B interact, the sharing of information and energy occurs within the empty space that separates the material elements of A and B. This space, according to quantum physics, is not really void of information and energy. Quite the contrary—it's filled with it.

Quantum physics tells us that what we experience as physical objects are mostly space, albeit full of energy and information.

If you imagine that an atom is the size of the Empire State Building, do you know how large the nucleus inside the atom is? Ten stories high? One story high? The size of a brick? Quantum physics tells us that it is just the size of a grain of sand.

The vacuum of space allows information from A to B and B to A to flow freely, traveling in circulating flows between A and B. Since the distance between A and B is mostly "non-material," this means that it is possible for the info-energy to circulate as well *within the space between A and B*. Hence, what happens *between* A and B is mirrored *within the space* between A and B. I term this an info-energy system. Just as we experience with our limited senses the external A-B system as dynamic and alive, so this "living vortex" within A and B is dynamic and alive.

It follows that if the material objects of the A-B system are removed, the information and energy in the vacuum of space will still be intact. What must remain is the circulating info-energy system that represents the history of that which was once matter—including memory for the "boundaries" that kept the info-energy within the system in the first place.

We can re-envision A and B as the scaffolds that help build living info-energy systems. A and B become the tools that help build and evolve the living energy universe.

Since everything in a physical body is interconnected energetically—for example, all cells and molecules are interconnected by electromagnetic energy traveling though the ubiquitous water in the body—all cells and molecules are storing a record of the energy history that defines the totality of who we are.

Moreover, not only does this information and energy extend out into space as we physically live, but, in addition, it continues to circulate within our bodies, accruing ever more structure. Hence, when our physical bodies decompose, the living info-energy systems within us are now "freed" beyond their physical scaffolds and will have all the consciousness, intent, and personality—for better or worse—of everything that has occurred in our lifetimes. Scientifically, this can be viewed as the "soul" and "spirit" of our physical beings—as seen through new eyes.

Of course, what we have outlined above is just a theory, a scientific "story" that may or may not be correct. However, because this particular story is based on the foundation of contemporary physics and systems science, if we are willing to be true to logic, this story deserves our serious consideration.

(The phrase "true to logic" was originally suggested by Lonnie Nelson, an inspired graduate student at the University of Arizona, whose interests bridge conventional and frontier science. As Lonnie puts it, being true to logic means that we follow the logic where it takes us, even if it takes us to areas we do not like or even frighten us because the predictions challenge our current world views.)

Being true to logic is a prerequisite to being true to data.

And being true to data is the heart and soul of science.

## CHOOSING "TRUTH RATHER THAN PEACE OF MIND"

If I am to be true to data, I must acknowledge the information from our own experiments, whether I like some of the predictions or not. Even if I consider some of the predictions ludicrous (and I sometimes do), I must be willing to entertain them to the extent that the data point in their direction.

At least this is what one is supposed to do if one is practicing science with integrity.

It is for this reason, that I have included the PeeWee gift and the Michael Senior death stories in this book. Though I am uncomfortable with this level of "psychic" possibility, the data suggest that I must be open to the possibility that "pre-cognition" plays a role in research of this kind.

As mentioned earlier, Chet Raymo, in his book *Skeptics and True Believers: The Exhilarating Connection Between Science and Religion,* maintains that scientists must always "chose truth rather than peace of mind." It is in this spirit that we conduct research in the Human Energy Systems Laboratory. Our number one question in presenting our data and results is "What's going on in these experiments?"

What are these seemingly superstar mediums actually doing in the laboratory? What do these findings mean?

If the explanation is not fraud, cold reading, picking up subtle psychological cues, or statistical coincidence, then what precisely is going on?

Is it telepathy with the living?

Is it reading memories in the vacuum of space?

Are the mediums getting information from their invisible "guides"?

Are they connecting to the living info-energy systems of our departed?

Is it a combination of all those things, and more?

The facts suggest, as we playfully describe them, that some combination of FACTs may be involved: Fundamental Anomalous Communication Telepathically.

It may be a Type P FACT, for telepathy with the physically living.

It may be a Type V FACT, for telepathy with the totality of information and energy stored in the vacuum of space.

It may be a Type G FACT, for telepathy with one's "guides."

It may be a Type D FACT, for telepathy with the departed.

The process may involve all of these FACTs, and more.

Whatever the answer or answers turn out to be, we must be willing to choose truth over peace of mind.

What if the truth science discovers doesn't bring peace of mind?

Depending upon the outcome—no or yes for the living soul hypothesis—some people will experience peace of mind, while others will not. This seems unavoidable.

What if the belief in an afterlife is the mistaken creation of our minds to help us cope with the fear of death and the loss of our loved ones?

What if science were to establish, beyond a reasonable doubt, that the living soul hypothesis is most likely a fantasy, a mental opiate to deaden our terror of death?

To the non-scientist who is more than just open to the belief of survival but desperately wants it to be true, such a conclusion could be devastating. Though it is impossible for science to prove that something does *not* exist (in statistics it is said that one can not prove the "null hypothesis"), science can lead us to strongly question the belief that something does exist.

If the hypothesis of a living soul was seriously questioned by scientific research, this could have the devastating impact of refuting for many people the dream that there is purpose and meaning to our universe, leaving the religious faithful as the only people still able to find peace within themselves. And would this mean that our capacity to love is, in the grand scheme of things, a fleeting emotion that dies with the decomposition of our physical bodies?

Negative findings concerning the living soul hypothesis would not bring peace of mind to people who strongly believe in life after life.

However, based on the experiments and findings obtained to date, integrity requires that we conclude that the data are strongly consistent with the hypothesis that some sort of anomalous information retrieval is going on with the deceased.

Evidence supportive of the living soul hypothesis will not, at least in the short run, bring peace of mind to people who wish to believe that (1) the universe is basically dust to dust, ashes to ashes, (2) consciousness is an adaptive side effect of a material brain, and (3) in the absence of functioning physical neurons, there is no mind—no thought, no memory, no feeling.

This is part of the reason why, as more findings emerge that are consistent with the living soul hypothesis, peace of mind will be in short supply for those individuals who prefer to dismiss the findings as due to accident, inadvertent misperception on the part of the investigators, or experimenter fraud.

When confronted with data that challenge one's familiar and preferred world view, there is a tendency among scientists and laymen alike to distrust the experiments, and even the experimenters, rather than believe the data. This is an understandable defense mechanism, since the more we deeply believe something, the more we will resist giving it up.

However, there is another reason why conservative science will first choose to distrust the experiments, and even the experimenters, before accepting extraordinary data. I applaud this reason. The truth is that scientists sometimes make mistakes, and we are all human. We must be open to all interpretations, including possible experimental and experimenter mistakes.

There is a saying in emergency medicine: "When you hear hoofbeats, don't think zebras." In emergency situations, it is essential that one consider the most likely explanation or cause of a problem first, and then go down the list. One must think "horses" first and "ponies" second, and only later consider zebras or camels after horses and ponies have been ruled out. When it comes to saving a physical life, it is critical to make the right choice as quickly as possible.

In a similar fashion, when a scientist hears about strange data, the "horse" and "pony" hypotheses to be entertained first are experimental error, experimenter bias, and even experimenter fraud. In fact, as any well-trained undergraduate in psychology knows, there was a famous horse known as "Clever Hans" that could apparently do math but was discovered to be "calculating" via subtle cues inadvertently provided by the human experimenter.

Raised on the "Clever Hans" story, and trained in both experimental psychology and evidence-based medicine, I'm sensitive to the wisdom of attempting to make the right choice without wasting time on dead ends.

Depending on one's point of view, metaphorically one could conclude that the data we have collected so far strongly suggest that "Clever Hans" is not the explanation—there are no humans creating the phenomenon.

As scientists conducting research in this area who believe strongly in letting the data speak, obtaining findings that (1) not only suggest that the survival hypothesis is true but (2) actually point to the possibility of proving it "beyond a reasonable doubt" (which is all science can ultimately do, one way or the other), is something of a mixed blessing.

One of the more vocal members of our Friendly Devil's Advocates committee said to me one day, "Gary, you've taken a ride on a moving train that will be impossible to get off."

I explained to this person, a well-respected psychology professor, that if the totality of the data had been negative or inconclusive, it would have been easy for me to get off the train and leave this research.

I reminded him that what led me to get on the train in the first place was the theoretical possibility of the phenomenon—the systemic memory hypothesis described above—and Linda's dream to know scientifically, one way or the other, whether her deceased father is still here. If the experimental data did not support the hypothesis, I would be free to get off the train. In fact, integrity would *require* that I get off the train, or at least seriously question where it was going.

However, I went on to explain that what keeps me on the train—which, parenthetically, seems to be moving faster and faster these days—are the efforts of the Dream Team of mediums we have had the privilege to work with, and the often inexplicable data that keep coming through them.

To jump off the train now would mean that I lacked integrity. I would have to be willing to ignore extensive provocative, if not profound, information revealed in the experiments to date.

As one student, David Meuhsam, aptly put it, "You were willing to collect the data. Now you're stuck with them."

David is right. The data suggest that our loved ones, their "info-energy systems," may be with us. And we are stuck with the data.

The question then arises, as the song says, "What's love got to do with it?" It turns out that it is not only the mediums who claim that love has everything to do with it; contemporary science, as well, is consistent with the vision that love truly matters.

If energy matters, as physics suggests, the number one energy may be love.

# The Energy Is Love

*The following is derived in part from scientific articles developed with Linda Russek.*

When people ask me "Why are you conducting research on the survival of consciousness hypothesis?" I explain that there are two primary reasons:

Reason 1: I am *pushed* by theory and data in science. Science provides the foundation for conducting research on the living soul hypothesis.

Reason 2: I am *pulled* by the force of love—first, by Linda's love for her departed father, second by Susy's love for her deceased mother, third, by my love for the Lindas and Susys of the world who understand that what matters, more than anything else, is our remarkable capacity to love.

While science pushes us to consider the living soul hypothesis, the pull of love gets us there as well. The combination of both science and love provides a compelling conceptual and experiential team for understanding the living soul hypothesis.

Our capacity to love is our greatest gift as well as our greatest challenge.

It's not news that love is anything but easy. The expression of love brings with it not only the full spectrum of positive emotions but a complementary spectrum of negative ones as well.

The question arises: If the living soul hypothesis is true, does the full spectrum of our emotions—our pleasures and pains, conflicts and joys—continue with us after physical death, as systemic memory predicts?

To address the question of the fundamental relationship between love and the living soul, let's first consider the complex nature of love itself and its role in human relationships.

### THE MYSTERY AND MAJESTY OF THE HUMAN CAPACITY TO LOVE

The potential scope of human love is vast. We can love virtually everything, from the profound to the profane. Human beings have the potential to love people, pets, plants, pianos, politics, and the planet as a whole. Scientists are no exception—their professional passions extend from A to Z, from astrophysics to zoology.

I know the gift and challenge of loving "too many things" firsthand.

As a child, I developed a passion for animals of virtually every size and shape. I had a small zoo in our home, including a dog and a cat; multiple tanks of freshwater fish, tropical fish, and salt-water fish; snakes and huge snapping turtles in outside pools; as well as guinea pigs, hamsters, and even a family of white rats.

I also developed a passion for science. I created electronics, physics, chemistry, and biology laboratories in my family's basement and my bedroom.

Fortunately, my parents appreciated the significance of encouraging love, and they fostered it whenever they could. I developed such a deep love for learning that one of my Yale Ph.D. students fondly described it as an "overdeveloped sense of wonder." My love for learning reflects a living legacy instilled by my parents and theirs.

From an evolutionary point of view, peoples' individual loves and desires to protect their special loves—from saving killer whales and redwood trees to people and even ideas—not only define us as a species but point to the extremely intelligent, highly adaptive, and potentially loving nature of the universe.

However, the powerful motivating force to save our loves also leads many to save in excess.

We sometimes overprotect in the name of love, and even massacre others who do not share our loves. Often we fail to love wisely, not because learning to love wisely is so difficult but because it has not been a high priority for our society to do so.

Although science knows relatively little about this ultimate motivating force, it is not inherently controversial to posit the pervasive role that love plays in human relationships at all levels of society.

The pervasive presence of our capacity to love is evident at birth. Most parents have witnessed firsthand that when babies come into the world, they often behave like little love machines. Virtually everything that babies come in contact with becomes an opportunity for them to explore.

If infants are raised in safe and trusting environments, their propensity for play and their overriding instinct of curiosity promises the development of a child who will grow up with the potential to love, within reason, everyone and everything in nature.

When people think of love, they often associate it with the concept of attraction—from the physical, through the emotional and mental, to the spiritual. Love can be said to be a powerful attractive force that binds human relationships—not only "here" but between "here" and "there" as well.

The idea of an attractive force is not limited to psychology. The concept of attraction is discussed in hard sciences such as physics and chemistry. Examples include the attraction of opposite poles of a magnet in physics, and the chemical bonding that occurs between two elements, such as hydrogen and oxygen, as they join forces to create the foundational chemical that makes physical life possible.

A question immediately arises when we speak of love as reflecting an attractive force: Are we using the word *force* merely metaphorically, or is there actually a force associated with love?

Do some people, both intuitively and literally, experience an energetic relationship between themselves and the ones they love?

Is the concept of love a universal concept, a generic "biophysics" of info-energy that ranges in complexity from the subatomic to the astronomic?

Speculations about the breadth and depth of love as reflecting a universal, and unifying, force in the cosmos purportedly go back to a time before recorded history. Yet, that it is old does not make it correct.

However, when we reframe the concept of love and describe it in bioelectromagnetic terms, we discover that specific predictions can be formulated and put to experimental test.

Research at the Human Energy Systems Lab suggests that love can be studied as a bioelectromagnetic energy as real as Newton's gravity. Love can be investigated as an invisible attractive force that, not unlike gravity, can transcend most boundaries and barriers—including the apparent separation from our loved ones that occurs at physical death.

Before we share with you some of this frontier research, we must first consider why it is that mediums believe the ultimate purpose of the living soul and after-death communication is the universal potential for love.

## WHO SEEKS MEDIUMS? THE COMMON DENOMINATOR APPEARS TO BE LOVE

What percentage of people who typically seek a medium hope that they will make contact with a deceased person whom they dearly love?

To the best of my knowledge, no one has addressed this question scientifically. However, it is not unreasonable to estimate that the percentage is well above 90 percent.

Conversely, though it also has not been established scientifically, it seems reasonable to predict that people who have not loved deeply, and have not lost a loved one, will probably not seek a medium.

Unless one has a strong motivation to do so, it takes too much effort and expense to pursue professional mediums. This is especially the case for the mediums who have collaborated with us in our research. The most visible members of our Dream Team of mediums have waiting lists that extend beyond a year, and they sometimes receive more than a $1,000 for a single one-hour reading.

If you happen to be someone who has lost loved ones, believe there's a chance you can find out that they are okay, and feel there is a possibility that you may receive a personal message from them, then you might choose to seek out a medium. Hence, it is reasonable to anticipate that mediums' clients, on the whole, represent a special subgroup of people. We must keep this fact in mind when we attempt to understand the kinds of observations reported by experienced mediums based on their professional practices.

Another way of saying this is that professional mediums, especially well-known mediums, in all likelihood do not see a random distribution of the population. A defining description of the people they see is probably an overriding desire to reconnect with one or more deceased love ones.

According to national polls, 75 percent of the population believe in the existence of an afterlife. Peoples' love for their friends and relatives is likely the inspiring force that allows people to hold on to this dream, especially given the scientific controversy that surrounds this belief.

## THE HEART'S ENERGY TRAVELS IN SPACE FOREVER

Physics defines energy as the capacity to do work and overcome resistance. Energy is force. Magnetism, electricity, heat, and gravity are all examples of energy.

As discussed earlier, a system is defined as a set of components or parts that interact recurrently. The components share information and energy with one another. In the process of connecting and sharing, the parts join and become a whole whose novel properties are termed emergent.

When we combine the concept of energy with the idea of a system, the resulting conceptual system is termed dynamical energy systems theory. The info-energy system hypothesis predicts that everything in nature—yes, *everything*—not only has a physical body (what we experience as the material), but also has an internal invisible soul (information) and spirit (energy) that continuously extend into space at the speed of light.

Let's consider the heart, the largest generator of electromagnetic signals in the body.

The heart's electrocardiogram—its dynamically changing electrical charge created with each heartbeat—can be readily recorded with electrodes placed on the surface of the skin. Our bodies, containing 70 percent to 80 percent water constituting the blood and lymph (which includes salt and other minerals), are very good conductors of electricity. As a result, with each beat of the heart, the electrical signal travels to every cell in the body. This means not only that each cell is bathed in the blood circulated by the heart, but every cell is also bathed in the electromagnetic energy produced by the heart.

The patterned electrocardiographic signal, or cardiac info-energy, can be recorded from anywhere on the body. This includes the tips of the fingers and the toes, the nose, and even the top of the head. In fact, when doctors want to record brain waves, muscle tension, or any other bioelectromagnetic signal, they first must filter out the heart's electrocardiogram.

Therefore, at any given moment in time, as long as your heart is beating, all of this bioelectromagnetic information and energy is mixing and interacting throughout your body, in a constantly circulating manner.

Now, what happens to the cardiac (and other electromagnetic) signals once they reach the surface of your skin?

Are we encased in an electromagnetic shield that would keep the signals from leaving the body? No.

A moment's reflection will tell you that the signals keep traveling and go into space at the speed of light, which is approximately 186,000 miles per second. Physics tells us that the heart's electrocardiogram, like all electromagnetic signals, is actually a form of invisible "light," or photons.

So as our cardiac energy leaves the body, it radiates out into the vacuum of space.

Imagine that you standing outside in the evening, looking at the stars in a clear sky, and now consider the following:

One second after your heart beats, or your loved one's heart beats, or even your dog's heart beats—it actually doesn't matter which—the heart's electromagnetocardiogram will have traveled approximately 186,000 miles in space.

Physics tells us that it must be out there because it is an electromagnetic signal. It is similar in nature to electromagnetic signals generated by distant stars or cell phones. Of course, our electrocardiographic signals are weaker in comparison to these signals, and they will continue to get weaker as they expand out into the vacuum of space. However, despite the relative weakness of these signals, physics tells us, in no uncertain terms, that they are traveling in the "vacuum" of space.

Two seconds later, your heart's signal will be 372,000 miles out into space, and once out there, it will keep going and going. Think about it—once your heart's signal is out in space, there is no way to get rid of it.

The science of astrophysics is based on the fact that once a star is born, it begins emitting and radiating electromagnetic fields, some of which we call visible light, and they will keep going and going, like that advertising animated toy, the Energizer Bunny—except these signals are *truly* eternal.

Long after the physical star has "died," its energy and information keep traveling, eventually reaching earth where you're standing. The photons that have traveled billions of miles to make their way into your pupils are not much larger than the head of a pin. The retinal cells in your eyes detect information from thousands of stars that can be millions of light-years away.

What then, are you looking at when you see the stars "in the sky?" Physics tells us that what you are actually looking at is the history of the stars reflecting the way they used to be when they emitted their energy ions ago.

Though the philosophical implications of this fact are typically ignored, the truth is that light has a kind of immortality. This light, composed of infinitesimally tiny photons, supposedly contains information that goes all the way back to the Big Bang and presumed by most contemporary physicists to have been created at the beginning of the known universe.

What is called the background radiation, which has been documented over the last few decades, is the "electromagnetic noise" that is believed to reflect the history of the universe going back 12 billion or more years ago.

And these are tiny photons indeed.

Care to guess how many biophotons it takes for our retinal cells to fire? Millions? Thousands? Ten?

Science tells us it takes just one.

Care to guess how many biophotons are being emitted from your heart alone with each beat? Millions and millions.

Once our cardiac biophotons get into space, all this information and energy is preserved in space. Hence, our heart's info-energy has a kind of immortality too, just like the stars themselves.

## EXPLANATIONS OF LOVING SYNCHRONICITIES: THE ENERGY CARDIOLOGY PREDICTION

In connection with our follow-up work on the Harvard Mastery of Stress Study, Linda asked each of the men we gathered data from whether they had ever experienced synchronicities, or meaningful coincidences, in their life. Virtually all of them reported they either had experienced them personally or witnessed one or more of their family member having them. Examples included having the identical thought as their wife, or a daughter sensing that her mother or father was ill and calling home.

The men offered three possible explanations for these seeming coincidences.

Approximately one third of the men said the reason was simply statistical coincidence; the synchronicity happened by chance.

Another third of the men attributed the coincidence to the fact that over the years, they and their wives had come to know each other's likes and dislikes, or the daughter knew her parents' habits and concerns.

However, a third of the men said they believed it had something to with "vibes." Each of these three hypotheses is plausible.

I then told the men our energy cardiology hypothesis—about how our heart's energy theoretically extends into space and interacts with our loved ones. After hearing the energy cardiology hypothesis, they were intrigued by the possibility that there might be some sort of neural recognition between people's electrocardiograms, even over long distances.

This hypothesis becomes even more plausible when we realize that most of us typically have spent many thousands of hours with our family members and loved ones, beginning from the intimate time we spent bathed in our mother's electrocardiogram in her womb, to the thousands of hours per year many of us spend in close contact with our spouses sleeping in bed.

The capacity for us to build up a systemic memory of our loved one's electrocardiogram requires that each heart have different features so we can know whose cardiac energy pattern or cardiac energy "signature" we are recognizing.

It turns out that each person's heart does have a unique pattern, which can be likened to the similarities of faces.

In one sense, all healthy faces look the same. They have two eyes, a nose, and a mouth. However, experience tells us that no two faces are exactly the same. The subtle differences in the shapes and colors of the eyes, nose, and mouth are what enable us to distinguish one face from other. The better we know people, and love them, the easier it is to recognize their faces in a crowd.

It's the same with the electromagnetic signature of the heart. All healthy hearts look the same. They all have what is called a P wave, a Q R S complex, and a T wave. However, when we look more closely, we discover that no two electrocardiograms are the exactly the same. There are subtle differences in the shapes of the P waves, QRS complexes, and T waves, and these differences enable us to distinguish one electrocardiogram from another. Each heart's unique anatomy, much like a snowflake, allows it to have a different energy signature that can develop a unique systemic memory. Contemporary quantum physics suggests that such energetic differences can, in theory, be detectable over long distances.

Is it possible that we can consciously distinguish between such subtle differences? Here is a simple example that illustrates the possibility. Have you ever been at a party, or in a loud restaurant with a lot of background noise, and someone quietly speaks your name, and you're aware of it despite the noise?

Even when we're not paying attention, we're nonetheless very good at pattern recognition, especially for patterns that have been repeated thousands of times and are meaningful to us, such as our own names.

Systems can come to recognize one another, like a tuning fork that resonates when another nearby tuning fork vibrates. In this sense, it is possible that our bodies as well as our minds remember the people we have come in contact with the most. Our tuning forks, so to speak, may become tuned to one another because we share a common systemic memory bond.

## From Cardiac Energy to High-Frequency X Rays and Gamma Rays

If this isn't enough to raise an eyebrow or two, let us briefly share a recent discovery Linda and I made with colleagues in our laboratory.

We have been recording what are termed gamma rays, which are very high-frequency signals that typically come from distant stars. Gamma rays pass not only through bodies and walls but even through lead shields.

These studies have shown that the human body spontaneously absorbs and/or scatters high-frequency gamma rays and simultaneously emits high frequency X rays. It appears that our bodies are continually emitting high-frequency X rays as we absorb and/or scatter the even higher-frequency gamma rays. Most of the energy studied in our laboratory to date is from the heart and hand regions. However, as far as we know, the entire body participates in this process. It is important to remember that gamma rays and X rays are actually photons; when they originate from the body, they are called bio-photons.

New research ongoing in our lab suggests that during times when people intentionally send energy to a person, especially a loved one, there is a detectable increase in the absorption and/or scattering of the gamma rays and an increase in the emission of high-frequency X rays.

When we put all these findings together, they strongly add up to the possibility of a biophysical linking between love, the heart, and energy. Some of my colleagues have even been so bold as to posit that the gamma rays may be interpreted as reflecting loving energy coming from the universe, which when absorbed is slowed down by the body and redistributed to people around us at a lower frequency, observed as high-frequency X rays.

What would happen if we were to take these observations and inferences even further? What if the loving energy that a mother shares with her child while it is in the womb actually affects the infant's DNA structure and development? If the electromagnetic signals from cell phones can supposedly do this in a disease-promoting way, why couldn't our body's own electromagnetic signals do so as well—hopefully in a life-affirming way?

You may be wondering: How can we make predictions about things we cannot see, smell, taste, or touch? Electrocardiograms, brains, X rays, and gamma rays share a fundamental property—they are all invisible to our normal senses. Could some of these invisible forces reflect the connective power of universal love?

Such an idea is by no means novel. In fact, a similar debate took place when Sir Isaac Newton decided to address the question of the universal law of gravity.

## Gravity as an Invisible Universal Attractive Force: Is This Evidence for the Existence of the Unconditional Love of God?

Whenever I lose faith in humankind, nature, or the cosmos as a whole, I conduct a little experiment.

I drop things.

Keys, erasers, dog bones—whatever objects I have in my hand that will not break when they fall, I drop them. Right now, as I take a moment to reflect, it's my dog Sammy's bone.

I have conducted this little experiment thousands of times. Every time I have dropped an object, it has fallen to the ground. Of course, I realize that *theoretically* it is not impossible that someone might be able slow down the speed with which a given object falls, or even cause an object to float in mid-air. However, when I drop things, what happens is totally predictable. The object falls.

When I go to sleep at night, I don't worry that when I awake I might find my body floating up near the ceiling. The truth is, after having conducted the experiment many thousands of times, and having witnessed my body safely in bed every morning, I put my faith in Newton's force called gravity.

The deep question, however, is, what is the explanation for this replicable observation? Seriously, can we "measure gravity?"

The truth is, we cannot measure gravity directly. What we do is observe objects, or dials moving on a scale, and we *infer* the existence of an invisible force that cannot be seen or heard. This mysterious forces even acts at a distance. Everyone knows that the moon pulls on the earth, the earth pulls on the sun, the sun pulls on the moon, the moon pulls on the sun, and the earth pulls on the moon. The truth is, it is profoundly mathematically difficult to calculate the effects that three "bodies" have on each other as they engage in mutual attractive feedback interactions.

In Newton's time, he infuriated some people with his proposal that we had to hypothesize the existence of something we couldn't see or hear, and could observe only indirectly. This sounds a lot like mediumship, doesn't it? We infer the existence of our loved ones by observing what a medium says, or by having an indirect experience of them. You and I can't see or detect them ourselves.

My dear friend Paul Pearsall has suggested that gravity and ghosts share the identical conceptual problem—they can be known only indirectly through their inferred effects on objects or beings.

It is curious that physics lectures and textbooks typically fail to mention that in addition to being a physicist and a mathematician, Newton was also a mystic. A deeply religious and spiritual man, he studied alchemy and philosophy, and some scientists frankly considered him to be a flake.

Here is what Newton actually believed. He proposed that every physical object has mass, and that this mass has a gravitational pull that exerts its force in all directions. This means that every object in the universe, to various degrees, is pulling in all directions on every other object. Through the universal force of gravity, everything is literally connected to everything else. According to Newton's view, the universe is a gigantic interconnected feedback system.

In order for any one object to move, it has to affect every other object in its immediate environment to some degree. The universal force of gravity requires that everything is dependent on everything else—nothing in the universe that has mass is independent of the interconnecting force of gravity.

For Newton, this force was truly unconditional—be it white or black, male or female, Eastern or Western, good or bad—it didn't matter. The unconditional force of gravity was totally non-prejudicial and dependable. In fact, gravity was the force that literally held the universe together. If Newton had lived to see *Star Wars*, he would have loved the phrase "May the force be with you."

Here is the amazing part of the story—the part most physics classes fail to teach. It turns out that Newton viewed the universal, unconditional attractive force of gravity as an expression of the unconditional love of God for the universe as a whole.

According to Newton, love is the universal energy, and the existence of gravity is one of the most fundamental and far-reaching illustrations of this unconditional loving process. The loving heart of God is literally expressed through the universal attractive force of gravity.

The persistence of gravity, like the persistence of light, points to the enduring if not eternal nature of information and energy. To the extent that consciousness is a fundamental property of an interconnected feedback universe, like energy itself, it cannot be destroyed but can only be transformed.

## So What Does Mediumship Have to Do with Love?

Let us now return to mediumship and imagine that we have deceased loved ones. Like the light from distant stars, physics suggests that our loved ones' info-energy is still there, and the medium can register their info-energy.

Now let's add the history of loving attraction, and let's allow for the possibility that our and their individual info-energy patterns have created a systemic memory bond that does not simply vanish with physical decomposition. If love, as an energy, is indeed enduring, as contemporary physics suggests, this provides a reason to believe that people who have experienced love in life will want to maintain their loving relationships in what is called the afterlife.

Most of the mediums we have had the privilege to work with are obsessed with love. They come to this obsession from many different ways. However, they all see their work as a blessing and a gift, helping people connect with their departed loved ones.

One of the criticisms skeptics sometimes have of mediums is that they often report receiving the same "boring" information. The people on the other side often seem to communicate the same general message: that they want their friends and family to know they are still alive and still have love for those they were closest to.

Earlier in these pages, we addressed the skeptics' question "Why do the deceased waste their brief encounter with a medium sharing a message of love with their family?"

Again, we believe the answer is simple.

Imagine that you're a deceased person, and you've been waiting for months or even years to contact someone you dearly love. After all this waiting, you have but a few precious moments to connect with your loved one through the medium.

What will you want to share with your loved one?

The latest physics and chemistry from the other side?

The current book you're reading, or planet you're visiting?

If you've been waiting for months or years to connect with your loved one, and the reason you wish to communicate is your love for them, what are you going to do?

You are going to want to prove that you are really here by identifying yourself. And you are going to want to share some of your special feelings. You may also want to comment about certain current events that are taking place in your loved one's life.

In the "from here to there and back again" picture experiment with Laurie Campbell described earlier, she purportedly contacted four departed people to find out about their pictures. As you will recall, Laurie had a hard time getting the pictures because she was flooded with messages of love and concern

Imagine for the moment that some mediums are genuine, and you are a medium.

To get accurate information, you must first get your own consciousness out of the way. You must also get other distractions out of the way, including electromagnetic activity in the air from TVs, phones, radios, and so on, so that you can tune into the messages provided by a given deceased person. Maybe your client has specific questions for this deceased person, but it's hard to receive the answers, not because there's no contact but because the deceased person is focused on getting his or her messages of love across and would rather not answer your particular questions.

As you can imagine, this is not an easy task. If mediumship is genuine, the truth is that we have very little idea how mediums actually do it. A lot of the miracle and majesty about all this is that it is totally confounded by love.

## A Concluding Note About the Potential Role of Love in the Life of the Super Skeptic

You have to wonder, why is it that certain people are so cynical and negative about mediums?

Is this simply the fault of the mediums, particularly the disingenuous and fraudulent ones?

Or does the source of the negativity arise deeply within the skeptics themselves?

Do extremely negative opinions about the living soul hypothesis stem from the skeptics' own personal love histories, or lack thereof?

What kind of person would prefer to believe that mediumship is completely a mistake, a coincidence, or a downright fraud?

Is it possible that the extreme skeptic's own love history encourages him or her to prefer a universe that would allow the light from distant stars to last forever, but not the info-energy patterns of human love?

As you can see, we can raise many more questions than we have answers for at this time.

However, just as it is important for humankind to come to understand what mediumship is and why people choose careers in mediumship, it is also important for humankind to come to understand the root of super skepticism, especially when the evolving data from controlled scientific experiments strongly encourage us to at least keep an open mind about the possibility that all this, and more, may be real.

Our working hypothesis is that we will never understand the answers to these and related questions unless we come to understand the nature and role of love in human existence and the cosmos as a whole. One of the great surprises in addressing the question of the living soul hypothesis is that it stimulates new visions about the nature of love and its role in the universe.

May the surprises continue.

# · APPENDIX C ·

# Journal Article on Accuracy and Replicability of After-Death Communication

This report of the HBO experiment was published in the *Journal of the Society for Psychical Research*, 2001, Vol. 65.1, No. 862, pages 1–25.

## ACCURACY AND REPLICABILITY OF ANOMALOUS AFTER-DEATH COMMUNICATION ACROSS HIGHLY SKILLED MEDIUMS

Gary E. R. Schwartz, Ph.D., Linda G. S. Russek, Ph.D., Lonnie A. Nelson, B.A., and Christopher Barentsen, B.A.

## Abstract

When multiple mediums attempt to receive after-death communications (ADCs) from a single individual (the sitter/subject) who has experienced multiple losses, will accurate and replicable ADC information be obtained? Five highly skilled mediums were flown to the Human Energy Systems Laboratory for research on ADC. An Arizona woman, unknown to all of the mediums, who had experienced six significant losses over the past ten years, served as the primary subject. She filled out detailed pre-experimental questionnaires about her losses. Each medium met individually with the sitter. There was no communication between the mediums about the sessions. Two chairs were placed side by side, a few feet apart, separated by a screen that eliminated visual cues. Except for an initial greeting, the only communications allowed from the sitter were simple yes or no responses to possible questions from the mediums. Nineteen channels of EEG and the ECG were recorded simultaneously from both the mediums and the sitter. Two video cameras recorded the sessions. Verbatim reports were obtained from complete transcripts of the sessions. A second sitter was tested with two of the mediums.

The mediums' average accuracy was 83% for sitter one and 77% for sitter two. The average accuracy for 68 control subjects was 36%. In a replication and extension experiment, mediums' average accuracy an initial ten-minute period that did <u>not</u> allow yes/no questioning was 77%. The data suggest that highly skilled mediums are able to obtain accurate (p less than one in ten million) and replicable information. Since factors of fraud, error, and statistical coincidence can not explain the present findings, other possible mechanisms should be considered in future research. These include telepathy, super psi, and survival of consciousness after death.

## Introduction

Empirical research on mediumship has been limited by a number of factors:

(1) availability of experienced mediums willing to collaborate in research.
(2) availability of subjects (sitters) willing to engage in careful scoring of transcripts,
(3) and funding to investigate these questions.

The research reported here became possible through unique circumstances. A major US television network decided to produce a documentary on after-death communication (ADC) and the plausibility of survival of consciousness after physical death. When the producer/director (Lisa Jackson) approached Schwartz and Russek about possibly participating in the documentary, we proposed that if they were seriously interested in the science of mediumship, they should fund a first-ever laboratory experiment with well-known mediums to examine possible inter-medium replicability of information obtained during readings under controlled circumstances. Moreover, thanks to the interest and cooperation of the mediums whose data are reported here, it was possible to record 19 channels of EEG and ECGs from each of them as well as from one of the sitters.

The data were collected in the Human Energy Systems Laboratory at the University of Arizona in Tucson. Preliminary analyses were reported at the June 1999 meeting of the Society for Scientific Exploration and were shown in the HBO special "Life Afterlife" which was broadcast in October 1999. Subsequent detailed scoring and analyses are reported here.

A replication and extension experiment was conducted. Four of the five original mediums were able to coordinate their schedules to participate in the research. Unique circumstances occurred again. The husband of the sitter featured in the HBO documentary died a few days before the replication and extension experiment was to be conducted. The design of the second experiment made it possible to collect data in such a way that the mediums would not be able to identify the sitters. The sitter agreed to be "re-read" to see if information could be replicated and extended to include the death of her husband. Hence, replicability of information was addressed not only across five mediums (Experiment I, the HBO experiment), but over time as well for two of the mediums (Experiment II, the Miraval experiment). The replication and extension experiment was made possible by support from Canyon Ranch Resort, the Miraval Resort, the Susy Smith Project from the University of Arizona, and the Family Love and Health Foundation. The data were collected at Miraval in Tucson.

In Experiment I, mediums were permitted to ask questions that allowed yes or no answers. In Experiment II, mediums were not permitted to ask any questions for ten minutes in Part I; Part II replicated Experiment I, which permitted yes/no questions. The experiments were primarily designed to minimize the plausibility of psychological and statistical interpretations (e.g., fraud and chance); they were secondarily designed to indirectly address two possible anomalous interpretations (telepathy with the sitter and direct communication with the departed).

## Experiment I (The HBO Experiment)

### Purpose

The primary purpose of Experiment I was to determine whether mediums could independently obtain accurate and replicable information from a sitter under controlled naturalistic conditions. These findings are reported in the body of the paper.

The secondary purpose was exploratory. The purpose was to examine possible ECG/ECG and ECG/EEG synchrony between mediums and a sitter during baseline and reading periods. We hypothesized that if mediums were engaged in either psychological (focused attention) and/or parapsychological reading (telepathy) of the sitter (i.e. the physically living), increased evidence of ECG/ECG and ECG/EEG medium-sitter synchrony might be observed during the readings compared to resting baselines (Russek and Schwartz, 1994; Song, Schwartz, and Russek, 1998). However, if the mediums were focusing their attention away from the sitter (e.g., attending to communication from the departed), decreased ECG/ECG and/or ECG/EEG midum-sitter synchrony might be observed during the readings compared to resting baselines. Given the technical complexity and preliminary nature of the EEG/ECG analyses, the findings are briefly summarized in Appendix A. They will be more fully presented in a separate publication.

### Mediums

Four internationally known mediums agreed to come to Tucson to collaborate in the research: listed alphabetically, George Anderson, John Edward, Anne Gehman, and Suzane Northrop. The fifth, Laurie Campbell, had previously participated in mediumship research conducted in our laboratory (Schwartz et al, 1999; Schwartz and Russek, 1999). The mediums were fully informed that the Human Energy Systems Laboratory was collaborating with HBO, that the research would be professionally filmed and aired internationally, that the research required they be blind to the identity of the sitters selected for the research, and that the research required the highest integrity of all involved—the laboratory, HBO, the mediums, and the sitters.

## Sitters

Each of the five mediums had an experimental session with one sitter, a 46-year-old woman who lives north of Tucson. She was selected because she had experienced the death of at least six loved ones in the past ten years. The sitter was recruited by HBO. The sitter was recommended to HBO by an ADC researcher who knew of her case. HBO informed the sitter that it was essential that her identity be kept secret from the mediums until after the experiment was completed. Moreover, she was told that her identity would be kept secret from the researchers until the day before the experiment was to be conducted. A second woman personally known by G.E.R.S. and L.G.S.R. (a 54-year-old woman who lives in Tucson who had also experienced the death of at least six loved ones in the past ten years) was invited to serve as the second sitter. The identity of this sitter was kept secret from HBO as well as the mediums. Time permitted collecting experimental sessions with the second sitter and two of the mediums.

Both sitters signed statements indicating that they had no verbal or written contact with any of the the five mediums prior to the experiment. Information about the sitters was kept secret from the mediums. They only knew that each of the sitters had experienced the loss of multiple loved ones in a ten-year period.

## Measures

Pretest information was obtained about each of the six deceased individuals that each sitter predicted might be received by one or more of the mediums (Appendix B).

During the experimental readings, the sitters took notes. Immediately after each reading, they completed numeric ratings from −1 to +5 (Appendix C).

Each of the five mediums and one of the sitters was fitted with an electrode cap containing 19 EEG electrodes and a ground. Linked ear electrodes were attached as well as ECG recorded arm to arm. The electrodes were attached by one of the authors (L.N.) and Mercy Fernandez, Ph.D. using standard electrode paste and impedance reducing procedures; all electrode resistances were less than 5 K ohms.

The EEG and ECG signals were recorded on two Lexicor Neurosearch 24 systems and processed by PCs, one system for the medium and a second system for the sitter. The signals were sampled at 256 Hz. The ECG signals from the mediums and the sitter were recorded in both systems. Using specially designed software, it was possible to examine ECG-triggered signal-averaging within the mediums and sitter (intrapersonal ECG/EEG interactions) and between the mediums and sitter (interpersonal ECG/ECG and ECG/EEG interactions) (Russek and Schwartz, 1994; Song, Schwartz, and Russek, 1998).

A few months after the data were collected, each of the sitters was invited back individually to the laboratory to carefully score transcripts of each of the mediums obtained from the video recordings. Every possible item uttered by each of the mediums was placed in one of six categories (name, initial, historical fact, personal description, temperament, and "opinion") and rated by the sitter using a numeric scale (−3 definitely an error, −2 probably an error, −1 possibly an error, 0 maybe an error or maybe correct, +1 possibly correct, +2 probably correct, +3 definitely correct).

The sitters were required to explain and justify each accuracy rating that they made for the items. Justification of accuracy ratings, particularly +3s, could be as simple as "my deceased son's name was Michael" (name category) to as complex as "my grandmother did have false teeth, and she did take them in and out in public, which greatly embarrassed my mother" (historical fact category). The sitters were also required to indicate whether the information could be independently verified by another living family member or friend (only the "opinion" category contained items that could not be independently verified). Each item was read out loud by G.E.R.S.; the ratings were recorded in Excel files by C.B. The experimenters repeatedly emphasized the research requirement of rating accuracy and possible verification (given the specific nature of the content, none was performed).

Note that ratings of accuracy do not discriminate between differences in degree of specificity. For example, accurate information such as "M" (initial), "Michael" (name), "committed suicide" (historical fact), "thin" (personal description), "playful sense of humor" (temperament), and "does not blame you for his decision to kill himself" (opinion) differ in their degree of specificity, but they were all correct and received accuracy ratings of +3 by a sitter.

## Procedure

Seven data collection sessions (five for sitter one and two for sitter two) were collected in the energy cardiology laboratory of the Human Energy Systems Laboratory in the course of a single day. The data were collected in February 1999. Each session took approximately one hour (including lead connecting and disconnecting, file naming on the computers, baselines, and readings). The room was arranged to accommodate the experimental design as well as the needs for filming. The two EEG/ECG systems were placed furthest from the door (run by G.E.R.S.). The sitter sat in a comfortable chair adjacent to the recording equipment, in view of G.E.R.S. and two video cameras run by the HBO filming team. Each medium entered the room, one per session, and sat down in a comfortable chair which was separated from the sitter's chair by a large floor-standing cloth-covered screen. The screen was approximately 6 feet high by 4 feet wide. Though the medium was never visible to the sitter during the reading, and vice versa, the medium was visible to both video cameras, as was the sitter.

Each medium was run individually, the order of their participation selected by agreement from all five mediums. The mediums waited their turn in the courtyard behind the laboratory and were closely and continuously monitored throughout the day by one of the senior investigators (L.G.S.R.) plus a research assistant (Carolyne Luna) to insure that no communication about the sessions occurred during the day of data collection. As mentioned previously, the mediums understood that integrity was absolutely essential in this research, and that fraud would not be tolerated during the experiment.

When each medium entered the room, their ECG and EEG leads were connected to the Lexicor. A two-minute eyes-closed resting baseline was obtained for both the medium and the sitter. Following the resting baseline, each medium briefly explained to the sitter how she or he conducted a reading. Then the medium was allowed to conduct the reading in her or his own way, with the restriction that they could ask only yes or no questions. The mediums varied in the number of questions they asked. The actual reading lasted for approximately 15 to 20 minutes.

After the reading was completed, the medium left the experimental room and returned to the courtyard. The experimenter reminded each medium not to discuss the reading (s) until the experiment was completed, and that they would be continuously monitored by two experimenters. The sitters then made their immediate ratings as displayed in Appendix C.

*Results:*
## Sitter 1 (5 Readings): Immediate Ratings

The immediate ratings, though important, are not primary, and therefore are noted only briefly here. The major findings are the detailed scoring results reported in the next section.

The number of departed persons identified by the sitter (based upon her original list of 6) for each of the five mediums were 5, 4, 3, 3, and 4, respectively; the resemblance ratings ranged from 4 to 5+ (verifiable names, dates, causes of death, personal characteristics, etc.). The average percent identification was 63%.

Interestingly, according to the sitter, each of the five mediums independently communicated specific information from 2 of the 6 departed individuals on her original list (the sitter's mother and son). Hence, one third of the anticipated departed persons were independently replicated 100% across all five mediums. In addition, anomalous information from 9 other departed individuals (not on the original list of 6) was also documented. The numbers of additional departed persons identified by the sitter from her readings with each of the the five mediums were 5, 6, 1, 5, 4; the resemblance ratings ranged from 4 to 5. According to the sitter, specific information identifying two of these individuals (the sitter's grandfather, and a dog beloved by her deceased son) were independently communicated by four of the five mediums. Hence, two of the unexpected departed individuals were replicated 80% across the mediums.

In light of these initial summary observations, careful item-by-item ratings of the transcripts were conducted.

## Sitter 1 (5 Ratings): Item by Item Yes/No Answers

Figure 1 displays the total number of items per reading, the number of questions asked that received a yes answer, and the number of questions asked that received a no answer.

Figure 2 displays the percentage of questions asked to the total number of items generated.

It can be seen that the mediums varied in the number of total items they ob-

## Figure 1

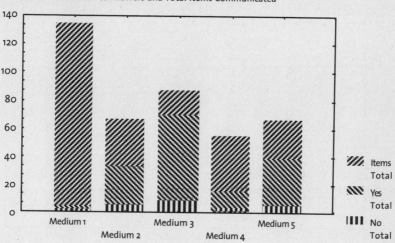

Number of No and Yes Answers and Total Items Communicated

## Figure 2

Percent Questions Asked to Items Communicated per Medium

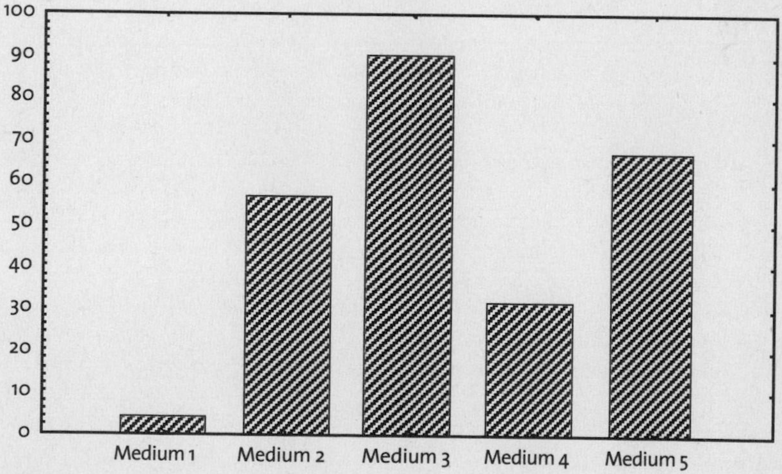

tained and the number of questions they asked. Medium 1, in particular, generated over 130 specific pieces of information yet asked only 5 questions, 4 of which (80%) were answered yes.

Figure 3 displays the percentage of yes answers obtained per medium. The

## Figure 3

Percent Yes Answers to Questions Asked by Mediums

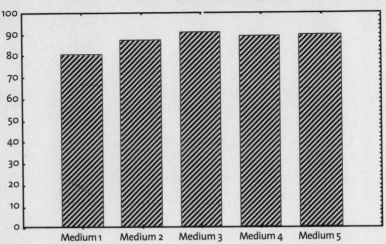

five mediums ranged in percent yes answers; the average accuracy was 85%. Medium 1, who obtained the lowest score (80%), only asked a total of five questions. Hence, it is impossible to claim that medium 1's percent accuracy ratings (see below) were due to "cold reading" and "fishing for information."

However, the question arose, did the other mediums obtain their high accuracy scores because they asked more questions? To address this question, the data were analyzed just for the first five questions asked. The results are displayed in Figure 4.

It can be seen that accuracy ranged from 80% to 100%; the average was 88%. A chi square comparing the number of yes versus no answers for the first five questions, compared with a simple, binary (yes/no) estimate of chance (50%) was $p < 0.006$. It is unclear whether the use of a simple binary 50% estimate over- or underestimates chance in this experiment. A careful analysis of the content suggests that the 50% figure may be an over-estimation. The first thirteen questions of medium 3 are presented verbatim in the general discussion to illustrate the nature of the content of the yes/no questions and their degree of specificity and precision.

The data suggest that according to the sitter's ratings, the mediums were receiving accurate information.

### Comparison to Base Rate Guessing: The Numeric Accuracy Ratings

The question arises, can intelligent and motivated persons guess this kind of information by chance alone? Some items were yes/no (e.g., is your son alive or dead?); other items were less susceptible to probability estimation (e.g., does your son's first name begin with the letter ____?). Since it was impossible to estimate

## Figure 4

Percent Yes Answers to the First Five Questions per Medium

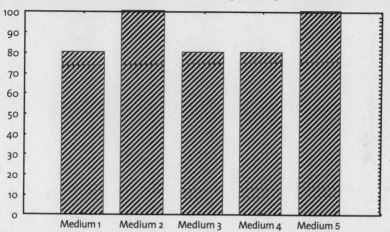

ahead of time base rates per item, we selected a large range of representative items, both correct and incorrect, and obtained control subject's guessing rates for sitter 1's data empirically.

A questionnaire containing 70 representative items was created, based on the content provided by the mediums (Appendix D). Some items were yes/no; others required that subjects provide content answers. It was administered to a control group of 68 male and female undergraduate students at the University of Arizona (average age 21 years, 70% female). Since it would have been preferable if control ratings were made by a large group of middle-aged female subjects who were matched to the demographics of the sitters, the control findings reported here should should be viewed with some caution. The control subjects were challenged to try and guess as well as the mediums did. As an incentive, they were told that after they completed the questionnaires, they would be told what the actual answers were, and then they would be able to watch the HBO documentary.

The data are displayed in Figure 5.

Their average accuracy for the 70 items was 36%, ranging from 20% to 54%. The mediums' average accuracy score (+3 ratings out of the total number of items receiving a rating per medium) was 83%, ranging from 77% to 93%. Especially significant is that medium 1, who asked only 5 questions, received 83% ratings of +3 out of medium 1's total of 130 items. A *t* test comparing the performance of the mediums versus the control group was p less than one in ten million.

### Analysis of Categories of Content

Figure 6 displays the percent of +3 scores for the six categories of content collected over the five mediums. Not surprisingly, percent accuracy for names was least accurate. Interestingly, percent accuracy for initials and especially tempera-

## Figure 5

Comparison of Guessing Performance of Controls (n=68) with Each Medium

Control Performance Ranged from 20% to 54%

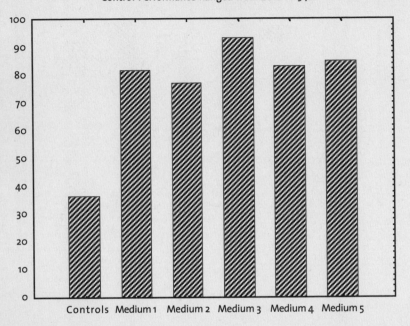

ment was most accurate. It is important to recognize that names, initials, descriptions, historical facts, and temperament could be confirmed by living relatives and friends of the sitter. Only the "opinions" category was "subjective" to the sitter.

### Replication with the Second Sitter: Item by Item Numeric Ratings

It was only possible to test the second sitter with mediums 1 and 3. Though the initial summary ratings, obtained for the purpose of examining replicability of information obtained across mediums, are not meaningful here (n = 2 mediums is insufficient to draw conclusions), the detailed analysis of her item by item numeric ratings is valuable as a comparison with the first sitter.

The first medium generated 103 items; the second medium generated 95 items. The first medium obtained 64% accuracy; the second medium reached 90% accuracy; the average was 77% accuracy.

Figure 7 displays the average percent accuracy for the six categories of information.

Accuracy for initials was again higher than for names, and accuracy for temperament was again higher than for historical facts. Note that for this sitter, the most subjective information ("opinions") was actually the lowest. The first

## Figure 6

Percent Sure Hits (+3s) per Category averaged over 5 Mediums

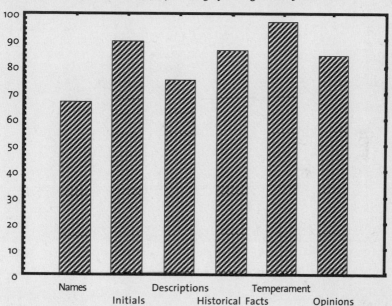

medium provided various "opinion" category statements that were rated less than +3 by the sitter, thus lowering this medium's average accuracy below 70%.

### Discussion

It appears that highly skilled mediums, in laboratory controlled yet supportive conditions, can receive specific categories of information that can be rated accurately by trained research sitters. One sitter had independent readings with five mediums. She also had her ECG and EEG recorded. The other sitter had separate readings with two of the five mediums. The average percent accuracy was 83% for the first sitter and 77% for the second sitter. Each of the mediums performed well above guessing rates. Control subjects who attempted to guess the information averaged 36% accuracy for all categories of information combined. The p value was less than one in ten million.

The percent guessing accuracy of the control subjects may be somewhat lower than the actual guessing accuracy because (1) the control subjects were substantially younger than the sitters (older subjects might have more extended information to guess from) and (2) they did not have the benefit of hearing the answers to the yes/no questions as the mediums did. On the other hand, the control subjects were shown a picture of the woman (the mediums did not see the sitters until after all the data were collected). Given the clearly specific nature of the represen-

## Figure 7

Percent Sure Hits (+3s) per Category averaged over 2 Mediums

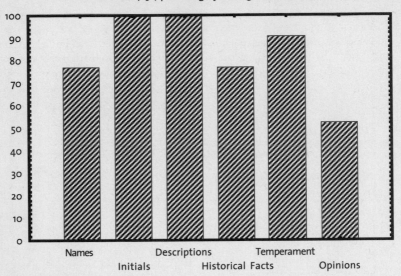

tative items reprinted in Appendix D, it seems improbable that a second group of control subjects who were matched for age, sex, and demographics, even given yes/no feedback per answer, would score as high as the mediums did in this experiment by guessing per se.

Though names were rated least accurately, the magnitude of the accuracy was still surprisingly high (67% for sitter one and 76% for sitter two). Initials received higher percent accuracy scores (90% for sitter one and 100% for sitter two). Personal temperament information was very accurately reported (95% for sitter one and 93% for sitter two).

The mediums varied greatly in the number of questions asked. Medium 3 generally asked more questions than medium 1, and tended to have higher accuracy ratings. However, it is significant that medium 1 only asked five questions of sitter 1, and was over 80% accurate for these questions. Moreover, medium 3's accuracy for the first five questions asked was also 80%.

The preliminary ECG and EEG findings summarized in Appendix A are intriguing and worth exploring in future research. No evidence was found for mediums' registering the sitters' ECG in their EEGs. Moreover, when the readings began, the degree of heart-to-heart synchrony between the medium and sitter changed—the medium's heart tended to beat when the sitter's heart was *not* beating. The combination of the ECG and EEG findings is not consistent with the telepathy hypothesis that the mediums were registering the energy or memories of the sitter. The pattern of findings is consistent with the hypothesis that these mediums may be disconnecting biophysically from the sitter as they attempt to receive anomalous communication, purportedly from departed individuals. Qualitative data presented in the general discussion also suggests that telepathy with the sitter does not satisfactorily account for all the findings.

The purpose of including the preliminary ECG/EEG data in this report is to illustrate the potential of using such techniques in future research to address possible biophysical mechanisms of anomalous information retrieval. Future research will require the use of appropriate control conditions comparing, for example, non-mediumistic versus mediumistic communication periods, to draw definitive conclusions about the meaning of the cardiac findings observed in Experiment I.

## Experiment II (The Miraval Experiment)

### Purpose

Experiment II was designed to attempt to replicate and extend Experiment I. The primary purpose was (1) to use a new group of sitters from various parts of the country who varied in age, sex, history of number of personal losses, belief in the plausibility of after-death communication, and depth of love for the departed, and (2) to add a new control condition that did not allow any verbal communication between the medium and the sitter.

### Mediums

Four of the original five mediums were able to come to Tucson to collaborate in the research: listed alphabetically, Laurie Campbell, John Edward, Anne Gehman, and Suzane Northrop.

### The Sitter

This report presents the findings from sitter one, whose husband died in a car crash a few days before Experiment II was to be conducted in June, 1999. She called L.G.S.R. to share her loss. L.G.S.R. suggested that she might consider being a sitter in the upcoming Experiment II, since Part I occurred in complete silence, and the sitters could not be seen by the mediums. This remarkable coincidence led to the replication data reported here. The sitter affirmed that she had no verbal or written contact with any of the mediums about the death of her husband and her subsequent participation in Experiment II.

### Procedure

The four mediums were housed at Canyon Ranch, which is located more than ten miles from Miraval. The sitter was housed in a separate hotel. Testing was conducted over two days. The four mediums were taken to four separate rooms; each room was separated by at least four other rooms. There were four experimenters (G.E.R.S., L.G.S.R, Carolyne Luna, and Patti Harada). The sitters were sequestered in a separate room, many rooms away from where the mediums were being tested. The mediums sat in a comfortable chair, facing a video camera and backup audio tape recorder, with their backs to the door. A given experimenter would enter the room and make sure that the medium was seated with her or his back to the door and facing the video recorder. The tape recorders would then be started. Next, the sitter was brought into the room and seated approximately six feet behind the medium. For the first ten minutes, the mediums were instructed to receive whatever information they could about the deceased and share this information out loud. They were not allowed to ask any questions of the sitters. The sitters were instructed to remain silent. After this Part I silent period, the mediums were allowed to ask yes/no questions, replicating the procedure used in Experiment I.

The sitter reported here was brought in to participate at the end of the two days; time permitted that she could be read by mediums 1 and 2 (as displayed in the figures, not as listed alphabetically) from Experiment I, who also participated in Experiment II. G.E.R.S. was the experimenter. The sessions were taped, and the verbal information transcribed.

## Results

The content of these two readings was dramatic. Information about the deceased son and dog were again replicated by both mediums. However, both mediums also received information about the recently deceased husband. Medium 2 reported being confused, saying "I keep hearing Michael times two, Michael times two." The father's name was Michael, the son's name was Michael, Jr.

A few months after these two sessions, after the transcripts had been prepared, the sitter returned to the laboratory for a detailed scoring session. The five-hour scoring session was recorded on video tape. G.E.R.S. again read the items out loud, and C.B. recorded the answers in an Excel file. The rating procedure was identical to Experiment 1, using numbers from −3 to +3.

Figure 10 displays the summary findings.

The two left bars display the percent +3 accuracy ratings for medium 1 and medium 2, combining the data for the silent (Part I) and questioning (Part II) periods. It can be seen that the average accuracy for the two mediums was 82%. Medium 1 generated a total of 127 items, medium 2 a total of 94 items.

The two right bars display the percent + accuracy ratings for the silent and questioning periods, combining the data for mediums 1 and 2. The average accuracy for the silent periods was 77% and for the questioning period, 85%. The total number of items received during the silent period was 64; the total during the questioning period was 157. The difference between the silent and questioning periods in percent accuracy was not statistically significant. The control subject's percent accuracy ratings from Experiment I are included in the center for comparison.

For completeness of presentation, figure 11 (page 306) displays a frequency histogram of the ratings of sitter 1 for the HBO (Experiment I) and Miraval (Experiment II), separately for the seven sessions (two each with mediums 1 and 2, one each with mediums 3, 4, and 5).

## Discussion

The accuracy of mediums 1 and 2 was replicated, including during a ten-minute silent period when no questioning was allowed. New information about the deceased husband was received by both mediums. More information was obtained during the questioning period than the silent period, and the accuracy rat-

### Figure 10

Percent Correct Communications for Medium 1 and Medium 2

Replicated in Silent and Questioning Periods

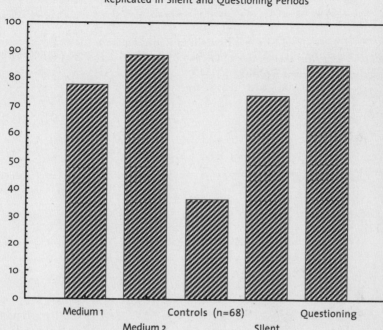

ings were somewhat higher. However, detailed information was obtained during the silent periods when no "cold reading" was possible.

Interestingly and surprisingly, neither medium reported guessing who the sitter was during or immediately following the yes/no questioning period (Part II). The experimenter (G.E.R.S.) would not allow the mediums to see the sitter until he pressed them repeatedly to guess who was behind them. Both mediums insisted that they had no idea who was behind them. They both stated that they conduct many readings per week in their busy professional lives and that it is difficult to keep specific readings straight in their minds, especially after many months. Both expressed profound shock when they were allowed to see the sitter and recognized her from Experiment I. It should be recalled that the mediums had not been told what had happened to this sitter by L.G.S.R. or G.E.R.S., and that they had not been told that they would be "re-reading" her in the replication and extension experiment. Their sadness visibly increased when they realized that it was her husband, Michael senior, who had recently died.

An anonymous reviewer suggested the interesting possibility that the mediums might have recognized the sitter's odor unconsciously, which triggered memories of their prior readings. This suggestion is creative but does not explain all of

Figure 11—Experiments I and II combined for Sitter One
This figure displays distributions of –3 to +3 ratings, separately for each medium in the two experiments (HBO and Miraval). It can be seen that each of the five mediums obtained mostly +3 complete accuracy ratings (average percentage is 83% over the seven readings), sporadic +2 to –2 scores, and a minority of –3 complete errors scores (average percentage is 10% over the seven readings).

Bivariate Distribution: Mediums in Both Experiments by Ratings

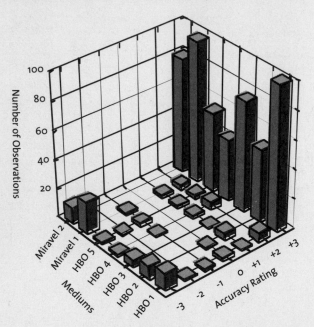

the data. For example, in Experiment I, medium 1 reported seeing a little brown dog. In Experiment II, medium 1 reported seeing a spotted beagle. After the session, the sitter explained that the mother of the brown dog experienced by four of the mediums in Experiment I was indeed a spotted beagle. At the rating session a few months later, the sitter brought photos of both the spotted beagle (the mother) and the little brown dog (her offspring).

## General Discussion: Quantitative Findings

These two experiments provide quantitative data that are consistent with the hypothesis that some form of anomalous information retrieval was occurring in these skilled mediums. Traditional hypotheses of fraud, subtle cueing, and statistical coincidence are improbable explanations of the total set of observations reported here. Adopting the William James metaphor, the particular mediums participating in this research may be examples of five "white crows" of anomalous information retrieval.

The experimenters have not ruled out definitively that HBO, with or without the cooperation of sitter 1, engaged in deception in Experiment I. Private detectives were not employed to attempt to independently verify confidentiality. However, it seems highly improbable that Lisa Jackson, an Emmy Award–winning producer who works for a multiple Emmy Award–winning production company, would risk her professional and personal reputation, as well as the reputation of her production company, to engage in fraud at the University of Arizona. Moreover, the experimenters had independently selected a second sitter whose identity was kept secret from HBO as well as from the mediums. Lisa Jackson and her team were well aware of the consequences of risking their integrity as well as the integrity of the laboratory. The experimenters were sensitive to the unique nature of this research and the need to eliminate, as best as possible, the occurrence of deception in the experiments. This included having the mediums watched at all times by two experimenters in Experiment I to insure that the mediums were reminded of the absolute requirement for integrity.

The present findings do not speak directly to the mechanism(s) of anomalous information retrieval observed. However, the apparent desynchrony of the medium's ECGs with the sitter's ECG during the reading periods compared to the baseline periods is inconsistent with a "telepathy with the sitter" interpretation of the findings. If telepathy with the sitter was involved, increased medium-sitter ECG/ECG synchrony might have been observed. Interpersonal medium-sitter ECG/ECG and ECG/EEG measurements may be useful in future research on possible mechanisms of mediumship phenomena (Russek and Schwartz, 1994).

## General Discussion: Qualitative Findings

The rich and extensive qualitative information conveyed in these readings could not be reported here. However, it is important to mention that the mediums spoke remarkably quickly and generated a surprisingly large number of specific facts.

The precise nature of the yes/no questions deserve some qualitative presentation. The first thirteen questions from medium 3 in experiment 1 are presented verbatim below to illustrate the nature of the yes/no questions and their answers.

It is clear that most of these questions provide unique information that is not implicit from previous questions. Questions were typically confirmatory of information received by the medium and passed on to the sitter. Questions did *not* typically request novel information from the sitter per se. Confirmatory examples illustrated below include that there was a young male who passed, the son's father was still alive, and that the sitter had a miscarriage.

Also note that the medium was very clear when he was asking a question that was possibly vague in his role as a research medium (he is known to do this professionally as well). This medium clearly did not want feedback from the sitter. For example, he says below "This I don't understand. If you do, say yes, you understand, but don't explain." and "So don't say anything, I want them to say it." The data are consistent with the suggestion that the statistical estimate of 50% binary chance may have been an overestimation.

MEDIUM: *Now, I don't know if they mean this by age or by generation, but they talk about the younger male that passed. Does that make sense to you?*

SITTER: Yes.

MEDIUM: *Okay, 'cause wherever he is is claiming he was the first one in the room. So I guess he wants the credit of coming first. He states he's family, that's correct?*

SITTER: Correct.

MEDIUM: *This I don't understand. If you do, say yes, you understand, but don't explain. He speaks about his dad, does that make sense?*

SITTER: Yes.

MEDIUM: *I don't know why yet. I don't know if he's trying to tell me his dad is there or if he's calling to his dad. So don't say anything, I want them to say it. Also, another male presence comes forward to you and says, "Dad is here." Is it correct your dad is passed?*

SITTER: Correct.

MEDIUM: *Okay, 'cause he's there. But this younger male, these are two different people, correct?*

SITTER: Correct.

MEDIUM: *Yeah, 'cause I don't, he's already explained "Don't get me mixed up." You know, they know each other but don't forget about him. Yeah, so your dad comes forward. Now your dad, okay, again, don't explain, just say you understand. Your dad speaks about the loss of child. That makes sense?*

SITTER: Yes.

MEDIUM: *Twice?*

MEDIUM: *'Cause your father says twice.*

SITTER: Yes.

MEDIUM: *Wait a minute, now he says thrice. He's saying three times. Does that make sense?*

SITTER: That's correct.

MEDIUM: *'Cause your father said, "Once, twice, thrice."*

SITTER: That's correct.

MEDIUM: *It . . . there's talk of the son that passed on. That is correct?*

SITTER: Yes.

MEDIUM: *Okay, he's claiming to be the first male who came in the room. That would make sense?*

> SITTER: Yes.
> MEDIUM: Okay. So him and his grandfather are together. Now your son's dad is still on the earth, I take it, yes?
> SITTER: Yes.
> MEDIUM: 'Cause he's . . . that's why I was hearing him talk about Dad. Now that's why I didn't want you to explain. Let him explain where his father is. His father is on the earth. Please tell Dad you've heard from me, whether he believes in this or not. Who cares? It's the message that's important, not the belief system. And as your son says, besides, he'll find that I'm right as usual someday anyway. Wait a minute now. There's talk of loss of another son, is that correct? Wait a minute now. Wait a minute, don't answer yet. Your father speaks aboout a miscarriage. Is it correct, you did have one?
> SITTER: Yes

Numerous examples indicate that not only was the qualitative information often accurate, but that paranormal interpretations such as telepathy with the sitter appear insufficient to explain the data. These novel qualitative examples curiously complement the quantitative medium-sitter ECG findings summarized in Appendix A.

Two qualitative examples from Experiment I are presented below to illustrate their potential conceptual significance for interpreting the quantitative findings. We include one that is somewhat subtle yet is potentially theoretically important; the other is straightforward and is especially significant.

*Qualitative Example I: Hearing initials and names for people and not pets.* For the first sitter, all five mediums obtained information about a deceased son. Three of the five mediums heard the initial "M" for the son, one said the name "Michael." None gave a false initial or name for the son. Also, none obtained information about a deceased daughter (her son did die; her daughter was alive).

The question arises, was this highly accurate information retrieved telepathically from the mind of the sitter?

Consider the following information: four of the five mediums obtained highly accurate details about a deceased dog. However, it turned out that none of the mediums heard the initial P for the dog, and none said "Peewee," the dog's name. No initials or names were heard and reported for the dog. Also, none of the mediums obtained information about a deceased cat (her dog did die and was very close to the son; the cat was alive). It is the *failure* to hear the dog's initial and name from the sitter that questions the plausibility of the interpretation of hearing the son's initial and name telepathically from the sitter.

The discrepancy between the mediums hearing the initial or the name of the sitter's deceased son, and not getting this kind of information for the sitter's deceased dog, is potentially significant because after the experiment was completed (during the debriefing and multiple scoring sessions), we observed repeatedly that whenever the sitter spoke of her deceased dog, she referred to him by name just as she did her son. We witnessed the sitter affectionately say her dog's name hundreds of times (e.g., "Peewee was so smart") in conversation just as she would affectionately say her son's name in conversation (e.g., "Michael and Peewee loved each other").

The question arises, if the mediums were "reading the sitter's mind," why did they *not* hear the name "Peewee" or the initial "P"? Was this simply a random or selective oversight with the dog? Or is this a common distinction in experiencing deceased persons versus deceased pets?

What the mediums said were things like "I see a little dog playing ball" (according to the sitter, "Peewee loved to play ball"), and "The dog is back! The dog is back!" The mediums reported experiencing the dog as if it was alive and non-verbal.

Subtle discrepancies like the above (and there are many in the qualitative data) lead one to question whether telepathy with the sitter is the sole mechanism of anomalous communication. These kinds of "anomalies in the anomalies" deserve systematic analysis in future research.

*Qualitative Example II: Receiving accurate information days before the readings.* One of the mediums purportedly received communication from the deceased mother of one of the sitters a few days before traveling to Tucson. The mother purportedly conveyed to the medium a favorite prayer that she had regularly recited to her daughter as a child. Moreover, according to the deceased mother, the daughter was secretly continuing to offer this prayer for her. An assistant to the medium was instructed to locate the prayer, and to have it laminated and gift-wrapped.

When the reading was about to begin with the sitter, the medium unexpectedly reported to the experimenters that he had forgotten to bring into the laboratory a present he had brought for this sitter from her deceased mother. Surprised by the claim of such a gift, we instructed the medium that he could have his assistant bring it in after the reading had officially ended and the formal data had been collected.

The gift was brought into the laboratory at the end of the session and passed around the screen to the sitter. Upon opening the present, the sitter, in tears, confirmed that this was a special prayer her mother had taught her as a child. Moreover, she shared that she silently continued to say this prayer for her deceased mother.

Since the medium purportedly did not know who the sitters were ahead of time, and also did not know who was behind the screen, the observation of the medium receiving anomalous communication three days before the experiment and giving this particular sitter this particular gift raises challenging questions. Careful examination of such unanticipated qualitative examples provides important clues that can be potentially replicated and extended in future research specifically designed to document their frequency and veracity.

The present findings suggest that systematic research on mediumship, documenting anomalous information retrieval and examining its mechanism(s), can be conducted in the laboratory. The collaboration of research-oriented mediums committed to the integrity of science and data is key. The mediums who collaborate with us have come to appreciate that our goal is to explore the phenomena, whatever they are, in an environment of respect and responsibility. We take their experiences, hypotheses, and feelings seriously, and attempt to foster a laboratory environment that can allow the purported phenomena to be uncovered. The emotional climate of the laboratory, and the comfort of all involved—mediums, sitters, and scientists—may be key in enabling the present observations to be revealed.

It is possible to conduct research long distance by telephone. By placing the medium's phone on mute during the silent data collection periods (so the sitters cannot hear the information on line) it is possible to keep the sitters "blind" to the information. This data collection procedure makes it possible to conduct post-session blind scoring of the transcripts, where each sitter scores not only their own transcripts, but the transcripts of other sitters as well, without having prior knowledge of which transcript is their transcript.

The mediums know that the motto of our laboratory is "let the data speak," whatever the data are—positive or negative, clarifying or confusing. It is mutually understood that if "mediums are willing to stand up and be counted, scientists should be willing to stand up and count them." The mediums also know that our laboratory is designed to achieve the following: "If it is real, it will be revealed; if it is fake, we will catch the mistake."

The challenge for the future is to make it possible to conduct systematic research, including multi-center trials, adopting the evolving philosophy of science of contemporary medical research. Just as the practice of medicine is becoming "evidence-based medicine," the practice of mediumship can become "evidence-based mediumship." Future research can also address the mechanisms of the anomalous information retrieval, including telepathy with the living (sitter), various super-psi interpretations, and telepathy with the departed (Braude, 1992; Cook, Greyson, and Stevenson, 1998; Schwartz, Russek, et al, 1999).

## Acknowledgments

We thank Robert Morris and Monty Keen for their comments on a preliminary version of the manuscript, Zofia Weaver and two anonymous reviewers of the manuscript for their important clarifications, the team of research assistants who helped with the experiments, and the mediums, sitters, and hypothesized family members for their active and responsible collaboration.

## References

Braude, S.E. (1992). Survival or super-psi? *Journal of Scientific Exploration.* 6,2: 127–144.

Cook, E.W., Greyson, B., and Stevenson, I. (1998). Do any near-death experiences provide evidence for the survival of human personality after death? Relevant features and illustrative case reports. *Journal of Scientific Exploration.* 12,3: 373–406.

Russek, L.G., and Schwartz, G.E. (1994). Interpersonal heart-brain registration and the perception of parental love: A 42-year follow-up of the Harvard Mastery of Stress Study. *Subtle Energies.* 5,3:195–208.

## Appendix C

Schwartz, G.E.R., and Russek, L.G.S. (1999). *The Living Energy Universe: A Fundamental Discovery That Transforms Science and Medicine.* Charlottesville, VA: Hampton Roads Publishing.

Schwartz, G.E.R., Russek, L.G.S., et al. (1999). Potential medium to departed to medium communication of pictorial information: Exploratory evidence consistent with psi and survival of consciousness. *The Noetics Journal,* in press.

Song, L.Z.Y.X.., Schwartz, G.E.R., and Russek L.G.R. (1998). Heart-focused attention and heart-brain synchronization: Energetic and physiological mechanisms. *Alternative Therapies in Health and Medicine.* 4,5:44–63.

## Appendix A: The ECG/EEG Findings

Figures 8a, 8b, and 8c display the averaged ECGs (–20 to +20 samples around the peak of the R spike in the ECGs) during the eyes closed resting baseline (left panels) and the first six minutes of the readings (right panels) for the first sitter.

Six minutes were selected because it represented the largest size of signal files stored on the computer (the averaging program only works on single files). 8a reflects the averaged medium's ECG signal triggered by the medium's ECG R spike (intrapersonal average). 8c reflects the averaged sitter's ECG signal triggered by the sitter's ECG R spike (also intrapersonal average). However, 8b reflects the averaged medium's ECG signal triggered by the sitter's ECG R spike (interpersonal average).

Since the left panels reflect eyes closed resting baseline, it is not surprising that the medium's averaged intrapersonal ECG (8a left) is similar in shape to the sitter's averaged intrapersonal ECG (8c left). When the medium begins talking during the reading period, the medium's averaged intrapersonal ECG (8a right) has clearly changed compared to the sitter's averaged intrapersonal ECG (8c right), which also has changed somewhat. Analyses of variance with condition (base versus reading) and time (± the R spike) reveal highly significant interactions for both the medium's intrapersonal ($p < 0.00001$) and sitter's intrapersonal ($p < 0.00001$) changes, as well as between each other ($p < 0.0001$).

However, what is theoretically important is the comparison of the pattern of the interpersonal ECG findings—when evidence for the presence of the sitter's ECG in the medium's ECG is examined. During the eyes closed resting baseline (8b left), the trend was for a peak in the medium's ECG to be present when the sitter's R spike occurred. The question was, would this "synchrony" be altered during the readings? A stronger synchronized peak would imply increased interpersonal connection; a weaker peak (or loss of synchronized peak) would imply decreased interpersonal connection.

The pattern in 8b right indicates that the medium's ECG peak virtually disappeared around the time of the sitter's ECG R spike and moved to right and left of the sitter's ECG R spike. In other words, the timing of the medium's ECG R spike shifted so that the medium's heart began to beat before or after the sitter's heartbeat. This shift in the timing of the medium's heart away from the sitter's heart was observed in each of the five mediums. Analyses of variance revealed a

## Figures 8a, 8b, 8c

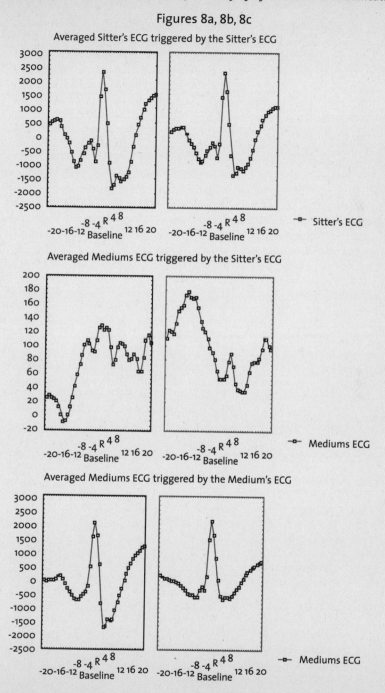

Averaged Sitter's ECG triggered by the Sitter's ECG

Averaged Mediums ECG triggered by the Sitter's ECG

Averaged Mediums ECG triggered by the Medium's ECG

highly significant condition (base versus reading) by time interaction (p < 0.0000001). The evidence suggests that at least concerning heart to heart synchrony, the medium's heart showed decreased synchrony (more precisely, a "dissynchrony") with the sitter's heart from the baseline to the reading period

The EEG findings can be summarized briefly. Only the medium's EEG was analyzed. Three sites (FP1, Figure 9a, C3, Figure 9b, and 01, Figure 9c) were analyzed during the baselines (left panel) and readings (right panel). The solid lines represent the averaged medium's ECG as expressed in the medium's EEG (interpersonal ECG-EEG). The dashed lines present the averaged sitter's ECG as expressed in the medium's EEG (interpersonal ECG-EEG).

The intrapersonal ECG-EEG patterns replicate previous findings (Russek and Schwartz, 1994; Song, Schwartz, and Russek, 1998). The synchronized ECG R spikes observed in the EEG are largest in O1 (9c) and smallest in FP1 (9a) during the eye closed resting baselines (solid lines, left panels). Interpersonally, there was little evidence for the sitter's ECG R spike in the medium's EEG during the baseline (dashed lines, left panels). During the reading period, the curves suggest that the medium's ECG R spike increased in its registration in FP1 (9a, right panel, solid line), as did the sitter's ECG R spike increase in its registration in FP1 (9a, right panel, dashed line). However, analysis of variance revealed that the condition (baseline versus reading) by time interaction was not significant (p > 0.40). There was no reliable evidence of the registration of the sitter's ECG R spike in the medium's EEG.

In sum, the medium-sitter ECG-ECG patterns indicate that during the readings, the medium's ECG shifted significantly; the medium's heartbeats decreased their temporal synchrony with the sitter's heartbeats as compared with the eyes closed resting baseline. The medium-sitter ECG-EEG patterns reveal no evidence that the mediums were registering the sitter's ECG in their EEGs, especially during the readings.

## Appendix B: Pretest Information Collected on All Six Deceased Persons

*Information about deceased friends and relatives*

Note–for ratings of Relationship, use the following:
0 = distant and cold
1 = moderately distant
2 = neutral
3 = moderately close
4 = very warm and close

Note–for ratings of Experience of Loss, use the following:
0 = relief at loss
1 = a little difficult
2 = moderately difficult
3 = very difficult and painful
4 = extremely emotionally painful

## Figures 9a, 9b, 9c

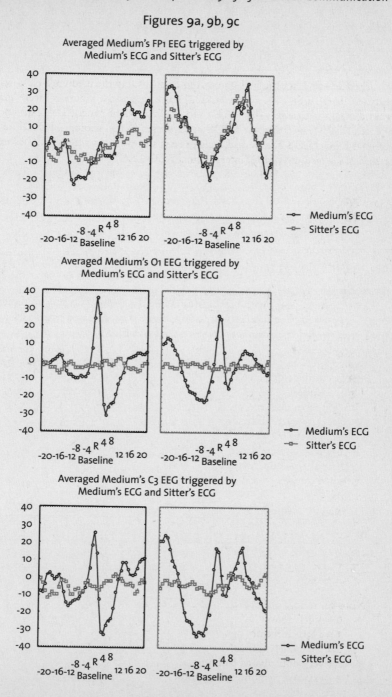

Averaged Medium's FP1 EEG triggered by
Medium's ECG and Sitter's ECG

Averaged Medium's O1 EEG triggered by
Medium's ECG and Sitter's ECG

Averaged Medium's C3 EEG triggered by
Medium's ECG and Sitter's ECG

Medium's ECG

Sitter's ECG

*Person #1*

Name _____ Sex _____ Relationship_____

Date of Death: Month_____ Year_____His/Her age at time of death _____years.

Cause of death _____

*Rating of Relationship* _____ *Rating of Experience of Loss* _____

Person's Height _____ Weight _____ Hair color _____

Occupation _____

Special Interests and Hobbies _____

Special memories:

Person's belief in survival after death (Circle one): Yes, Maybe, No, Don't know

Have you experienced a communication with this person after death? (Circle one):

Yes, Maybe, No, Explain

## Appendix C: Ratings During Experimental Sessions

### Instructions for "Sitters"

After each "sitting" with each medium, rate the medium on how accurate he or she was in receiving information from each of your deceased friends or relatives. Use the following numbers to rate your **overall impression** per deceased friend or relative:

    –1 Mistaken identity
     1 No mention
     2 Slight resemblance
     3 Moderate resemblance
     4 Strong resemblance
     5 Very strong resemblance
     6 Definite communication

| Deceased Person (fill in names) | Medium 1 | Medium 2 | Medium 3 | Medium 4 | Medium 5 |
|---|---|---|---|---|---|
|  |  |  |  |  |  |
|  |  |  |  |  |  |
|  |  |  |  |  |  |
|  |  |  |  |  |  |
|  |  |  |  |  |  |
|  |  |  |  |  |  |

On the following pages, please note any special signs, messages, memories, etc., below, for specific persons, when they happen, per medium.

## Appendix D: Control Subject's Questionnaire

*Note: Sixty-eight control subjects filled out the following questionnaire. The average accuracy for the first 11 questions, for the 68 subjects as a whole, was **56%**. Chance for yes/no questions is 50%. Performance on questions that required specific answers, such as question 12, was much lower than 50% (many questions were less than 5%). This questionnaire potentially overestimates actual guessing rates because it suggests areas where information should be requested. The mediums did not have these pointers.*

Name _____ Sex _____ Age_____

Can you guess information as well as a medium?

Please help us determine to what extent people can guess information about a person who is being "read" by a medium. Please answer each of the following questions. When you are finished, we will score your answers together and determine your overall accuracy.

The woman "sitter" is 46 years old; she experienced multiple deaths of loved ones during the past ten years. She lives in Arizona.

Check "alive" or "deceased" for each listing

|  | Alive | Deceased |
|---|---|---|
| 1. Husband | _____ | _____ |
| 2. Daughter | _____ | _____ |
| 3. Son | _____ | _____ |
| 4. Mother | _____ | _____ |
| 5. Father | _____ | _____ |
| 6. Mother-in-law | _____ | _____ |
| 7. Father-in-law | _____ | _____ |
| 8. Aunt | _____ | _____ |
| 9. Uncle | _____ | _____ |
| 10. Cat | _____ | _____ |
| 11. Dog | _____ | _____ |

Answer each of the following questions:

1. Who called the sitter "Patsy"?
2. Did sitter's child who died die after the father?
3. What is the sitter's child's initial?
4. What is the sitter's child's name?
5. What was the cause of the sitter's child's death?
6. Was the sitter's child happy?
7. Did the sitter's child have a sense of humor?
8. Did the sitter's child blame the mother (the sitter) for her/his condition?

9. Did the sitter's child blame the father for her/his condition?
10. Did the sitter's (her) mother die a long time ago?
11. Did her father die a long time ago?
12. Did her mother have any vices? If yes, what?
13. Did her father have any vices? If yes, what?
14. What was the cause of her mother's death?
15. What was the cause of her father's death?
16. Who named her (the sitter)?
17. Was she close with her father?
18. Was she close with her mother?
19. Was anything passed down from her father? If yes, what?
20. Did her father wear ties?
21. Did her father wear suits?
22. Did her father wear hats?
23. Did her father wear boots?
24. Did her father die slowly?
25. Who had false teeth?
26. What did she do with her teeth?
27. Who died first, mother or father?
28. Where did her father live?
29. Who gave a wedding band?
30. To whom was it given?
31. Where did her mother's parents live?
32. Who helped raise her?
33. Who was very good with her hands?
34. Who was very good with his hands?
35. Who loved to dance?
36. What kind of dancing did he/she do?
37. Who raised roses?
38. Who was a "pistol"?
39. Who received a family honor?
40. What was the honor?
41. Who did not meet the husband before the wedding?
42. Who attended the wedding purportedly from the spirit world?
43. Who could not walk well, from a stroke?
44. Who drove big vehicles?
45. Was her mother raised in the city?
46. What was her father's father's name?
47. Did her father wear a beard?
48. Was her mother a weak woman?
49. What male name was received by most of the mediums?
50. What is another male name received by most of the mediums?
51. What female name was received by most of the mediums?
52. What was the size of the dog?  small   medium   large
53. What was the color of the dog?  white with spots   brown   black and tan

54. What was the hair texture of the dog?   short hair   rough hair   fluffy hair
55. What was the aunt's name?
56. Did someone wear a military suit? If yes, who?
57. What strange thing happened in the house?
58. Who was believed to cause this event?
59. Who received a memorial?

How accurate do you think you were?   _____% (from 0 to 100%)
How accurate do you think the mediums were?   _____% (from 0 to 100%)
What is your belief about survival of consciousness after death? Circle one:
NO   Probably NO   Possibly NO   Maybe   Possibly YES   Probably YES   YES

# • APPENDIX D •

# Journal Article on Accuracy and Replicability of Anomalous Information Retrieval

This article on the Canyon Ranch experiment was submitted to *Journal of the Society for Psychical Research*, March 2001.

## ACCURACY AND REPLICABILITY OF ANOMALOUS INFORMATION RETRIEVAL: REPLICATION AND EXTENSION.

Gary E. R. Schwartz, Ph.D., Linda G. S. Russek, Ph.D., and Christopher Barentsen, B.A.

## Abstract

A century ago, William James and colleagues investigated a woman named Mrs. Piper who claimed to be able to receive information from departed individuals. James came to the conclusion that Piper was a genuine "white crow" who disproved the law that "all crows are black." Contemporary research appears to have uncovered more "white crows" that provide evidence of anomalous information retrieval. The present study investigated the ability of three research "mediums" (who purportedly receive the information) to obtain information regarding the deceased loved ones of five research "sitters" (subjects). The mediums were kept blind to the identity of the sitters. The mediums sat behind a floor-to-ceiling screen, with their backs to the screen facing video cameras. The mediums were not allowed to ask any questions, and the sitters never spoke. Transcripts were made from the recordings. The sitters scored all initials, names, historical facts, personal descriptions, and temperament descriptions (n = 528 items for 15 readings) using a −3 (definite miss) to +3 (definite hit) rating scale. When the sitters rated their own readings, the average percent +3 scores was 40%. When the sitters rated the readings of the other sitters (control readings), the value was 25% (p < 0.03). The findings replicate and extend James' hypothesis that information and energy, and potentially consciousness itself, can continue after physical death.

## Introduction

In the history of science, anomalous phenomena have sometimes played an important role in revising and expanding theories, methods, and applications in areas as wide ranging as physics, chemistry, biology, psychology, medicine, and astrophysics (Cardena, Lynn, and Krippner, 2000).

William James had a deep interest in anomalous phenomena in psychology and science in general. His volume *The Varieties of Religious Experience* is an acclaimed classic in academic psychology. However, James' empirical research on anomalous phenomena related to the possibility of the continuance of consciousness after physical death—one of the most challenging and controversial anomalous phenomena in psychology, science, and religion—is often ignored.

In Moore's *In Search of White Crows: Spiritualism, Parapsychology, and American Culture,* James' history of research on mediumship is succinctly reviewed:

> *In the fall of 1885, on the recommendation of his mother-in-law, James attended a séance conducted by a Boston medium, Mrs. Leonora Piper, who had only recently during the course of an illness, become aware of her powers. "My impression after this first visit," James wrote, "was that Mrs. P. was either possessed of supernormal powers, or knew the members of my wife's family by sight and had by some lucky coincidence become acquainted with a multitude of their domestic circumstances as to produce the startling impression which she did. My later knowledge of her sittings and personal acquaintance with her has led me* absolutely to reject the latter explanation, and to believe that she has supernormal powers." (italics added).

Moore goes on to write:

> *Mrs. Piper proved to be the white crow of a good many other people besides James. The SPR [S]ociety for Psychical Research› in effect hired her as a permanent object of research . . . there was no hint of fraud . . . Hodgson, when he started to arrange the literally thousands of sittings that she gave under the sponsorship of the SPR, had had her followed by a detective who reported that she was most certainly not part of any spy network through which mediums reputedly got information about prospective sitters . . . people who sat with her often came to her in disguise and always used false names. With few exceptions they agreed with Charles Eliot Norton, who after two sittings with Mrs. Piper in 1894, had said that "there was no question as to Mrs. Piper's good faith."*

One hundred years after James and SPR's comprehensive studies of Mrs. Piper, a group of new "white crows" has been investigated in a series of laboratory studies conducted at the University of Arizona (Schwartz et al, 1999; Schwartz and Russek, 1999; Schwartz, Russek, Nelson, and Barentsen, 2001; Schwartz and Russek, 2001). Given the controversial nature of the topic of mediumship and the possibility of the continuance of continuance beyond physical death, most conventional journals in the biological and behavioral sciences have been understandably reticent to publish papers in the area. For this reason, "alternative" journals such as the *Journal of the Society for Psychical Research* (published by SPR for over 100 years) (e.g., Schwartz, Russek, Nelson, and Barentsen, 2001) or the *Journal of Scientific Exploration* (e.g., Schwartz and Russek, 2000), have been the only avenues to date for such data to be published.

The experiment reported in this paper addresses the question of replicability of anomalous information retrieval in highly skilled mediums. Its methods and findings have important implications for consciousness studies, parapsychology, and the possibility of the continuance of consciousness after physical death.

## Methods

### Subjects

There were three "mediums" (people who purportedly receive information from individuals who have died; Laurie Campbell, John Edward, and Suzane Northrop). They had collaborated in two previous multi-medium experiments in the Human Energy Systems Laboratory (Schwartz, Russek, Nelson, and Barentsen, 2001). In addition, Campbell has collaborated in single- (e.g., Schwartz et al, 1999; Schwartz and Russek, 1999) and double-medium (e.g., Schwartz and Russek, 2001) studies in the laboratory as well.

[Note: these individuals are research mediums—they are willing to participate in studies that require substantial experimental control. No evidence of fraud or cold reading has been observed with these select research mediums.]

There were five "sitters" (all female, ranging in age from 20s to 50s). All had two or more deceased loved ones with strong emotional bonds. The identities of the sitters were kept secret from the mediums (described in more detail below). Moreover, the experimenters were kept blind to most of the specific information about the deceased loved ones of the five research sitters until after the data had been collected and the scoring of the transcripts had been completed by the sitters.

[Note: these individuals are research sitters who are willing to perform careful and time-consuming scoring of the transcripts. All have undergraduate degrees. Two have master's degrees and work as research coordinators at the University of Arizona.]

### Design

The single-blind research design consisted of two parts:

*(1) Sitter-Silent Condition:* During this ten-minute period, the mediums were requested to speak out loud whatever information they received about the deceased loved ones of the sitters. The mediums were not allowed to ask any ques-

tions of the sitters. The mediums were tested in separate rooms, facing video cameras and backup tape recorders. They sat with their backs to a floor-to-ceiling screen that separated them from the sitters and experimenters. The mediums could not see or hear the sitters. Hence, the mediums were blind to age, sex, appearance, non-verbal visual cues, and verbal cues.

(2) *Questioning Condition:* During this ten-minute period, the mediums were allowed to ask simple yes/no questions of the sitters. However, the sitters were still not allowed to speak. Instead, the sitters nodded their heads yes or no, and the experimenters spoke yes or no. Hence, the only voices the mediums heard during the course of the experiment were the voices of the experimenters.

Schwartz was the experimenter with Edward, Russek was the experimenter with Campbell, and Barentsen was the experimenter with Northrop. Hence, a given medium heard only the voice of one experimenter during the data collection.

Sitters were sequestered in a separate room. They were escorted to a given room by the appropriate experimenter. Since there were five sitters and three mediums, there were at least two sitters waiting in the sitter room at all times.

## Control for Blinding

The order of sessions (each sitter was tested with each medium) was determined the morning of the day the data were to be collected. Hence, even if the mediums had somehow obtained prior information about the identity of the sitters, the information would not have been useful during the sitter-silent condition, since the mediums would not know when to apply what information [Note: if the mediums had somehow obtained detailed information about each of the five sitters by phone tapping and detectives ahead of time, and since the mediums received yes/no feedback during the questioning periods, they could have possibly figured out, by the end of the fourth reading, who the last sitter would be.]

The most compelling data of anomalous information retrieval comes from the sitter-silent period. These are the data are reported here.

## Scoring of the Transcripts

The fifteen audio tapes (five sitters times three mediums) were professionally transcribed. The third author extracted all initials, names, historical factors, personal descriptions, temperaments, and "other" statements (e.g., purported opinions stated by deceased persons to the mediums), and placed them in Excel spreadsheets. The five sitters were required to score every item using a −3 to +3 scale, where −3 was a definite miss, −2 a probable miss, −1 a possible miss, 0 a maybe miss/maybe hit, +1 a possible hit, +2 a probable hit, and +3 a definite hit. Sitters were encouraged to give conservative ratings (i.e. to use less positive numbers unless they were sure of a given rating). If they did not know whether a given item was correct or not, they were to leave it blank. The three experimenters also scored the 15 readings as if the information applied to them.

## Results

### Total Items Averaged over Readings and Mediums

Figure 1 displays the total numbers of items generated by the three mediums during the sitter-silent condition, averaged over the five readings. Since the purpose of this paper is not to focus on the individual personalities and performances of the mediums, the mediums are simply referred to as 1, 2, and 3.

It can be seen that medium 1 generated substantially more items (approximately 60 items per reading on the average), compared with mediums 2 and 3, who averaged around 25 and 20 items each session, respectively. The total number of items generated during the silent periods for the three mediums over the 15 readings was 528.

Figure 2 displays the number of items over the course of the five readings (from the first of the day to the last), averaged over the three mediums. The mediums predicted that they would tire over the course of the five sessions. The data are consistent with their hypothesis.

### Accuracy of Ratings Comparing + 3 (Hits) and −3 (Misses)

When the percent number of hits (+3) and misses (−3) was examined comparing when the sitters rated their own three readings (called "readings" on the graphs)

## Figure 1

### Average Number of Items per Reading for Mediums 1 –3

### Medium Main Effect

$F_{(2,12)} = 14.07; p < 0.0007$

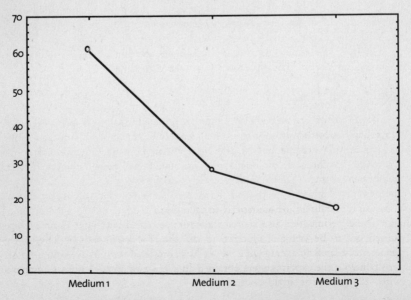

## Figure 2

Change over Readings in Number of Items Averaged over Mediums 1–3

Readings Main Effect

$F_{(4,8)} = 4.80; p < 0.0286$

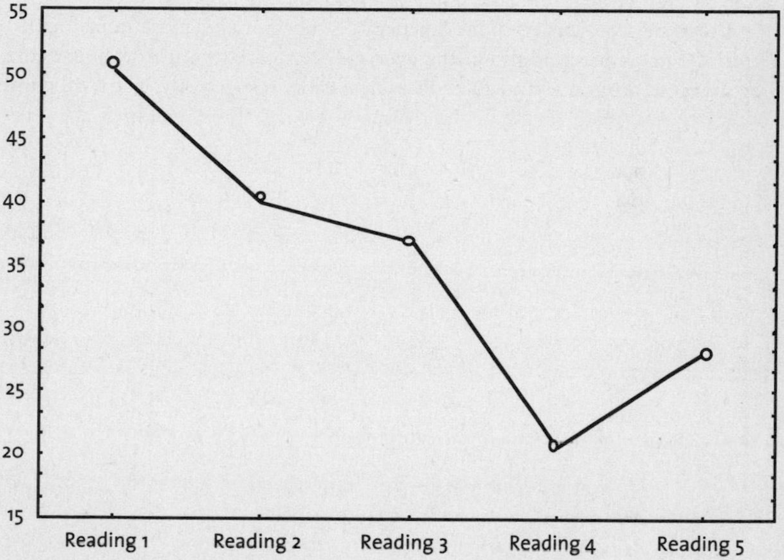

versus when the sitters rated the other twelve readings (called "controls" on the graphs), was there (1) a greater number of hits for their own readings compared to the controls, and (2) a reduced number of misses for their own readings compared to the controls?

As displayed in Figure 3, it can be seen that the percent hits (shown on the left) was higher for the actual readings (40%, circles with solid lines compared to 25%, squares with dashed lines) than for the control readings, and this pattern was reversed for the misses (29% versus 42%). The total difference was 28% (15% increase for hits and 13% decease for misses).

In terms of actual numbers of items per reading, the average number of +3 hits was 12 for the actual readings versus 6 for controls. The average number of –3 misses per reading was 7 for actual readings versus 13 for controls. Interestingly, the number of blanks (unscorable items as perceived by the sitters) was almost identical for readings and controls (6 in each case.)

The experimenters also scored the entire set of 15 readings. Their averages turned out to be virtually identical to the sitters' control ratings. The experimenters obtained an average of 25% +3 hits compared with 25% +3 hits for sitter's controls; the experimenters obtained an average of 55% –3 misses compared with 42% misses for sitters' controls.

## Figure 3

Comparison of Readings and Controls for Percent Hits and Misses

2-way Interaction

$F_{(1,23)} = 5.34; p < 0.0302$

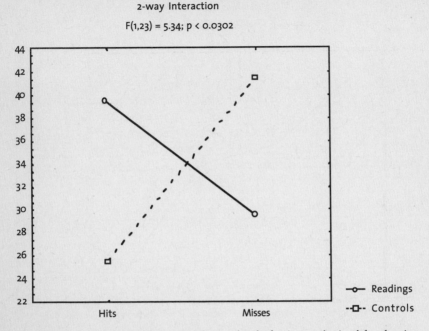

In sum, increased accuracy was observed only for items obtained for the sitters' own readings. This effect was observed to various degrees across the categories of information.

The mediums varied in their percent accuracy. Medium 1 averaged 40% accuracy, medium 2 averaged 28% accuracy, and medium 3 averaged 54% accuracy. Since medium 1 had more than twice as many items as the other two mediums, and medium 3 had the least number of items, it appears that the mediums' accuracy is not a simple function of sheer number of items generated per se.

Nonetheless, each medium showed discrimination in terms of reading versus control ratings. These findings are displayed in Figure 4.

It can be seen that +3 hits were consistently higher for the sitter's own readings compared to control ratings (solid versus dashed lines, right box), and −3 misses were consistently lower for sitter's own readings compared to control ratings (solid versus dashed lines, left box).

When the data are averaged across the three mediums, every sitter has higher ratings scores for their own ratings compared to the controls.

### Strings of Hits: Information Packets
The ratings of individual items do not address the observation that the mediums sometimes obtained strings or chains of hits that represented themes and mean-

## Figure 4

Comparison of Readings and Controls

for Mediums 1 - 3

for Percent Hits and Percent Misses

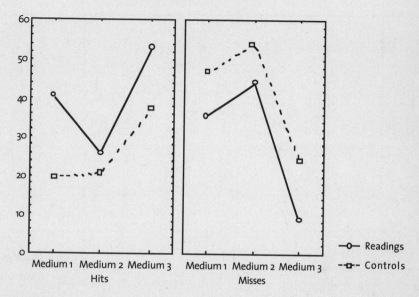

ingful content. A new scoring procedure was implemented where sitters and experimenters searched for three or more consecutive hits that reflected a meaningful theme or content group.

For the experimenters, the category "readings" referred to the five readings for the specific medium they served as experimenter. The "control" category referred to the ten readings for the other two mediums. This made it possible to look for potential *subtle* expression of information reflecting the experimenter's deceased loved ones entering into their respective medium's readings.

As can be seen in Figure 5, the primary effect appeared for the sitters themselves (solid lines). Sitters (blue lines) detected approximately two information packets per reading on the average for their own readings (left circle) compared with approximately 0.5 information packets per reading on the average for the control readings (right circle) (interaction $p < 0.01$). To make sure that the sitters and experimenters used the same criteria, each person (five sitters and three experimenters) had to (1) present to the entire group every possible information packet they scored in all 15 readings, and (2) justify inclusion or exclusion. The group as a whole pushed the sitters to include as few information packets as possible (to deflate their scores), and pushed the experimenters to include as many information packets as possible (to inflate their scores). Despite these efforts, the experi-

## Figure 5

**Number of Information Packets in Readings and Controls for Sitters and Experimenters**

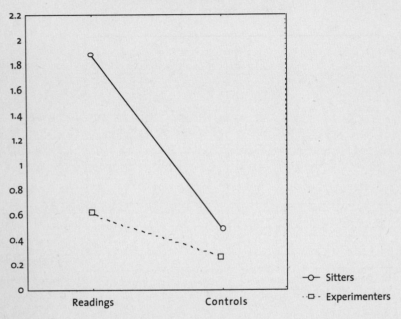

menters clearly detected a minimal number of possible information packets (dashed line, left and right squares), even during their "readings."

### Supplementary Analyses: Potential Parallels Between Sitters and Experimenters

There appeared to be an interesting trend in the experimenters' data. Given the small sample size (three experimenters), the analyses presented below should be viewed as possible suggestions for future research.

The experimenters scored an average of 0.6 information packets per reading (which turns out to be more than one information packet for every two readings) for the readings they witnessed with the mediums they supervised, versus 0.3 information packets per reading (which turns out to less than one information packet for every three readings) for the readings of the other experimenters' mediums.

Since information packets were composed of individual items, a subsequent analysis was performed comparing the sitters' percent +3 hits and –3 misses with the experimenters' percent +3 hits and –3 misses, separately for readings and readings and controls.

In Figure 6, the left box displays the data for the sitters (a smaller version of Figure 3 previously); the right box displays parallel the data for the experimenters.

## Figure 6

Comparison of Sitters and Experimenters

for Readings and Controls

for Hits and Misses

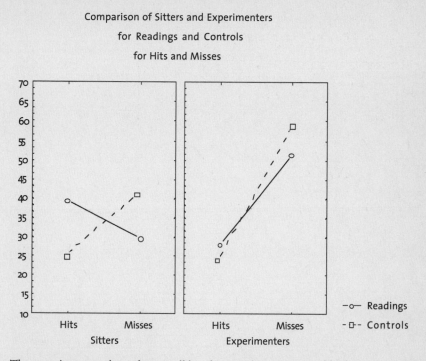

The experimenters show the overall low hits (mid 20s range) and high misses (mid 50s range) mentioned previously.

However, when the percent scores for the controls are subtracted from the percent scores for the readings, separately for the sitters (left) and experimenters (right), it can be seen that the pattern of subtractions is similar (though clearly smaller) for the experimenters compared with the sitters.

Figure 7 indicates that the solid line, for the hits, is higher than 0 for both the sitters and the experimenters, and the dashed line, for the misses, is lower than 0 for both the sitters and the experimenters.

Does this apparently replicated pattern for both the sitters and experimenters reflect a subtle scoring bias? Or was anomalous information "bleeding" through from the minds of the sitters and the experimenters (telepathy with the living) and/or from the "spirit" world (the continuance of consciousness hypothesis) occurring for both sitters and experimenters? This is an important question for future research.

## Discussion

The present findings suggest that under controlled experimental conditions where research mediums are (1) blind to the identity of sitters and (2) they are not al-

## Figure 7

Change in Percent Responses: Readings minus Controls

for Sitters and Experimenters

for Hits and Misses

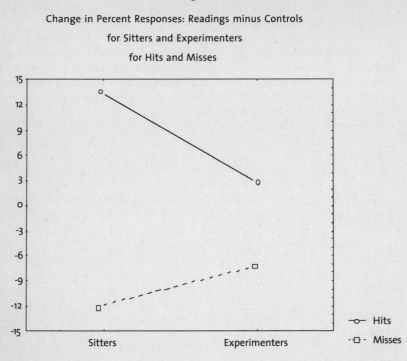

lowed to ask questions of the sitters, they can obtain information that is consistently scored as more accurate (higher percents of +3 hits, lower percents of –3 misses, and higher numbers of information packets) when sitters score their own readings compared with when they score the readings of other sitters (i.e. controls).

The percent accuracy scores for the readings (40% for +3 hits) are higher than the percent accuracy scores for the controls (25% for + 3 hits). The 40% for +3 hits is also higher than the 29% for the –3 misses. However, the averages do not express the richness of the actual transcripts and "anomalies within the anomalies." The following example illustrates some of the novel observations that emerge in this area of research.

### Example of Actual Content

For the third sitter, medium 2 reported receiving information about a deceased grandmother who was very loving (general information that could apply to most people). However, medium 2 also reported (1) that the grandmother brought "daisies to the sitter's mother's wedding" (a unique set of specific information that was true), (2) that the grandmother had two dogs, a large black poodle and a large white poodle (highly specific information that was true), and (3) that the "white one tore up the house" (unusual information that was true). The accuracy of the information concerning the grandmother (the primary deceased person in this reading) was rated by the sitter above 80%.

More interesting is the information obtained during the fourth sitter's reading. Medium 2 received *nothing* for this sitter (i.e., 0%, which obviously lowered the average percent +3 accuracy for the entire experiment as well as medium 2's overall accuracy score of 28%). Medium 2 reported that he could not receive any information for this sitter. Instead, Medium 2 reported that he was receiving continued information for the previous sitter!

Medium 2 said that "the grandmother is still here." Medium 2 proposed that the previous sitter was not with another medium at that moment (it turned out he was correct), which was his explanation for why the grandmother was still in his presence. Medium 2 reported hearing the song "On the Good Ship Lollipop" and "Sabrina, the teenage witch."

After the fourth (and seemingly failed) reading was completed, the experimenter (Schwartz) brought the sitter back to the room where the sitters were sequestered. To his surprise, he discovered that the previous sitter was still there.

When he questioned this sitter, she informed him (with emotion) that (1) she had curly brown hair as a child, and sang and danced Shirley Temple songs with her grandmother, including "On the Good Ship Lollipop." (2) the sitter's name was Sabrina, and (3) when she was a teenager, some kids teased her about being "Sabrina, the teenage witch," and she went to her grandmother for solace.

Medium 2's specific prediction and information were confirmed. The only information previously known by the experimenter was that the third sitter's name was Sabrina and that she had a deceased grandmother. This is only one of numerous remarkable and convincing examples of apparent genuine anomalous information retrieval in the current experiment.

## Future Research

It is possible to extend the sitter-silent paradigm to create double-blind and even triple-blind studies. A multi-center, triple-blind study has been approved by the University IRB committee, and the pilot study is currently being conducted. Sitters are selected by their respective universities, and only the investigators in each center know the identities of their respective sitters. The mediums are located in various parts of the country. A research coordinator works with the investigator to schedule long distance phone appointments.

At the appointed time, the research coordinator calls the investigator. The research coordinator's phone is then placed on mute, and the sitter is asked to hold the silenced phone to his or her ear for the duration of the sitter-silent reading. The medium is then called. The medium speaks into the phone for ten to fifteen minutes. The information is tape recorded. Note that the medium never sees or hears the sitter, and the sitter never sees or hears the medium (they are blind to each other). Also, note that although the research coordinator is not blind to the identity of the medium, he or she is blind to the identity of the sitter (hence triple-blind).

When all the data are collected, the sitters are mailed two sets of transcripts. One set is of the transcripts obtained from their personal readings with the various mediums; the other set is of someone else's set of readings with the various mediums. Hence, the sitters are blind to which readings are theirs. All items are scored. In addition, the sitters are asked to select which readings they judge to be their personal readings.

If positive findings are obtained, possible conventional explanations of cold reading (magician tricks used by fake mediums), sitter rater bias (though possible in the previous studies, is highly improbable—e.g., consider the grandmother information reported above), experimenter bias, and guessing, will be ruled out in the triple-blind studies. Anomalous information retrieval will require consideration of alternative hypotheses, including (1) telepathy with the physically living, (2) so-called "super-psi" hypotheses such as precognition (Braude, 1992) and extended systemic memory resonance (Schwartz and Russek, 2001), and (3) continuance of consciousness after death.

### Integrity of Research Mediums, Past and Present

As stated above, after many investigations with Mrs. Piper, William James came to the conclusion that "I should be willing now to stake as much money on Mrs. Piper's honesty as on that of anyone I know, and I am quite satisfied to leave my reputation for wisdom or folly, so far as human nature is concerned, to stand or fall by this declaration."

As a result of conducting multiple experiments with Laurie Campbell, John Edward, and Suzane Northrop (who have been putting their professional careers on the line to be investigated in a university laboratory) over the past three years, we should be willing to follow James and state that concerning their behavior in our laboratory, we are "willing now to stake as much money on Campbell, Edward, and Northrop's honesty as on that of anyone we know, and we are quite satisfied to leave our reputations for wisdom or folly, so far as human nature is concerned, to stand or fall by this declaration."

The challenge for contemporary psychology, neuroscience, and consciousness studies is to consider the implications of such findings for understanding mechanisms of consciousness and their implications for the continuance of consciousness hypothesis.

## References

Braude, S.E. (1992). Survival or super-psi? *Journal of Scientific Exploration.* 6,2:127–144.

Cardena, E, Lynn, S.J., and Krippner, S. (2000). *Varieties of Anomalous Experience: Examining the Scientific Evidence.* Washington, DC: American Psychological Association.

Russek, L.G.S., Schwartz, G.E.R., Russek, E., and Russek, H.I. (hypothesized) (1999). A possible approach for researching purported spirit communication: An empirical-anecdotal investigation. *Advances in Mind-Body Medicine.* 15,4: 295–301.

Schwartz, G.E.R., and Russek, L.G.S. (1999). *The Living Energy Universe: A Fundamental Discovery That Transforms Science and Medicine.* Charlottesville, VA: Hampton Roads Publishing.

Schwartz, G.E.R., Russek, L.G.S., et al. (1999). Potential medium to departed to medium communication of pictorial information: Exploratory evidence consistent with psi and survival of consciousness. *The Noetics Journal.* 2,3: 283–294.

Schwartz, G.E.R., and Russek, L.G.S. (2001, in press). Evidence of anomalous information retrieval between two research mediums: Telepathy, network memory resonance, and continuance of consciousness. *Journal of the Society for Psychical Research* (Reprinted in this book as Appendix E.)

Schwartz, G.E.R., Russek, L.G.S., Nelson, L.A. and Barentsen, C. (2001 in press). Accuracy and Replicability of Anomalous After-Death Communication Across Highly Skilled Mediums. *The Journal of the Society for Psychical Research.* 65, 862:1–25. (Reprinted in this book as Appendix C.)

# · APPENDIX E ·

# Journal Article on the Campbell "White Crow" Readings

This report of the Campbell "White Crow" readings is in press for publication in the *Journal of The Society of Psychical Research*, 2001.

### EVIDENCE OF ANOMALOUS INFORMATION RETRIEVAL BETWEEN TWO RESEARCH MEDIUMS: TELEPATHY, NETWORK MEMORY RESONANCE, AND CONTINUANCE OF CONSCIOUSNESS

*Gary E. Schwartz, Ph.D., and Linda G. Russek, Ph.D., Human Energy Systems Laboratory, University of Arizona.*

## Abstract

Can mediums receive highly accurate and specific information under laboratory-controlled blind conditions: (1) prior to the scheduled time of the reading and (2) during the reading in the absence of visual, auditory, or other potential sensory cues? A medium who for the last three years has been participating in the research conducted at the Human Energy Systems Laboratory at the University of Arizona took part in a novel experiment with a unique sitter she did not know. The medium was in Tucson, Arizona; the sitter (also a medium) was in Los Angeles, California. The experimental design involved three phases: Phase 1, a pre-reading contemplation period where the medium attempted to receive information about the sitter's deceased loved ones before the reading began; Phase 2, a sitter-silent period where the telephone was on mute so that the sitter could not hear the information received by the medium; and Phase 3, an actual telephone reading involving dialogue between the medium and the sitter. Specific and accurate information regarding names and relationships was obtained during Phases 1 and

2, while information obtained during Phase 3 included four pieces of specific information unknown to the sitter and later confirmed. The number of names and other striking details provided in the reading rules out the possibility that the results are due to chance (p less than 1 in 2.6 trillion), even on the most conservative estimate. Stringent precautions were taken to rule out fraud, cold reading, vague information, statistical coincidence, selective sitter memory, and sitter rater bias. It is postulated that three anomalous mechanisms may be involved: telepathy with the living, network memory resonance with the living (a super-psi hypothesis), and the existence of intentional, organizing consciousness.

> *In order to disprove the law that all crows are black, it is enough to find one white crow.*
> WILLIAM JAMES, M.D.

## Introduction

Contemporary research on anomalous information retrieval has been advanced through the cooperation of research-oriented mediums with exceptional talent and integrity and scientists open to exploring their abilities (Schwartz et al, 1999; Schwartz and Russek, 1999; Schwartz, Russek, Nelson, and Barentsen, 2001; Schwartz, Russek, and Barentsen, 2001).

In order to establish anomalous information retrieval, it is essential to rule out (1) conventional sources of information (e.g., visual and auditory) obtained intentionally (e.g., through fraud or cold reading) or unintentionally (e.g., via subtle cueing associated with the sitters breathing); (2) experimenter bias or error; and (3) rater bias on the part of the sitters (e.g., selective memory effects or inflated ratings of information) (reviewed in Gauld, 1984).

Research in the Human Energy Systems Laboratory (HESL) has employed single-blind experiments where in the first part of the session, research mediums (i.e. mediums who engage in controlled research studies) are completely blind to the sitters (e.g., Schwartz, Russek, Nelson, and Barentsen, 2001; Schwartz, Russek, and Barentsen, 2001). The mediums do not see or hear the sitter. The mediums must report information out loud in the first ten minutes with no knowledge of the sitters' age, sex, appearance, tone of voice, personal history, and beliefs. Double-blind experiments where the sitters (1) do not hear the readings when they are performed and (2) later score blinded transcripts (containing their personal readings and control readings of other sitters) are ongoing in HESL.

In Schwartz, Russek, Nelson, and Barentsen (2001), five mediums were investigated. We suggested that "the particular mediums participating in this research may be examples of five 'white crows' of anomalous information retrieval." Extending James's metaphor further, we suggest that the particular research design and reading reported here may be an example of a "white crow" reading in mediumship science. We also believe that the present findings are consistent with the frequently quoted recommendation that "extraordinary claims require extraordinary evidence."

The single blind sitter-silent paradigm (termed the Russek procedure in

HESL) was extended by Laurie Campbell (LC), chair of our mediumship research committee. LC began doing private readings in the summer of 2000 and wished to extend the Russek procedure to her private practice. It occurred to LC that, during her pre-reading contemplation sessions (the term "contemplation" was proposed by Stanley Krippner; LC calls them "meditations"), which regularly occur approximately one-half hour before a scheduled reading, she could request information purportedly from the sitter's departed loved ones *before the reading began.*

LC noticed that she typically received specific information—names, relationships, causes of death, personal description—that she could record prior to each reading and then confirm or disconfirm, item by item, with the sitter in the first part of the actual reading. At the time this report was written, LC had recorded data on over 100 readings using this pre-reading contemplation procedure (termed the Campbell procedure in HESL), her accuracy ratings ranging from 50% to 95%.

We learned of her procedure in December 2000 and decided to conduct a controlled blinded laboratory experiment to investigate her claims. The design of the experiment is described below, followed by the data from one reading with a unique sitter whose evidence is so extraordinary as to deserve special scrutiny.

A full report summarizing group statistics is in preparation. Statistically significant evidence for anomalous information retrieval was found for each of the three sitters investigated in the experiment. However, it is the uniqueness and extraordinarily evidential nature of the particular reading highlighted in this detailed report that justifies focusing on this "white crow" research reading. We have tried to report all potential sources of error and/or fraud in the conduct of this experiment, letting the reader reach his or her own conclusion about possible sources of contamination in the design.

## Experimental Design

### Selection of Sitters

Sitters chosen by the experimenters (the authors, GERS and LGSR) needed to meet the following criteria: (1) experience of significant personal losses of beloved individuals; (2) sincere interest in the possibility of a spiritual reality and the survival of consciousness hypothesis; (3) maturity, integrity, and committment to the rigors of experimental research; and (4) willingness to score information collected in both the single-blind and double-blind conditions after the readings were conducted and transcripts were prepared.

The medium (LC) was blind to the selection and identities of the specific sitters.

The particular sitter whose data are reported here, George Dalzell (GD), is (1) professionally trained as a psychiatric social worker in Los Angeles County in California, (2) comes from a highly educated academic family, (3) is deeply interested in research, and (4) has validated data from four deceased individuals (described below). Moreover, he has secretly been a medium for the past few years since the death of a dear friend, Michael (M), who was one of the four persons GD invited to serve as "departed hypothesized co-investigators" in the present experiment (Schwartz et al, 1999; Russek et al, 1999).

This last fact is especially important, because GD has extensive data documented in a forthcoming book (Dalzell, 2001) that provides evidential support for the continued existence of M.

At the time of testing, LC and GD had never met (in person or by telephone, letter, or e-mail). The mediums were willing to have their phone records examined, although the possibility that they could have used phone booths or phones of friends cannot be eliminated.

LC had been told of GD's existence (the authors of this report mentioned to her GD's interest in HESL's research a few months earlier). However, she was not informed that GD would be one of the sitters selected to participate in this experiment, nor was she ever informed that GD would be considered to serve as a sitter in any laboratory investigations. LC had not been shown GD's manuscript (Dalzell, 2001). The manuscript was kept out of sight of LC. A number of details obtained by LC in the readings were not only absent from the book, but they were unknown to GD prior to the readings. Hence, the contention that LC somehow read the manuscript cannot explain the evidence.

GD knew of LC's existence (GD had read reports from the laboratory describing research with LC; Schwartz et al, 1999; Schwartz and Russek, 1999; Schwartz, Russek, Nelson, and Barentsen, 2001). GD was told that LC *might* be the medium in this experiment (he knows HESL is working with a number of research mediums). Given GD's academic background and professional standing, as well as his personal interest in this research area, the opportunity to participate as a research sitter in this experiment was of professional and personal significance to him. Engaging in fraud in the laboratory, if detected, would greatly jeopardize his career as a social worker as well as a medium. He was made aware (as are all mediums and sitters) that if fraud was detected, it would be exposed.

## Design

The experiment was conducted in Tucson, Arizona. LC was flown in from Irvine, California, to participate in the research. The sitters were located in Arizona and California. All readings were conducted over the telephone. Distances between the medium and the sitters ranged from approximately ten miles to greater than one thousand miles.

The sitters were telephoned by GERS and LGSR and invited to participate. The procedures were described in detail, including the pre-reading contemplation periods and the sitter-silent periods. Sitters were encouraged to attempt to personally connect with their deceased loved ones and invite them to communicate with LC prior to their scheduled appointment times with LC. Sitters were told that, as in our previous experiments (Schwartz et al, 1999; Schwartz and Russek, 1999; Schwartz, Russek, Nelson, and Barentsen, 2001; Schwartz, Russek, and Barentsen, 2001), LC would be completely blind to their identity.

The sitters were reminded of the need for absolute integrity, and that they would be required later to carefully score transcripts from the readings. They understood that some of the transcripts they would recognize, and others they would not (Phases 1 and 2 described below). We explained that they would not be told ahead of time which of the blinded transcripts were their transcripts until they had completed the scoring and we had analyzed the data.

LC stayed at the home of GERS and LGSR for the weekend of the experiment. When one of the experimenters was speaking with a potential sitter on the telephone in a given room (to schedule an appointment), the other experimenter was with LC in another room, thus ensuring that LC was not overhearing the phone conversation. From the time that sitters were selected to the completion of the experiment, LC never left the home except when she was in the company of the experimenters.

Since the exceptional nature of the data reported here was not anticipated ahead of time, the experiment did not include additional desirable controls such as independent observers of all the procedures to establish that the experimenters were not engaged in conscious or unconscious deception. However, the experimenters are exceptionally sensitive to the possibility of unconscious "leakage," if not conscious collusion. It was deemed more effective to watch LC in order to rule out any possibility of the LC communicating with the sitters—the sitters were contacted only one day before data collection to participate in the experiment—than to have LC staying in a hotel away from the experimenters.

Readings were scheduled for specific times (e.g., 2:30, 4:30, 6:00 P.M.). The procedure for each reading was as follows:

## Phase 1: Pre-Reading (Campbell) Procedure

One-half hour before a scheduled time, LC would conduct her contemplation period, in seclusion and silence. She would write down the information she received during the pre-reading period. This phase eliminates all possible visible and auditory cues (as well as olfactory cues) and therefore definitively eliminates conventional explanations of cold reading, subtle cueing, and medium fraud, as possible explanations of the findings.

## Phase 2: Sitter-Silent (Russek) Procedure

At the appointed time, depending upon the specific sitter, either the sitter telephoned the experimenters (GESR answered the phone) or the experimenter telephoned the sitter. A Sony digital video tape recorder was used to record the initial reception of the sitter and the conduct of the Russek Procedure.

The sitter was reminded that the telephone would be placed on mute (hence the sitters would not be able to hear LC speaking) and that they were to hold the telephone to their ear for the duration of the ten-minute sitter-silent period. We confirmed empirically that the mute button worked effectively, and that the sitters could not detect words spoken by GERS before he handed the muted telephone to LC. Moreover, LC sat a few feet from the answering machine that contained the mute button. She held the phone with her left hand and wrote notes with her right hand. *There was no possibility of her secretly attempting to manipulate the mute button.*

When the telephone was placed on mute, it was handed to LC. Since the sitter's telephone was not placed on mute (not all sitters had a mute button, and we wanted the sitters to focus their attention as if the telephone was being used in this phase of the reading), sporadic noises generated by the sitter and his or her environment could sometimes be heard by LC if she held the telephone in a normal listening and speaking position. The sporadic noises were distracting to LC. Hence, LC held the telephone with the instrument turned away from her ear, thus minimizing potential distractions.

One reviewer suggested that LC could have used cues such as breathing coming from the phone as feedback for cold reading. However, since the sitters could *not* hear LC, the "feedback" would have to be from sitters *unconsciously receiving information from LC via telepathy*, and then communicating agreement through subtle changes in breathing. This speculation would be a novel super-psi cold reading–type hypothesis.

The camera recorded the Russek procedure, during which time LC shared out loud the impressions she was receiving. At no time did the experimenters refer to the sitters by name, and LC had not yet heard the sitter's voice. Phase 2 lasted approximately 15 minutes. The blind sitter-silent phase eliminates possible visible and olfactory cues (and hence cold reading, subtle cueing, and fraud) as well as useful auditory cues, since the sitter could not hear LC, and LC was not using sporadic distracting auditory cues to shape her responses.

## Phase 3: The Actual Reading Procedure

When the sitter-silent period was completed, the experimenter took the telephone from LC, turned off the mute button, and started a Radio Shack telephone tape recorder that recorded both LC's voice and the sitter's voice. With the telephone on mute, LC's voice could not be recorded on the telephone tape recorder. However, LC's voice was recorded via the auditory channel of the video tape recorder.

The experimenter explained to the sitter that she or he would now hear LC's voice, and that LC would explain how she conducted a normal reading. LC then introduced herself and explained how she conducted a normal medium-sitter dialogue reading. LC then read, item by item, the content received during the pre-reading contemplation, and asked the sitter to confirm, question, or deny the information. Hence, the sitter was not blind to the pre-reading contemplation content (the Campbell procedure) in this experiment.

However, we requested that LC not read the sitter-silent period content (the Russek procedure) in this experiment. This material was to be saved for later blind scoring by the sitters.

As will be discussed below, the pre-reading (Campbell) procedure can be used for blind scoring by sitters as well. However, this was not the purpose of the present experiment. The purpose was to document whether the pre-reading procedure generated discrete and specific accurate information under single-blind laboratory conditions.

The material obtained during Phase 3 (the actual reading) is obviously complicated by the dialogue established between the medium and the sitter. However, as will be clear, the content received during the actual reading complemented and extended the content received during Phases 1 and 2, thus providing compelling supportive evidence for anomalous information retrieval by LC.

## Results for GD

### Names and Relationships for Phases 1 and 2

The experimenters knew that GD planned to invite M as a departed hypothe-sized co-investigator. However, the experimenters were blind to the other individ-uals whom GD purportedly invited to participate in the research.

Subsequently, according to GD, he invited four specific individuals: (1) M, (2) a deceased aunt named Alice, A, (3) his father, Bob, B, and (4) another close friend, Jerry, J.

During Phases 1 (pre-reading) and 2 (sitter-silent) combined, LC reported:

(1) that she was being told that this reading was for someone named George (GD),
(2) that there was a deceased friend named Michael (M),
(3) that there was a deceased person named Bob (B) (relationship not specified),
(4) that there was a deceased friend named Jerry (J),
(5) that there was someone with a strange name that sounded like "Talya," "Tiya," and "Tilya" (T) (LC's phonetic spellings of the name she heard),
(6) that there was a deceased person named Alice (A) (relationship speci-fied in Phase 3)
(7) that there was a deceased dog whose name began with an S.

However, LC ended Phase 2 with a statement indicating that the primary de-ceased person for this particular sitter was a male named Michael (M). [In further discussion, names will be indicated by initials.] LC provided full names, not ini-tials, for these individuals in Phases 1 and 2.

Table 1 lists all names and initials recorded in writing by LC during Phases 1–3 (save for three scientists' names, mentioned for completeness in the Dis-cussion section). The sitter used a 0–3 ratings scale: (0) unknown to sitter (pos-sibly a mistake, e.g., Joyce), (1) known but not close—e.g., GD knows of a Shermer but doubts that Sherm (LC's spelling) is important to the reading, (2) known and moderately close—e.g., sitter knows a Fred and LC might be refer-ring to him, and (3) known and close (e.g., the names GD, M, B, A, J, Talya, S, and K).

The names of the four people specifically invited by GD—M, A, B, and J—were received by LC during Phases 1 and 2. In addition, it turned out to be factu-ally correct that GD had a friend with the unusual name that sounded like Talya (T) (GD called her Tallia) and that GD had a beloved dog with an S name (LC's guess about the actual name was similar in sound but not precisely correct).

## Table 1. Summary of Names, Relationships, and Ratings

| Name | Relationship | Living/Decesed | Rating (0–3) |
| --- | --- | --- | --- |
| **PRE-READING** | | | |
| George (G) ** | Self | Living | 3 |
| Jerry (J)** | Friend | Deceased | 3 |
| John | Great-grandfather | Deceased | 2 |
| B name | | | |
| (Becky, Barbara, Betty) | Friend | Living | 1 |
| Maureen | Friend | Living | 1 |
| Robert/Bob (B) ** | Father | Deceased | 3 |
| Talya/Tily/Tilya (T)** | Friend | Living | 3 |
| S (Suzane) (S)** | Dog | Deceased | 2+ |
| Sherm? (LC spelled) | Known | Living | 1 |
| | | | |
| **SITTER-SILENT** | | | |
| Michael (M)** | Friend | Deceased | 3 |
| Jerry (J)** | Friend | Deceased | 3 |
| Joyce | —— | —— | 0 |
| Fred | Friend | Living | 2 |
| Francis ** | Friend | Living | 3 |
| Albert or Alfred ** | Friend of friend | Deceased | 3 |
| Alice (A) ** | Aunt | Deceased | 3 |
| Elaine | —— | —— | 0 |
| | | | |
| **ACTUAL READING** | | | |
| Michael (M)** | Friend | Deceased | 3 |
| Marcus ** | Friend | Living | 3 |
| Jerry (J)** | Friend | Deceased | 3 |
| Albert ** | Joel's friend | Deceased | 3 |
| Alice (A)** | Aunt | Deceased | 3 |
| George (G)** | Self | Living | 3 |
| Arthur | Friend of friend | Deceased | 2+ |
| name suppressed for | | | |
| privacy (K)** | Granddaughter of Alice | Living | 3 |
| Joe/Joseph | —— | —— | 0 |

**Refers to people or pets of special significance to GD.
——Means that no information was provided by LC.

It is unfortunate that we did not think to have GD write down the names of the people invited 24 hours before the reading, and have this document notarized. It has been suggested that GD may have been deceiving us and/or himself about the people he invited to the reading so as to help the sales of his book when it was published. This speculation has no basis in fact and is entirely inconsistent with GD's professional and personal history. It also could not explain other facts in the data, such as the four pieces of information obtained by LC, unknown to GD, that he subsequently confirmed after the readings.

LC reported receiving other names; three were not recognized by GD and therefore could be scored as errors (listed in Table 1 as Joyce, Elaine, and Joe/Joseph). However, both experimenters do have close relationships with a Joyce, an Elaine, and a Joseph.

For the purpose of scoring in Phases 1 and 2, we limited our analysis to the specific names, relationships, and details of the four people invited by GD (M, B, J, A) plus two other clearly important individuals (a person and a pet) close to GD (T, S).

As will be clear from the actual reading (Phase 3) described below, not only were each of the four primary people described accurately by LC, but *four additional facts not known by GD and later confirmed by sources close to GD* indicated that exceptionally accurate information was obtained for GD's deceased family and close friends.

### Additional Content during Phases 1 (Pre-Reading) and 2 (Sitter-Silent)

LC reported meaningful content during Phases 1 and 2 that was clearly relevant to GD and his deceased loved ones. It has been suggested during the reviewing process that many of these items were, by themselves "vague" and could apply to many people. However, what make this information important is the *constellation* of descriptions, specially when the more vague information is interspersed with highly specific content. Just because a medium reports vague information at times does not necessarily imply that the mechanism is "cold reading." The information, though general, may still apply to the individual in question.

During Phase 1 (pre-reading) LC wrote that the sitter (who had yet to be telephoned) was concerned with "truth that is held within the soul's journey—journey of the soul's path—truth from someone with an M name" and that the sitter was preparing to "stand up and be counted." GD is preparing to stand up and be counted with the publication of his book (Dalzell, 2001). The names G, M, B, T, and a small dog were mentioned.

LC saw "candles burning." GD informed us that he had lit a candle just prior to the beginning of the experiment, an act seldom practiced by GD.

During Phase 2 (sitter-silent), LC reported East Coast and California (both correct—GD comes from the East Coast, and he currently lives in California), seeing science and books associated with the sitter and his deceased father (both true), new discoveries with radio and television in the future (all true), recent advancement with new directions (true), father deceased (true), the name "Michael" key to the reading (true), and Jerry.

Other material received by LC was more general and could apply to many people (e.g., that the sitter was loving and caring). It should be noted that LC said that GD's mother was deceased; GD informed us that this was an error; his mother was living and in good health at the time of the experiment.

As in the previous research (Schwartz et al, 1999; Schwartz and Russek, 1999; Schwartz, Russek, Nelson, and Barentsen, 2001; Schwartz, Russek, and Barentsen, 2001), it was during the actual reading (Phase 3), that the most extensive and detailed information was retrieved and which replicated and extended the information obtained during Phases 1 and 2.

### Phase 3 (Actual Reading)

Content was outlined as it emerged, including four examples of information not previously known to GD. After reviewing Phase 1 with GD, LC began the reading by focusing on M. She also mentioned that J had passed recently (in the past 6 months, which was true), and that A was also strongly present. LC described M as a partner (which was true) and that M was GD's "muse" (an interesting phrase—remember that LC was blind to the identity of the sitter, though she now knew that the sitter was male and that the names she had received previously were accurate and important to the sitter).

She described M as seeing the "world" through "lots of glass." She returned to this fact at various points in the reading. LC could not interpret what M was "showing" her. It turned out that M was an international purser and flight attendant for Lufthansa Airlines. He flew all over the globe, literally seeing the world through the glass windows of airplanes.

She described M's personality accurately—not only as loving and caring, but obsessively neat and "pristine" (true).

LC then moved to J. She saw him as being from the East Coast, Brooklyn area (true), and that he was "drinking and smoking" (true).

It is important that GD did *not* know at the time of the reading that J had lived in Brooklyn; this was confirmed afterward by a friend of J and GD. She saw him as often "intoxicated" and sitting on "bar stools" (he was an alcoholic for more than half of his life). She also said that he had "stopped" drinking before he died (true).

After describing an "A" named male (details that were true), she returned to M. She saw M in a white kitchen that was "cozy" with "stone" (true).

LC said that M showed her where he lived: somewhere in Europe, and his parents have a "heavy accent" (M was German). LC reported that M was showing her a big city, and then M was traveling through the countryside to his home. Along the road to his house LC was shown a river and "centuries old stonework" (true).

LC claimed that M showed her an old, stone "monastery" on the edge of the river on the way to his parent's home. This information was *not* known to GD prior to the reading. After the reading, GD telephoned M's parents in Germany and learned that there is an old abbey church along the river's edge on the way to their house, and that they had held a service for M in this monastery-like stone building a few weeks prior to the experiment.

LC then described the older Aunt A, her great sense of humor (true), but related that A was experiencing "compassion and sorrow" for her granddaughter K (true), who was having difficulties and was "uncontrolled." LC indicated that K was currently receiving "healing." This detail was *not* known to GD prior to the reading. After the reading, GD telephoned K's mother, who informed him that K was indeed having serious difficulties and had sought psychological counseling in the week prior to the experiment because she was in crisis.

Also interesting was the fact that GD originally thought that LC had misspelled K's name. GD later learned that LC was correct.

LC described A's cottage in more detail, and then moved back to GD himself. LC said she was being shown by M that GD's life was about to become "noisy" and be "turned upside down." This is true. With the publication of GD's book, his secret life as a medium will become a matter of public record, and he may have to face professional complications in his role as a psychiatric social worker in good standing with the Los Angeles county Department of Mental Health, as well as his role as Psychiatric Admissions Coordinator at a Hospital in Glendale, California.

The experimenters found it interesting and evidential that LC reported M showing her GD and "white coat"/clinicians in a hospital prior to the reading. It turned out that GD had performed psychological evaluations in the emergency room of a Los Angeles hospital, and he had been there just prior to the reading.

The experimenters also found it interesting and evidential that LC saw the small dog (colors and personality description reported by GD to be accurate) being near a favorite tree and water. GD later informed us that he and his dog spent many hours at a special tree near the water, where his deceased dog was buried after living to be eighteen years old.

The complete reading lasted more than one hour, and substantial information was received. Space precludes reporting the complete reading. [Note: the full transcript with detailed commentary from the sitter will be placed on a web site for future scholars to examine.]

Some of the information received by LC can be labeled as general and is applicable widely (e.g., that Aunt A was loving, or M was compassionate). GD estimated that the information was at least 90% accurate. Though this information accurately portrayed the deceased and living family and friends of GD, given that this kind of information is general and widely applicable, it is not considered evidential in the context of the present report.

However, much of the information received by LC was highly specific and clearly organized for specific individuals (e.g., the pattern of "partner," "M," "world through glass," "small house in Europe," "old stone monastery," "on the river's edge," "lived life to the fullest"). GD said this kind of specific information was also at least 90% accurate. Because this information is so highly specific and precisely organized, it is decidedly evidential.

## Discussion

The design of this experiment is unusual because of the pre-reading contemplation period, the sitter-silent period, the special qualities of both the medium (e.g., Schwartz, Russek, Nelson, and Barentsen, 2001; Schwartz, Russek, and Barentsen, 2001) and the sitter (Dalzell, 2001).

The pre-reading contemplation condition in this experiment is especially important because it supports LC's hypothesis that she is able to receive information *before readings actually begin*. Since her private clients schedule appointments months in advance, it gives some plausibility to LC's hypothesis that their hypothesized deceased loved ones will be waiting for the scheduled moment in time when they can communicate through her to their loved ones (super-psi hypotheses are discussed below).

Future experiments can be designed to explicitly investigate the "scheduling variable" and determine if LC is more accurate during pre-reading contemplation periods if (1) appointments are scheduled and (2) sitters invite their deceased loved to communicate prior to the reading.

### Integrity of the Sitters, Procedures, and Experimenters

Having conducted research with LC for three years under increasingly controlled laboratory conditions, we find it highly improbable that LC has engaged in fraud with her private clients. Speculation that LC might be using the internet or an investigator to get information about her private clients before the readings, and then using the pre-reading information to impress her clients, has no foundation in evidence.

As mentioned previously, extreme care was taken to ensure that only the experimenters knew of the selection of the three sitters (their names, sexes, ages, and locations). The sitters were selected after LC arrived in Tucson. She stayed at the experimenters' home (and therefore was under close scrutiny). LC did not have a cell phone. Telephone records can document that one brief telephone call was placed to GD on December 16th, 2000 (he was not home then); one call was made by GD that evening returning the experimenter's call to discuss the upcoming reading (he spoke only with GERS; LGSR was with LC in a separate room while GERS spoke with GD); and one call was made by the experimenters at 6:00 P.M. on December 17, 2000, for the session.

Paraphrasing William James and his opinion of Mrs. Piper's integrity, we are "willing now to stake as much money on Laurie Campbell's honesty as on that of anyone we know, and we are quite satisfied to leave our reputations for wisdom or folly, so far as human nature is concerned, to stand or fall by this declaration."

GD has indicated that he would be willing to undergo a professional lie detection test to help establish her personal integrity. LC and the authors would be willing to do the same if it would help address the concerns of the critics of this research.

We mentioned in the Experimental Design section that in this experiment we set out to evaluate the significance of the contemplation (pre-reading) period, and did not anticipate observing such an extraordinary reading. Had we done so, we would have included additional procedures to establish the integrity of the experimental procedures (e.g., we would have had independent observers witness all of the procedures).

At our laboratory we are very conscious of the importance of integrity in science in general, and mediumship science in particular. The concept of integrity, as well as the consequences of being caught in fraud, are fully explained in a statement which all participants in our work are expected to sign. We emphasize this point particularly in view of the unexpected and unusual nature of the findings presented in this paper, although of course we realise that signing a piece of paper will not deter a determined "fraudster." However, we are well informed about the potential of deception, and will report evidence of it when it is observed in the laboratory (Schwartz, Russek, and Nelson, 2001).

### Possible Rater Bias

The specific information received during both the pre-reading contemplation condition (Phase 1) and the sitter-silent condition (Phase 2) cannot be explained as being due to rater bias in GD's scoring of the information. These findings compliment and extend Robertson and Roy (2001).

Details regarding names and relationships are discrete and precise, and can be independently verified by living family and friends. The fact that GD has conducted independent research attempting to discover if his friend's consciousness continues (reported in Dalzell, 2001), and that GD's family and friends provide independent confirmation of the facts reported by LC, serves as essential cross-validation of the information received by LC, and appears to preclude telepathy and super-psi in some cases (see below).

In Schwartz et al (2001), the average accuracy of information scored by the sitters from the transcripts was 83% for the actual readings and 77% for the silent periods. These studies were conducted proximally (i.e. locally)—the medium and sitter were in the same room.

However, the present experiment was conducted "long distance" (i.e. non-locally)—from Tucson, Arizona to Los Angeles, California, a distance of over one thousand miles. The accuracy of the specific information obtained during the actual reading (Phase 3) was estimated by the sitter to be above 90%. Moreover, the combined accuracy of the names and relationships obtained during the pre-reading contemplation (Phase 1) and sitter-silent (Phase 2) conditions was also estimated to be above 90%.

As mentioned in the Results section, none of the six primary names received by LC during the pre-reading and sitter-silent periods *in the context of their specific relationship to the sitter* applied to either experimenter. Curiously, the three names received by LC without relationship information, which GD rated as "0" (unknown and therefore possible errors)—Joyce, Elaine, and Joseph—were names of people close to the experimenters (and would have been scored highly had we been sitters).

Note that by comparison, neither author has (1) a deceased person B, or (2) a deceased close friend M, or (3) a deceased close friend J, or (4) a deceased person A, or (5) any known person named Tallia, or (6) a deceased dog S. Clearly, some people will have one or more of these name-relationship pairs, but virtually no one (except GD) will have the complete pattern of all the name-relationships received by LC in Phases 1 and 2. These results cannot be obtained by chance. This hypothesis was also investigated empirically with a control group and is reported in Appendix A. One possible way for conservatively estimating conditional properties is reported in Appendix B (value calculated was p less than 1 in 2.6 trillion).

One curiosity is noted for the sake of completeness and integrity. In the actual reading (Phase 3), LC brought up the names of three well-known deceased scientists in context of GD: Albert Einstein, David Bohm, and Carl Jung. In LC's notes taken during the actual reading, their names were mentioned in the context of words such as "group," "inspire," science exploration," "work with Einstein," and "agreement." In the process of reading a draft of this paper, GD informed us that in addition to the four primary individuals, he also invited "spirit scientists to help facilitate the experiment." The fact that LC mentioned Einstein, Bohm, and Jung in this particular reading (and she has never mentioned three senior scientists in the context of any previous research reading conducted over the past three years) is interesting in the context of GD's declaration.

GD recognizes that whereas most of the data can be readily confirmed by independent sources (e.g., by Michael's family or Jerry's friends), other information cannot (e.g., that in his role as a medium, he invited "spirit scientists to help facilitate the experiment").

### An Integrative Triune Approach to Anomalous Information Retrieval

Since fraud, selective memory on the part of the sitter, and sitter rating bias have been essentially ruled out in this research, it becomes meaningful to consider possible alternative/anomalous/paranormal hypotheses.

There are three primary alternative (anomalous/paranormal) hypotheses that can account for the present findings (Gauld, 1984; Schwartz et al, 1999; Schwartz, Russek, Nelson, and Barentsen, 2001). We suggest that all three may be involved in anomalous information retrieval, and that they share a common dependence on info-energy systemic resonance relationships (described in Schwartz and Russek, 1999). Other hypotheses may also be possible, including novel hypotheses that have yet to be conceived (a position recommended by Michael Shermer).

The first hypothesis is telepathy with the living. The premise is that the medium is reading the conscious mind of the sitter (locally and/or nonlocally). Given the level of awareness and experience of the sitter in the present experiment, telepathy with the sitter needs to be seriously considered.

However, the inclusion of Phases 1 and 2 in this experiment, coupled with the observation that *four pieces of specific information were not known to the sitter prior to the reading:*

(1) the stone church along the river (for M),
(2) Aunt A's living granddaughter's crisis (K),

(3) the correct spelling of K's name (GD thought it was spelled with a C), and

(4) J's living on the east coast in Brooklyn,

make the simple telepathy hypothesis insufficient to account for all the information retrieved by LC.

The second hypothesis is often termed "super-psi" (e.g., Braude, 1992). One version of the super-psi hypothesis can be thought of as an extended unconscious telepathy/systemic resonance mechanism with everyone presently living (Schwartz and Russek, 1999). Simply stated, (1) LC resonates with the experimenters, (2) the experimenters resonate with the sitter (e.g., the senior author has spoken with GD numerous times and met him three times in person), (3) the sitter resonates with his living family members and friends (including family members and friends of M, A, B, and J), and (4) the information is retrieved unconsciously through systemic memory resonance (Schwartz and Russek, 1999). The network of dynamic info-energy relationships is accessed unconsciously by LC. The majority of the present findings are consistent with such a network memory resonance hypothesis.

Given that the telepathy hypothesis (1) and the network memory resonance hypothesis (2) (one example of a super-psi hypothesis, Braude 1992) are both plausible in principle, the question arises, do hypotheses 1 and 2 together account for all the data in this research reading? We suggest that they do not.

Close examination of the *language used by LC* indicates that she is not simply reporting memories and images. LC is also reporting intentions and interpretations reflecting the information processing of "entities" (her words), or dynamically changing info-energy systems (our words, Schwartz and Russek, 1999).

When LC describes how M is interpreting future changes in GD's life, for example, the language not only implies that M is living, *but the precise way the information is being organized is recognized by GD as reflecting M's mind and personality.*

In other words, it is the specific *intentional and organized* way the information is received by LC and reported to GD that suggests that LC is not simply reporting the conscious or unconscious memories of GD and his extended network of family and friends. Given the blind conditions employed in Phases 1 and 2, it is also unlikely that LC might be role-playing and impersonating discarnate entities. We thus believe that it is valid to postulate hypothesis 3—the organizing consciousness (or soul) hypothesis, reflecting the fact that it is the precise details of the organizing nature of the information that implies the continued existence of an intentional, living consciousness (soul).

In view of the decades of substantial and replicated experimental research in parapsychology (e.g., meta-analyses reviewed in Radin, 1997), it is prudent to consider the possibility not only that all three hypotheses may be true, but that hypotheses 1 and 2 (telepathy and super-psi) may be prerequisite mechanisms for the involvement of an organizing consciousness (hypothesis 3). Hypotheses

1 and 2 may thus be intimately involved in the discovery of evidence for formulating hypothesis 3. In other words, we propose that *hypotheses 1 and 2 may provide the mechanistic foundation that allows hypothesis 3 to be documented (e.g., mediums claim that they engage in "telepathy" with the deceased)*. Together, they reflect an integrative triune approach to dynamic anomalous information retrieval.

### Implications for Future Research

Future research can exploit the power of the pre-reading contemplation (Campbell) and sitter-silent (Russek) procedures in both single-blind and double-blind experiments. Stimulated by the present findings, we are currently using the Campbell procedure (Phase 1), combined with the Russek procedure (Phase 2), with sitters who do not receive an actual medium-sitter dialogue condition (i.e., no Phase 3). Hence, the mediums never hear the sitters' voices and the sitters' never hear the mediums' voices. Information obtained from both the Campbell and Russek procedures is then mailed to the sitters under blinded conditions. The transcripts for the sitter (the sitter's own transcript) and another sitter's transcript (which serves as a "placebo" control) are scored, item by item. If the sitters can accurately determine which of the two transcripts belong to them, this establishes anomalous information retrieval under strict double-blind conditions.

In one ongoing double-blind experiment, five mediums are serving not only in the role of mediums, but they are also serving in the role of sitters. Double-blinding the Campbell and Russek procedures makes this kind of experimental design possible.

After this report was written, GD, in the role of a medium, attempted the LC pre-reading contemplation paradigm with a sitter. He reported receiving accurate information of name, cause of death, age at death, and personal descriptions that matched the primary person invited by the sitter. The approximate accuracy was 85%. GD is currently serving as one of the mediums and sitters in the above double-blind experiment.

Future research can determine if characteristics of the sitter matter. For example, when mediums and spiritually open people serve as sitters in a double-blind experiment, is more specific and detailed information retrieved than when disbelievers and skeptics serve as sitters?

### Publishing White Crow Research Readings

It is likely that future findings will not be substantially greater (in terms of accuracy) than are the present findings. Clearly, future experiments can replicate the basic observations reported here and confirm that they can be generalized to other mediums, with other sitters.

It is hoped that this paper, focused on the findings of a "white crow" research reading, will encourage other investigators to explore the potential of these experimental procedures and replicate the findings. Future papers using these procedures, replicating evidence of such readings, can help firmly establish the existence of anomalous information retrieval, and potentially the continuance of consciousness (Schwartz, 2001)

## Acknowledgments

We thank Laurie Campbell, Chairperson of the Mediumship Research Committee, the Human Energy Systems Laboratory, and George E. Dalzell, Psychiatric Social Worker, Department of Mental Health, County of Los Angeles, California, for their dedication to research on the continuance of consciousness hypothesis. The constructive questions and critiques of Stanley Krippner, Ph.D., Charles Tart, Ph.D., Zofia Weaver, Ph.D., James Randi, Andrew Harter, Michael Shermer, Ph.D., and three anonymous reviewers, are gratefully acknowledged. It should be noted that the most skeptical reviewers of this manuscript (JR and MS), despite the data and the safeguards, persisted in their personal belief that fraud must somehow be involved in mediumship research of this kind.

## REFERENCES

Braude, S. E. (1992). Survival or super-psi? *Journal of Scientific Exploration.* 6,2: 127–144.

Dalzell, G.E. (2001, in press). *Messages: Evidence of Life After Death.* Charlottesville, VA: Hampton Roads Publishing.

Gauld, A. (1984). *Mediumship and Survival: A Century of Investigation.* Chicago, IL: Academy Chicago Publishing.

Radin, D. (1997). *The Conscious Universe: The Scientific Truth of Psychic Phenomena.* San Francisco, CA: HarperCollins.

Robertson, T.J., and Roy, A.E. (2001). A preliminary study of the acceptance by non-recipients of mediums' statements to recipients. *JSPR.* 65,863: 91–106.

Russek, L.G.S., Schwartz, G.E.R., Russek, E. and Russek, H.I. (hyp) (1999). A possible approach for researching purported spirit communication: An empirical-anecdotal investigation. *Advances in Mind-Body Medicine.* 15,4: 295–301.

Schwartz, G.E.R., and Russek, L.G.S. (1999). *The Living Energy Universe: A Fundamental Discovery that Transforms Science and Medicine.* Charlottesville, VA: Hampton Roads Publishing.

Schwartz, G.E.R., Russek, L.G.S., Watson, D.E., Campbell, L., Smith, S., Smith, E.H. (hyp)*, James, W. (hyp), Russek, H.I. (hyp), and Schwartz, H. (hyp) (1999). Potential medium to departed to medium communication of pictorial information: Exploratory evidence consistent with psi and survival of consciousness. *The Noetics Journal.* 2,3: 283–294.

Schwartz, G.E.R., Russek, L.G.S., Nelson, L.A., and Barentsen, C. (2001). Accuracy and replicability of anomalous after-death communication across highly skilled mediums. *JSPR.* 65, 862: 1–25.

---

*[Hypothesized; a deceased person who appeared to take part in the experiment. Ed.]*

Schwartz, G.R., Russek, L.G., and Nelson, L.A. (2001, submitted for publication). Purported anomalous perception in a highly skilled individual: Observations, interpretations, compassion.

Schwartz, G.E., Russek, L.G., and Barentsen, C. (2001, in press). Accuracy and replicability of anomalous information retrieval: Replication and extension. *JSPR.*

Schwartz, G.E., with Simon, W.L. (2001, in press). *The Afterlife Experiments: Breakthrough Scientific Evidence for Life After Death.* New York, NY: Pocket Books.

## Appendix A: Actual Estimates of Names and Relationship Data

To examine actual rates of names and conditional probabilities, a sample of students (n = 88, mean age 20.6 years) at the University of Arizona were asked a set of questions concerning first names of family members and friends.

One question requested that they list their father's first name. Among the 88 names provided, there were three Roberts (one Robert, one Bob, and one Bobby). Three students listed the name Michael, one listed the name Jerry, and none listed the name George.

Table 1 lists the percentages for the four male names obtained from the class data, as well as percentages and rankings based upon 3,003,954 male subjects from the U.S. Census Bureau available on the web for 1990 (the sample provided for this purpose by the Census Bureau).

### Table 1

| Name | Class Percentages | Census Percentages | Census Rankings |
|------|-------------------|--------------------|-----------------|
| Robert | 3.41% | 3.14% | 3 |
| Michael | 3.41% | 2.63% | 4 |
| Jerry | 1.14% | 0.43% | 16 |
| George | 0.00% | 0.93% | 39 |
| Average | 1.86% | 1.78% | 15.5 |

It can be seen that the class data (n = 88) generally replicated the 1990 census figures (n = 3,003,954) for percentage of male names in the general population. According to the actual data, the average for these four names is approximately 1.8%, or 1 in 56. The highest value, 3.41%, would be only 1 in 29.

The students were also asked to list their favorite aunt's first name. None gave the name Alice, Katherine, or Talia. However, when they were asked if they knew someone with an unusual T sounding name, two subjects claimed that they knew people that sounded like Talia. Table 2 lists the student percentages as well as the data provided by the U.S. Census Bureau.

## Table 2

| Name | Class Percentages | Census Percentages | Census Rankings |
|------|-------------------|--------------------|-----------------|
| Alice | 0.00% | 0.31% | 51 |
| Katherine | 0.00% | 0.36% | 61 |
| Talia | 0.02% | 0.00% | 1,797 |
| | | | |
| Average | 0.01% | 0.22% | 636 |

It can be seen that the class data (n = 88) generally replicated the 1990 census figures (n = 3,184,399) for percentage of female names in the general population. According to actual data from the census, the average for these two names is approximately 0.34%, or 1 in 298 (the average for the class data was 0%).

If the data provided by the class regarding the name Talia were used, the actual estimate would be 1 in 44. If the Census Bureau (0.003%) data were used, the actual estimate would be reduced to 1 in 33,333. On the whole, using actual estimates employing the average for the class, the value would be 1 in 10,000; employing the average for the census, the value would be 1 in 454.

It was possible to determine empirically the number of subjects who had various combinations of 5 names of family and friends. Since the sample of college students included females and males, we did not include the student's own name in the analysis (the sitter in the present experiment was male).

Students were asked to indicate if they had (1) an aunt named Alice, (2) a niece or cousin named Katherine, (3) a male friend named Michael, (4) a male friend named Jerry, and/or (5) a friend named Talia. We did not specify living or dead; this was done to increase the possibility of finding subjects (who were younger than the sitter) who might match the sitter for names and relationships.

Only six subjects out of 88 (1.14%) had one match. Three subjects reported a father named Robert/Bob, one subject reported a close friend named Michael, and two subjects claimed that they knew someone with a name that sounded like Talia. No subjects reported two matches (e.g., no subjects reported having a father named Robert *and* a close friend named Michael). None of the subjects had three, four, or five matches.

## Appendix B: Conditional Probability Estimates of Names and Relationship Data

If we estimate that there are at least 15 common American male names (e.g., common names of male people well known by the experimenters include Al, Bill, Bob, Edward, Gary, George, Harry, Howard, John, Larry, Michael, Mark, Sam, Steve, Tom), and 15 common female names (female names well known by the experimenters include Alice, Beverly, Cathy, Jane, Joyce, Joan, Kate, Karen, Linda, Lynn, Mary, Margaret, Martha, Rita, Susan), we can conservatively estimate that the probability of LC getting a specific name correct for a given sex is 1 in 15.

[Note: the number 15 was selected here to be a conservative yet fair number.

Obviously, other common names could be added to the list (e.g., additional common names of males known by the experimenters include Daniel, James, Paul, Ralph, Terry, and additional common names of females known by the experimenters include Ann, Judy, Lisa, Sara, Shirley). Increasing the estimated number of possible common names would only make the conditional probabilities all the more improbable by chance. For example, the conservative 1 in 2.6 trillion estimate would be multiplied by at least 5 x 5 x 5 x 5 x 5 x 5 (an increase of 15,625 for the six names given), to less than 1 in 41,000 trillion ). The specific examples of male and female names listed above were selected after the experiment was completed and the experimenters decided to attempt to calculate conditional probabilities for the findings. Actual analyses of first name frequencies at the University of Arizona and the U.S. Census bureau, reported in Appendix A, document that 1 in 15 is empirically a conservative estimate.

[Note: One reviewer suggested that once the sitter gets a single name correct, the p value should be reduced accordingly. For example, 1 in 30—male plus female—should be reduced to 1 in 29, with each name picked. However, this assumes that readings involve single names. In a recent experiment, a medium reported hearing "Michael times 2, Michael times 2"—not realizing that the name of the son who died, followed by the name of the father died, were Michael junior and Michael senior, respectively. The medium not only indicated that the son and father were both deceased, and the father died after the son, but he correctly implied that both had the name Michael (Schwartz, Russek, and Barentsen, 2001). Given that 1 in 30 is an underestimate to begin with, the assumption that the p value should be reduced will not alter substantially the overall value of the probabilities.]

Relationship can be conservatively estimated as 1 in 12 (e.g., mother, father, daughter, son, grandmother, grandfather, aunt, uncle, wife, husband, female friend, male friend).

[Note: ideally one might wish to give more weight to older persons such as grandparents and parents, and less weight to friends and children. For the present data, doing so would serve to make the conditional probabilities even more significant; we purposely adopted a relatively conservative procedure for this reading.]

The conditional probabilities were calculated as follows:.

LC said that this particular sitter was male (1 in 2) and his name was G (1 in 15). For this information, the probability would be 2 x 15 or 1 in 30 (p < 0.033). [Note: when a name is selected without a relationship given, the pool of possible names (male and female combined), as calculated here, would be 2 x 15, or 30 possible names].

LC said that the primary deceased person was a male friend and his name was M. A male friend (1 in 12) named M (1 in 15) would be 12 x 15 or 1 in 180 (p < 0.006). The combined probability of G and M, so identified, is 30 x 180, or 1 in 5400.

LC said that there was a deceased friend name J. Friend named J would be 12 x 15 or 1 in 180 (p < 0.006). The combined probability of G, M and J, so identified, is 30 x 180 x 180, or 1 in 972,000.

LC said that there was a deceased person named B. LC did not specify the precise relationship. Person named B would simply be 2 x 15 (p < 0.03). The combined probability of G, M, J, and B, so identified, is 30 x 180 x 180 x 30, or 1 in 29,160,000.

LC said that there was a deceased person named A. LC did not specify the precise relationship. Person named A would simply be 2 x 15 (p < 0.03). The combined probability of G, M, J, B, and A, so identified, is 30 x 180 x 180 x 30 x 30, or 1 in 874,800,000.

The combined probability value of 1 in 874,800,000 is an underestimate of the actual combined probability.

For example, consider what happens when we add the highly unusual T name, Tallia (LC spelled Tilya) to the conditional probability. LC did not comment what the relationship was. However, the question arises, what is the probability of spontaneously guessing the unusual name Tallia/Tilya by chance? A conservative estimate is 1 in 100 (p < 0.01). When we add T to the combined probability of G, M, J, B, and A this brings the conditional probability to 30 x 180 x 180 x 30 x 30 x 100, or 1 in 87,480,000,000.

Also important is the dog with an S initial. LC did not provide information about the sex of the dog, though she later described the dog accurately. If we estimate that of 26 letters in the alphabet, picking S by chance is conservatively 1 in 15 (clearly names starting with Q's, X's, and Z's are highly improbable, whereas names like Alice, Bob, Charles, Debbie, Edward, Frank, Gary, Harry, Jerry, Kathy, Larry, Mary, Peter, Susan and Tom and the selection of dog is maybe 1 in 2 (dogs and cats are the primary pets that mediums seem to mention), reporting a deceased dog with an S name is at least 1 in 30 (p < 0.03). Adding the S dog to G, M, J, B, A, and T brings the conditional probability to 30 x 180 x 180 x 30 x 30 x 100 x 30, or 1 in 2,624,400,000,000.

In sum, for these six names, one initial, and relationships per se, the conditional probability is at least p less than one in 2.6 trillion.

# • ACKNOWLEDGMENTS •

## FROM GARY SCHWARTZ

*The love of learning rules the world.*
PHI KAPPA PHI MOTTO, THE UNIVERSITY OF ARIZONA

*It is more important to be human than it is to be important.*
WILL ROGERS

The writing of this book was inspired by people who care about love and life.

Linda Russek and her deceased father, Henry I. Russek, M.D., are the reasons why this research began. If the data reported in this book turn out to be true, the late Dr. Russek has more than just a historical involvement with this work—he may be actively involved as a "departed hypothesized co-investigator" as well. This book hopefully honors Dr. Russek (a man I never met) and the gift of his remarkable daughter in my life (for a few years as a research and romantic partner, and hopefully forever as a friend).

We wish to acknowledge Elayne Russek, Linda's mother, for her appropriate balance of skepticism and caring openness in searching for the possibility of her husband's continued existence. Not only has Elayne helped nurture this research, she has even collaborated with us—albeit reluctantly—on an experiment examining possible spirit communication from Henry.

Bill Simon is a writer's writer. An open-minded skeptic, he agreed (with some reluctance) to consider this project at the request of Bill Gladstone, his literary agent as well as mine. Bill's magic with words, as well as his background in magic and "mind-reading," turned my ideas and experiences into a publishable manuscript, and I will be forever grateful.

# Acknowledgments

The inspiration to find Bill Simon as a writing partner came from Tracy Bernstein of Pocket Books. Tracy understands the power of the written word and, together with Bill, clarified and enlivened the story. Tracy is an editor's editor—she helped craft this book from the beginning.

Christopher Barentsen, a former student at the University of Arizona and a sitter in the Miraval experiment, has a deep feeling for both science and mediumship and was a great help to us in initially assembling the material for this book.

Our research on mediumship began in part because Richard Lane, M.D., Ph.D.—who completed his medical research fellowship with me at Yale University, then moved to the University of Arizona to join the faculty in the Department of Psychiatry, and ultimately completed a Ph.D. with me in the Department of Psychology—happened to read an article about Susy Smith in the *Arizona Daily Star* in 1995 and suggested we want might to contact her. The rest, as they say, is history. We thank you, Richard, for caring to introduce us to Susy.

This research would not exist without the devotion and talents of a "dream team" of mediums who range in age from their thirties to their sixties. The oldest, the late Ms. Susy Smith, has been called by Linda the "matriarch of survival research." Susy devoted the last forty-five years of her life to parapsychology and the topic of survival. The last of her thirty published books, *The Afterlife Codes* (Hampton Roads Publishing, 2000), includes a $10,000 reward to the person who correctly guesses the secret phrase that she hopes to communicate from the "other side." In 1971 Susy created the Survival Research Foundation, a small nonprofit organization, to foster research in this area. Susy was a teacher, a collaborator, and the inspiration for this work. She became our adopted grandmother, and she considered Linda and me to be her "illegitimate grandchildren." In 1997 Linda and I created the Susy Smith Project in the Human Energy Systems Laboratory to honor Susy's dream to understand how communication with departed loved ones is possible.

Laurie Campbell, the chair of our Mediumship Research Committee in the Human Energy Systems Laboratory, has repeatedly dropped our jaws over the years. Laurie and Susy showed us that there are mediums who have integrity and believe in the scientific reality of life after death. We came to know Laurie through Dr. Donald Watson, a brilliant psychiatrist who has become a dear colleague and friend. Together with Patricia Kubis, the woman who initially brought Don and Laurie together, they have played a critical role in the evolution of this work.

John Edward and Suzane Northrop are extraordinary mediums. Their integrity for this work is matched only by their passion for the mission. Like Laurie Campbell, they have scientific minds and appreciate the requirement for experimental validation. Not only have they have encouraged us to conduct controlled research, they have helped us share the discovery process in this book.

Like Suzane Northrop, George Anderson and Rev. Anne Gehman have been doing professional mediumship for many decades. They are deeply spiritual people who believe that their talents reflect a divine gift from the Source. They have brought a unique level of reverence to this work and to our laboratory. Their visions and skills are documented in this book; together with Laurie, John, and

Suzane, the results of their research on the HBO experiment have been published in a scientific journal and cited in the reference section.

Many people helped make this research possible. Lisa Jackson, the producer/director of the HBO documentary *Life Afterlife,* and Linda Ellerbee, the head of Lucky Duck Productions, which produced the documentary, dreamed of doing a serious film about life after death. When Linda and I proposed that HBO fund an experiment to bring five purportedly exceptional mediums to Tucson for a first-ever energy cardiology mediumship experiment, Lisa and her colleagues saw the potential and enabled it to happen. She and her production crew were a delight to work with. They made it possible to have professionally recorded raw video footage of the entire experiment.

Our two courageous sitters in the HBO experiment, Patricia Price and Ronnie Nathanson, were remarkable to work with and come to know. They volunteered many hours to carefully score the transcripts of their sessions. Students and staff at the University of Arizona who actively collaborated on the HBO research included Mercy Fernandez, Ph.D., Carolyne Luna, and Lonnie Nelson. Funds to conduct the research in the laboratory was provided in part by the Family Love and Health Foundation, by a gift from the National Institute of Discovery Science, and from our personal funds.

The Miraval Experiment was made possible by the generous support of both the Canyon Ranch and Miraval Resorts in Tucson. Canyon Ranch provided room and board for the mediums; Miraval provided the space to conduct the research and the transportation between Canyon Ranch and Miraval. We thank Jerry Cohen, Gary Frost, Carrie Thompson, Tony Vuturo, and Mel Zuckerman of Canyon Ranch, and Joseph DeNucci and William O'Donnell of Miraval, for their vision and support. Our ten sitters were a remarkable group of people who care deeply about the survival question. Their opinions range from seriously skeptical to strong believers. They are Marie Smith, Heather Rist, David Weinstock, Jim Coan, Christopher Barentsen, Patricia Price, Elayne Russek, James Levin, M.D., Diane Goldner, and Elizabeth Duffy, M.D. Students and staff who actively collaborated on the HBO study included Jim Coan, Patti Harada, Carolyne Luna, David Weinstock, and Heather Rist. Funding for transportation to Tucson and other expenses were provided by the Family Love and Health Foundation (now the Heart Science Foundation), a gift from the Bigelow Foundation, and personal funds.

The Canyon Ranch Experiment involved the collaboration of five research sitters: Lynn Ferro, Terry Raymond, Sabrina Geoffrion, Janna Excel, and Juliet Speisman. Funds for this experiment were provided by Canyon Ranch, by the Family Love and Health Foundation, by a gift from the National Institute of Discovery Science, and from personal funds. Canyon Ranch also graciously supports a graduate research fellowship program in energy medicine in the Human Energy Systems Laboratory.

I also wish to thank the many organizations who have funded my basic and clinical research at Harvard, Yale, and the University of Arizona. They include the National Institutes of Health, the National Institute of Mental Health, the National Science Foundation, the Advanced Research Projects Agency of the Department of Defense, and the Veterans Administration. Though none of these organizations have funded research on the continuance of consciousness hypothesis to date, it is hoped that as the research becomes better known, these organizations will come to recognize the importance of the findings for their respective missions.

Many remarkable scientists and colleagues from the United States and abroad have directly or indirectly influenced the design and interpretation of this research. They include Deepak Chopra (who graciously wrote the Foreword), Robert Morris, Dean Radin, Rupert Sheldrake, Charles Tart, Stanley Krippner, Suzan Blakemore, Dana Zohar, Robert Kall, Joel Martin, Arthur Berger, Frank Tribbe, Larry Dossey, M.D., James Levin, M.D., Paul Pearsall, Dennis Stillings, Donald Watson, M.D., Donald Morse, Roger Nelson, Brenda Dunn, Robert Jahn, Raymond Moody, M.D., Maralyn Schlitz, Melvin Morse, M.D., David Charlmers, Bruce Moen, Deborah Delaney, Daryl Bem, Elmer and Alyce Green, Jeanne Achterberg, Frank Lawlis, Suki Miller, Fred Allen Wolfe, Stuart Hameroff, Dick Bierman, David Bressler, Marty Rossman, M.D., Ken Wilber, Karl Pribram, M.D., David Loye, Thom Hartmann, Erwin Laslow, Lee Lipsenthal, M.D., Robert Kall, Monty Keen, Alan Gauld, Marcello Truzzi, Zofia Weaver, Loyd Auerbach, Joie Jones, Beverly Rubik, Alex Imich, Uri Geller, Rustum Roy, William Tiller, and John Alexander. Their ideas and questions live on in this book. We also wish to thank our local psychic magician advisor, Ross Howoritz, for sharing the secrets of illusory magic with us so that we could uncover the real magic of mediumship.

It is with special appreciation that we acknowledge a group of colleagues and students at the University of Arizona who continually encourage us to pursue the scientific dream of discovering whether survival of consciousness is real. Jill and Memo Grassman are colleagues and extended family, and their dreams complement ours. Colleagues who have served in the Program in Integrative Medicine, including Iris Bell, M.D., David Rychener, Tracey Gaudet, M.D., John Turrant, Lynn Ferro, the majority of the M.D. Fellows in the program, and Andrew Weil, M.D., have encouraged us to be brave and follow the data whereever they lead. The head of the Department of Psychology, Lynn Nadel, and the dean of the College of Social and Behavioral Sciences, Holly Smith, have been steadfast in their support of academic freedom, and they have encouraged us to address this question with scientific responsibility.

Our anonymous Friendly Devil's Advocate committee of distinguished skeptical faculty and students (the size of the committee has ranged from five to fifteen) has actively helped raise the kinds of questions that honor the complexity and challenge of conducting this kind of research. We also thank the most vocal critics of the living soul hypothesis, especially James "the Amazing" Randi, Andrew Harter, Michael Shermer, and "Pierre," who never let us forget their concerns.

The greatest encouragement has come from the young minds who look to their professor to be a scientific role model who steadfastly follows the data where ever they take him. In particular, Lonnie Nelson, Shauna Shapiro, David Weinstock, Sabrina Geoffrion, Craig Santerre, Patti Harada, Shamini Jain, Daniel Lewis, Sabrina Lewis, Summer Swanick, Michael Kaufman, Mishele Woods, and Juliet Speisman—thank you for your support and guidance. Also, steadfast encouragement has come from new research-oriented mediums who have fostered the work of the laboratory, including Lynn Gardner, Mary Ann Morgan, Allison Klupar, JoAnn Ruhl, Willow Sibert, George Dalzell, and Joel Rothchild, as well as the loving research teams focused on Johrei (Pat Starron, Bob Starron, Carol Martin, Francine Jamison), the biomagnetic touch healing (Paul Bucky, Jennifer Phelps, and Tod Zelickson), and after-death researcher and author Judy Guggenheim.

Three university professors played a pivotal role in encouraging me, when I was a young student, to be brave and open-minded in science. Harold Johnson, my undergraduate honors thesis advisor at Cornell University, was beloved by his students and encouraged them to pursue their scientific dreams with creativity and care. David Shapiro and Bernard Tursky at Harvard University, my dissertation advisors, were a constant source of guidance and inspiration as they modeled the philosophy "let the data speak." Many other teachers, including over fifty Ph.D. students and post-doctoral fellows at Harvard, Yale, and the University of Arizona who have completed dissertations with me, have supported this philosophy as well. These students include Daniel Goleman, Richard Davidson, Miriam London, Daniel Weinberger, William Polonski, Geoffrey Ahern, and John Kline. Space precludes listing all your names. You know who you are, and that your teachings live within me. However, I wish to especially honor William Bowen, who passed away shortly after completing his Ph.D. with me at Yale University.

We thank William Gladstone, our senior editor and agent, for his efforts in enabling this work to be published in book form; Anne Hardy and Jon Feldman, our spiritual science publicity team, for their conviction that this work needs to be known and discussed widely; and James Levin, M.D., Natalie Cederquist, and Peter and Lynn Karlen, for their behind-the-scenes efforts in fostering this research. And special thanks to Harris Dienstrey, the editor of *Advances in Mind-Body Medicine,* for his longstanding interest in our research that bridges mind-body medicine, energy medicine, and spiritual medicine, and for publishing this work in his journal.

If the conclusions from this research are supported by future research, then we must conclude that many individuals from "the other side" have actively collaborated in our research program. Most explicit are our four original "departed hypothesized co-investigators," who are listed as "hyp" (hypothesized, meaning deceased but apparently taking part in the experiments), co-authors of the published scientific paper: Henry Russek, M.D., Howard Schwartz, Betty Smith, and William James, M.D. Though we sometimes shake our heads in disbelief as we contemplate this possibility, the data suggest that our head-shaking may ultimately become nodding, indicating "yes" to their collaboration. Future research will tell, one way or the other.

If the answer turns out to be yes, then the memories and personalities of my deceased parents, Howard and Shirley Schwartz, other beloved family members, and friends—including Louis and Dora Levin, and Sam—are alive and evolving too, and they will know that they are always a part of my heart.

Also, if the answer turns out to be yes, then we should warmly acknowledge the participation of the many departed loved ones of our research sitters whose continued existence is strongly suggested by the research.

Finally, if the answer turns out to be yes, then it is our special privilege to honor the late Michael Price, Sr., Patricia's husband, who witnessed the HBO experiment in the flesh, then passed on, and subsequently appears to have participated in the Miraval Experiment in spirit. It is scientifically possible that Michael's unanticipated "validating of the validation" will evolve into the kind of data that ultimately prove the reality of survival.

The truth is, if the answer turns out to be yes, they are the real heroes of this work.

## FROM BILL SIMON

My wife, Arynne; our daughter, Victoria; and our son, Sheldon Bermont, all agree that I am accurately described as having both feet firmly planted on *terra firma*. So they were surprised by a decision I made some time back.

One morning, my wise and perceptive agent Bill Gladstone called to say he had a project—something out of the ordinary—but wasn't sure I'd be interested. What he had was a book project that most writers would either discount out of hand or find themselves becoming enthralled with, in the rush of magic and amazement. He expected that my skeptical attitude and predilection for hard truth could add a needed solid dimension. Bill convinced me that this might be an engaging challenge, and was sure I could keep my intellectual distance while writing about the amazing happenings going on in Tucson, Arizona.

So I agreed to talk to Gary Schwartz, who impressed me from the very first, both in terms of his credentials as a scientist and for his overflowing enthusiasm. He made clear that he wanted my fierce determination to get at truth and accuracy. I believed him. My wife, Arynne, laughed; she is now delighted to have been so wrong, for I have had a wonderful experience working on this book. I have been jolted into thinking and caring about ideas I had in the past willfully dismissed.

How lucky I am to have been introduced to Gary Schwartz and his work. And this is a perfect opportunity to thank Bill Gladstone, a rare and exceptional agent. He knows me so well by now (he's been representing me for ten years and is the only literary agent I've ever had and ever expect to have). He keeps encouraging me to accept new opportunities and walk through the doors he opens for me.

Next to my wonderful Arynne, the sunshine that keeps me happily writing is the glow from my daughter, Victoria; my son, Sheldon; his Merrilee; and my twin grandchildren, Vincent and Elena. And I want once again to acknowledge the efforts of Josie Rodriguez, our housekeeper of twenty-eight years, who helps keep the household on an even keel.

At Pocket Books, the editor who brought this project into the house and has shepherded it and found so many ways to improve it is the steadfast Tracy Bernstein, to whom I am indebted.

If your jaw occasionally dropped as you read these pages, I will know that the work of Gary Schwartz has had its deserving impact. And if you found some enjoyment, I will know that my own effort has succeeded, as well.

# • RECOMMENDED READINGS •

The following twelve books provide a useful and enjoyable introduction to the science and art of mediumship. Together they represent a compelling overview to this emerging field.

Some of my favorites were not included because they were unfortunately out of print. For example, an excellent academic book in my personal library, listed on Amazon.com for special order, is Arthur S. Berger's (1987) *Aristocracy of the Dead: New Findings in Post Mortem Survival* (McFarland, Jefferson, NC). Berger is the president of the Survival Research Foundation, founded by the late Susy Smith, and he has been in the field a very long time.

For readers interested in hearing an audiotape on mediumship science, a lecture and dialogue with Deepak Chopra, M.D., and me (2001) *Science and Soul: The Survival of Consciousness After Death* provides a dynamic introduction to contemporary afterlife research (Hay House, Carlsbad, CA, ISBN: 1561708224).

## THE SCIENCE OF MEDIUMSHIP, AFTER-DEATH COMMUNICATIONS, AND PARAPSYCHOLOGY

Gauld, Alan (1984). *Mediumship and Survival: A Century of Investigations* (Academy Chicago; ISBN: 0586084290). This book is required reading for anyone who wishes to know the history of scientific research on mediumship. Most vocal critics of research on afterlife survival have not taken the time to read this seminal book. If they did, they would temper their criticisms accordingly.

Radin, Dean (1997). *The Conscious Universe: The Scientific Truth of Psychic Phenomena* (HarperCollins New York; ISBN: 0062515020). This book is a gem. Written for the general public, it reviews research on parapsychology in general and documents how far science has come in revealing replicable psychic phenomena. Radin includes sections on the history and mechanisms of biased skepticism and prejudice in the scientific and religious communities.

Schwartz, Gary, and Russek, Linda (1999). *The Living Energy Universe: A Fundamental Discovery That Transforms Science and Medicine* (Hampton Roads Charlottsville; ISBN: 1571741704). This book, written for the general public, combines scientific theory, integrating contemporary physics and systems analysis, with empirical research and personal experiences that enliven the information. It offers both reasoning and data indicating that everything in the universe, including light and energy itself, is eternal, alive, and evolving. It provides the scientific foundation for *The Afterlife Experiments.*

Morse, Donald (2000). *Searching For Eternity: A Scientist's Spiritual Journey to Overcome Death Anxiety* (Eagle Wing Books Memphis, TN; ISBN: 0940829274). Morse is a unique person with a D.D.S. as well as a Ph.D. in psychology, who is currently editor of the *Journal of Religious and Psychical Research.* He reviews his personal journey facing the fear of death and explains how he discovered that death is not the end but is a transition to a larger reality. His book reviews not only research but the history of belief in the afterlife in diverse religions throughout recorded history.

Martin, Joel, and Romanowski, Patricia (1998). *Love Beyond Life: The Healing Power of After-Death Communications* (Bantam Books New York; ISBN: 044022649X). This book is also a gem. Written for the general public, it reviews research and personal experiences about the role that afterlife communications can play in healing from grief. The authors' focus is on the enduring motivation of love, a theme repeated by all the mediums listed below. They have written several books about the distinguished medium George Anderson.

Guggenheim, Bill, and Guggenheim, Judy (1999). *Hello from Heaven: A New Field of Research* (Bantam Books New York; ISBN: 0553576348). This book is not about professional mediums but about people from all walks of life who have received after-death communications from their departed loved ones. This scientific study of thousands of individuals is illuminating and inspiring. The book provides messages of hope to bereaved survivors and points to the scientific reality of these profound experiences.

## THE ART OF MEDIUMSHIP: PERSONAL AND PROFESSIONAL

Smith, Susy (2001). *The Afterlife Codes: Searching for Evidence of the Survival of the Soul.* (Hampton Roads Charlottsville; ISBN: 1571741917). Truly inspiring, this book tells the life story of Susy Smith, the "matriach of survival research." Smith shows how it possible for skeptical laypersons (herself and others) to develop the capacity to make contact with deceased loved ones and test the communication for authenticity. Her thirtieth book, published shortly before she died, includes a detailed description of her remarkable afterlife codes experiment, offering a $10,000 reword for anyone who correctly receives her secret code.

Rothchild, Joel (2001). *Signals: An Inspiring Story of Life After Life* (New World Library Novato; ISBN: 1577311795). Rothchild is a medical miracle: the longest surviving person with AIDS. His book describes how after his dear friend Albert died of AIDS, Rothchild received repeated and compelling afterlife communication that provide strong evidence for life after death. The style of writing beautifully complements his inspiring story of the possibility of love and life-sustaining support from the other side.

Dalzell, George (2002). *Messages: Evidence for Life After Death* (Hampton Roads Charlottsville). This is the third book I recommend that documents how any person can potentially become a "lay scientist" and obtain strong evidence for life after death. Dalzell is a psychiatric social worker who, after the death of his dear friend Michael, discovered that he was receiving repeated and compelling after-death communications that could be documented definitively through contact with mediums. Dalzell has become a research medium who collaborates with the Human Energy Systems Laboratory at the University of Arizona.

Edward, John (2000). *One Last Time: A Psychic Medium Speaks to Those We Have Loved and Lost.* (Berkley New York; ISBN: 0425166929). Edward participated in three experiments in the Human Energy Systems Laboratory. His profound talents are demonstrated weekly on his successful television series, *Crossing Over with John Edward.* Edward's book is must reading for people interested in the art of mediumship and integrity in living.

Northrop, Susan, with McLoughlin, Kate (1996). *Seance: Healing Messages from Beyond.* (Dell Books New York; ISBN: 0440221765). Northrop is another remarkable medium who participated in three experiments at the University of Arizona. Her life story is powerful. She has lived with scorn, ridicule, and prejudice, yet continues to practice what she knows to be true through repeated experience. Northrop is outspoken about the reality of mediumship and its significance. Her book presents a striking and comforting vision of the power of mind to connect the visible with the living invisible.

Anderson, George, and Barone, Andrew (2000). *Lessons from the Light: Extraordinary Messages of Comfort and Hope from the Other Side* (Berkley New York; ISBN:.0425174166). George Anderson is one of the world's most distinguished and well-studied mediums. A deeply spiritual person, whose primary purpose is to bring through messages of love and forgiveness, he is also devoted to obtaining information that can be validated empirically. Anderson was one of the members of the "dream team" in the HBO experiment conducted at the University of Arizona. His book is moving and profoundly meaningful.

# • THE CONTRIBUTORS •

Gary Schwartz can be contacted through the Human Energy Systems laboratory website at www.openmindsciences.com

Dr. Linda Russek was co-founder and co-director of the Human Energy Systems Laboratory (1996–2001). She is currently president and director of the Heart Science Foundation, which is dedicated to providing educational programs on cutting-edge discoveries in mind-body, energy, and spiritual medicine designed to inspire and empower all ages to create more joyous, fulfilling, and healthful lives. Other services for groups include soul rejuvenation retreats and annual conferences. Dr. Russek states: "The Foundation's Center for Family Love and Health offers whole-person coaching, soul-family therapy, and integrative energy medicine treatments. The Foundation's research creatively blends new science with spritual reality and the human experience to explore an expanded vision of who we are as living energy beings and to make meaningful contact with the loving energy universe."

Dr. Russek can be contacted through the Heart Science Foundation website at www.heartsciencefoundation.com

# • THE RESEARCH MEDIUMS •

The research described in these pages would not have been possible without the participation of the five mediums who have graciously given their time to take part in the experiments.

Laurie Campbell—(949) 726 1042; http://www.lauriecampbell.net/
John Edward—(631) 547 6043; http://www.johnedward.net/
Suzane Northrop—(516) 676 7036; http://www.theseance.com/
George Anderson—(516) 285 5713; http://www.georgeanderson.com/
Anne Gehman—(703) 354 5767

# · I N D E X ·

# A Remarkable Experiment with Deepak Chopra

I was on vacation in California last summer, when, toward the end of a chance meeting with Deepak Chopra, he confessed a personal wish. He shared with me that his father had recently died, and that he deeply desired a reading with one of the Michael Jordans of mediumship, but he insisted it would have to be private and secret.

It was evident that Deepak deeply loved and respected his father, and he had never experienced so great a personal loss.

As a scientist, I had immediately jumped at the chance to do an experiment with this much admired, totally credible man. His request presented a remarkable opportunity, and I suggested that the reading be set up as an experiment, in which we would have not one but several mediums; this would let us see if information would be replicated, with some of the same facts being provided by more than one of the mediums.

I assured him I would tell no one, including my staff. For my part, I had a similar requirement: In order to insure the integrity of the experiment, it was essential to make certain there was no way that word could be leaked about who the sitter would be. Deepak would have to keep the experiment secret from everyone, including most of his staff (save for Carolyn Rangel, his administrative assistant, who coordinates the schedules).

It was also vital that I be kept completely uninformed as to details about his father; at the time, all I knew was that his father had been a famous cardiologist in India.

The key to quality research is integrity. The validity of mediumship research stands or falls on the honesty and responsibility of the experimenters, staff, sitters, and mediums. To know Dr. Chopra is to know what the word *integrity* really means.

### The Experimental Design

I decided I would seek the use of three mediums. One was to be the well-documented Laurie Campbell (described in many chapters in this book). The other two were new research mediums with whom I have had the privilege to work since the time covered in these pages: Allison DuBois, in Phoenix, Arizona, is the mother of three young children and is married to an aerospace engineer; Mary Occhino, in Shirley, New York, has been a professional medium for over twenty years but, like Allison, had never participated in mediumship research before meeting me.

All three agree to take part and abide by the terms of secrecy. The experiment, I explained, would be conducted long-distance, over the telephone. I shared with them that the sitter was a famous person, but nothing more—no details of the sitter's sex, age, location, or in what field the person was famous.

Similar to the White Crow experiment, these research readings took place in three phases.

First came a Pre-Reading, during which the medium attempted to contact the deceased Susy Smith (see chapters 2 and 4, which describe Susy when she was alive), and asked Susy to bring to them the deceased loved ones of the secret sitter. Note that the medium was attempting to receive this information before the designated times for the telephone call to be placed connecting the medium to the sitter.

In this first phase, the medium wrote down her impressions. At the end of this phase, I placed the telephone call to the medium, and she read out loud whatever information she had received so far.

Then came a Sitter-Silent phase, during which the medium attempted to contact the deceased relatives of the secret sitter, and report out loud, moment by moment, whatever impressions she received. I was in phone contact with the medium through this period; since the caller ID was blocked, she could not find out by that method that I was calling from the Chopra Center at the Rancho La Costa resort in California.

These two phases provided the actual experimental research data. The third phase, a normal telephone reading, was something I provided for Deepak, not for science. During this phase I allowed him to speak with the mediums. The information obtained during Phase III, though quite remarkable, was very personal and understandably will continue to be kept private.

### We Look at the Data

After the three readings were completed, the audiotapes were transcribed. I then returned to La Costa to videotape Dr. Chopra and me as we individually scored every item from Phases I and II, for each of the three mediums, using the -3 to +3 scoring procedure already described in these pages. Even as we conducted the ratings, I could see that the number of +3s was adding up in a remarkable way.

Readers of this book know by now that one of the favorite claims of skeptics is that the information is general and could apply to many people. In this case, I scored the data for myself while Deepak was scoring how well each piece of information fit his own circumstance. If the scores were similar, then the skeptic's claim would be valid.

Much of the information fit Deepak's father and not mine. One or another of the mediums said that the sitter's father was a man of stature, knew many politicians, was very handsome, came from an attractive family, and was surrounded by beautiful women. He had left the country and moved to the city, and had left his father's profession. He provided not only for his own immediate family, but for his extended family. Each of these details were accurate for Deepak.

For me, every one of these statements was completely wrong. My father was not a man of stature, he did not know any politicians, he was homely, he did not come from an attractive family, and he was not surrounded by beautiful women. He left the city and moved to the country, he followed in his father's professional footsteps, and he had difficulty providing for his own family.

All three mediums said that the name *John* was important to the sitter, and one said that the name *Jackie* was also important. I scored the common name *John* as +3, because John Edward is very important to me and the evolution of this research. However, I do not personally know any Jackies, living or deceased.

Deepak scored both items as +3. The late Jackie Kennedy was a close personal friend of Deepak; her husband, of course, was named John.

My favorite piece of information that can be shared is when the medium Mary Occhino said, "A close relative is showing a problem with his throat, and that his vocal cords were removed before he died."

What a novel statement. Vocal cords removed before he died? In the many hundreds of research readings I have witnessed, mediums have on a handful of occasions spoken about throat problems, but have never mentioned vocal cords being removed before someone died. In my own experience, I have never personally known anyone, living or deceased, whose vocal cords were removed.

To my great surprise, Deepak acknowledged that an uncle dear to him had developed throat cancer, and his vocal cords had been surgically removed before he passed. +3 and +3 for Deepak.

I considered this a dazzling shot—a three-pointer from midcourt.

### Bottom Line

For Phases I and II combined—the scientific portion of the effort—the three mediums together provided a total of 305 data items.

At the end of the scoring session, Deepak had given +3's to 77 percent of the data items, with the individual mediums ranging from 75 percent to 79 percent. This success rate was higher than ratings for the five silent-sitters in the Canyon Ranch experiment.

How well did the medium's statements apply to me? The average for the three mediums was just under 27 percent. This was consistent with the results for the control scoring in the Canyon Ranch Experiment.

I examined the scoring sheets very closely, and considered all possible explanations. I went over the results a second time, and found no errors.

The results were, to use a single word, *staggering*.

Though the level of detail was at times astounding, the skeptical mind might still question whether the same information could be obtained by a stage medium skilled in cold-reading techniques, cheating by the mediums, or rater bias.

Cold reading appears to be clearly ruled out; barely more than one in four of the data items were correct for me, while more than three out of four were correct for Deepak; cold reading relies on using statements that apply to many people.

Even if each of the three mediums had done research or hired detectives (it would have to have been independent, since none of the mediums knew who the others were), they had no way of tracking down who the "famous person" might have been.

### For More Information on the Deepak Experiment

As I write this, I have already completed a scientific paper describing the experiments and the stunning results, and submitted it for publication by a peer-reviewed scientific journal. The title is purposely written in the language of science: "Nonlocal Anomalous Information Retrieval: A Multi-Medium Multi-Scored Single-Blind Experiment."

Anyone interested can find a complete copy of this scientific paper at www.openmindsciences.com.